START YOUR OWN

PODCAST
BUSINESS

Additional titles in **Entrepreneur's Startup Series**

Start Your Own

Entrepreneur
MAGAZINE'S

 STARTUP

START YOUR OWN

PODCAST

BUSINESS

YOUR STEP-BY-STEP GUIDE
TO SUCCESS

The Staff of Entrepreneur Media, Inc. & Jason R. Rich

Entrepreneur Press®

Publisher: Entrepreneur Press
Cover Design: Andrew Welyczko
Production and Composition: Eliot House Productions

This publication is designed to provide accurate and authoritative information in regard to the subject
matter covered. It is sold with the understanding that the publisher is not engaged in rendering legal,
accounting, or other professional services. If legal advice or other expert assistance is required, the
services of a competent professional person should be sought.

Entrepreneur Press® is a registered trademark of Entrepreneur Media, Inc.

An application to register this book for cataloging has been submitted to the Library of Congress.

ISBN 978-1-64201-112-8 (paperback) | ISBN 978-1-61308-435-9 (ebook)

Printed in the United States of America

25 24 23 22 21   10 9 8 7 6 5 4 3 2 1

Contents

Chapter 3

Choosing Topic, Title, Format, Length, and Frequency . . . 41

Chapter 4

Define Your Audience 59

What Is a Podcast?

D o you have something to say? Do you have an intended audience in mind that you'd like to share that something with? Well, the internet provides you—and virtually everyone else—with a public and potentially vast global forum that allows you to create and distribute your original content in a variety of easily accessible formats.

Back in February 2005, YouTube launched and quickly became the world's largest collection of free, on-demand video content. Now accessible from smartphones, tablets, internet-connected computers, and smart television sets, YouTube allows virtually anyone to create and publish video-based content and potentially attract an audience that could grow larger than the viewership of a typical network television show.

The people who create and distribute original, video-based content offered on YouTube have become known as "YouTubers," "online personalities," and "social media influencers." Some of these content creators have become as rich and famous as mainstream celebrities from television, movies, and the recording industry.

Meanwhile, instead of recording, editing, and publishing video content, others have chosen to broadcast live via the internet, using a service like YouTube Live, Facebook Live, Instagram, YouNow, or Twitch. Some of the broadcasters who regularly turn a camera onto themselves to educate or entertain their audience have also become wildly successful, wealthy, and popular.

Content creators who are not interested in investing the time and money needed to create video-based content or broadcast live via the internet have the ability to publish a blog, using a service like WordPress, Blogger, Tumblr, or SquareSpace. A blog (or online-based publication) can include text, photos, video clips, graphic animations, and audio in a customized layout to convey your content to an audience.

There is yet another option for sharing content with an audience that's quickly growing in popularity: *podcasting*. Today, just about anyone with an internet-connected smartphone, tablet, computer, smartwatch, smart TV, or smart speaker has the ability to find and access podcasts via the internet on an on-demand basis. For the *podcaster* (the person or organization producing the podcast), this provides a tremendous opportunity, as well as a low-cost way to reach a potentially global audience. For the purposes of this book, a podcast is audio-based (as opposed to video-based).

fun fact

Currently more than 54 percent of podcast listeners access and enjoy podcast broadcasts via their internet-connected smartphones. This is mainly because Apple (for the iPhone and iPad) and Google (for Android-based mobile devices) have made it very easy to find, access, and download (or stream) podcasts using a specialized mobile app that now comes preinstalled on most mobile devices. Numerous third-party apps also allow smartphone users to access and enjoy their favorite podcasts for free.

Podcasting Offers a Way to Reach an Audience Using Audio

How to produce, distribute, promote, and generate revenue from an audio-based podcast is the primary

► Stats About Podcasts

According to Apple, as of late 2019, there were more than 750,000 active podcasts available via the internet and more than 20 million individual podcast episodes. This included content published in more than 100 languages. PodcastHosting.org reports that as of February 2021, there are over 1,750,000 podcasts in existence and upwards of 43 million podcast episodes.

Spotify, which is primarily a music streaming service that also offers podcasts, reports that more than 53 percent of its users between the ages of 12 and 24 have become regular podcast listeners. As of early 2020, Spotify boasted having more than 232 million active users (including 109 million paid subscribers). Approximately 72 percent of Spotify's users are millennials.

PodcastHosting.org reported that as of February 2021, 75 percent of the U.S. population is familiar with the term "podcasting," and upwards of 50 percent of all U.S. homes are podcast fans, with more than 155 million people actively listening to podcasts on a regular basis.

focus of this book. For someone (including a company or organization) with something to say, podcasting is a viable option that is quickly changing the media consumption habits of people from all walks of life and from all over the world. You're about to discover why!

In recent years, podcasts have gone mainstream. In other words, they're no longer something that just caters to technology-oriented geeks with expensive and specialized equipment. Podcasts are currently accessible to more people than ever before.

Research shows that as of early 2020, more than 70 percent of the U.S. population is already familiar with the concept of podcasting, and at least half of all Americans have listened to a podcast. In fact, 22 percent of the U.S. population listens to podcasts on a weekly basis—and that number is growing rapidly. Thus, there's probably an audience out there waiting to hear your podcast!

Regardless of what type of information you want to share with your intended audience, chances are this audience is already familiar with what a podcast is, and has the wherewithal to find, access, and experience the podcast episodes you plan to produce. Without doing too much research, you'll likely discover podcasting could be a viable method for you to reach a target audience in a way that gives you tremendous freedom when it comes to how you'll share your information and content.

While the overall audience for mainstream (terrestrial) AM/FM radio is quickly shrinking, more and more people of all ages are now using their internet-connected smartphones, tablets, smartwatches, computers, smart TVs, smart speakers, and the

► Subject Matter Limitations

Podcasts can focus on just about any subject matter whatsoever thanks to the First Amendment (in the United States), which grants Americans freedom of speech. Keeping this in mind, the online-based podcast hosting services and distributors (such as Apple Podcasts, Google Podcasts, Spotify, etc.) all have their own Terms and Conditions a podcaster must agree to which prevent podcasters from sharing certain types of content that promote hatred, violence, racism, or terrorism, for example.

You'll find Apple Podcasts' Terms and Conditions online at: www.apple.com/legal/internet-services/itunes/us/terms.html. Google's Content and Conduct Policies for Podcasts can be found at: https://policies.google.com/terms. Note that until recently, Apple Podcasts was referred to as iTunes/Apple Podcasts.

infotainment systems in their vehicles to access and enjoy audio podcasts on a regular basis.

What Exactly Is a Podcast?

A podcast is, according to the dictionary, "a digital audio file made available on the internet for downloading to a computer or mobile device, typically available as a series, new installments of which can be received by subscribers automatically."

While podcasts can be produced as videos, this type of content tends to fall within the realm of what's offered on YouTube and other video streaming services. Therefore, throughout this book, the focus is almost exclusively on audio-based podcasts.

For the purposes of this book, a podcast is an audio-based program that's made available to its audience on an ongoing and consistent basis via individual episodes. A podcast typically focuses on a specific subject matter and caters to a clearly defined (niche) audience. A podcast typically consists of separate episodes that get released over time, and each episode typically follows a specific show format.

fun fact

According to PodcastHosting.org, as of February 2021 (during the COVID-19 pandemic), 90 percent of all U.S. podcast listeners listen to their favorite podcasts from home, and the average podcast listener subscribed to six shows, but listened to an average of seven shows per week. Comedy, education, and news were the most popular podcast genres.

▶ Podcasting Potential

Depending on your objectives, producing and distributing a podcast can be used as a revenue-generating business opportunity unto itself. However, it can also be used as a powerful and highly targeted marketing, sales, and promotional tool for yourself, your product(s)/service(s), and/or your company (or organization).

Regardless of your objectives, understand that building an audience for your podcast will take time. Podcasting is *not* a get-rich-quick scheme or a way to make yourself instantly famous. If you're willing to invest the required time and effort into the creation, production, distribution, and promotion of your podcast, what's offered right away by becoming a podcaster is a vast amount of potential.

How you tap this potential, as well as your own creativity, will play a huge factor in whether your podcast ultimately becomes successful, attracts a large audience, and allows you to achieve the objectives you have in mind for it. One of those objectives may be to generate ongoing revenue directly from the podcast.

The first few chapters of this book will help you understand the potential that podcasting offers, and then assist you in defining realistic goals and expectations related to the financial benefits and other perks that exist for podcasters.

While podcasting does not offer overnight fame and fortune, thanks to the fast-growing global audience and demand for podcasts, both fame and fortune are potentially things that can be achieved over time—if you're able to create episodic content that stands out from your competition and that appeals to your podcast's target audience.

As a podcaster, your competition includes other podcasts (yes, there are a lot of them) as well as all other media formats that offer similar content to what you plan to offer. Using creativity and an understanding of your target audience, you'll need to "package" your content in a unique, interesting, informative, educational, and entertaining way, and then present it in a show format that appeals to your audience.

Keep in mind, the content of your podcast and its relevance to your intended audience is crucial. However, just as important is the production quality of your podcast. Chapters 7 through 9 focus on recording and producing a podcast and explain how to achieve consistent professional-level production quality.

Just like a radio show, a podcast can follow a wide range of potential show formats. For example, a podcast can be presented in a newscast style, as a talk show (that includes calls or questions from audience members), as an interview show (with special guests featured during each episode), as an audio drama, or as a storytelling medium featuring a narrator or host.

Once a podcast is published on the internet through a podcast hosting service, listeners can download or stream each podcast episode and can choose to "subscribe" to that podcast.

When someone subscribes to a podcast, the device they use to listen to their favorite podcasts will automatically alert the listener when a new episode is released, and in many cases, will automatically download each new episode as it becomes available to listeners. The audience can then access and enjoy their favorite podcasts and podcast episodes on-demand.

The goal of a podcaster is to attract an audience to their podcast and ideally get listeners to subscribe (for free) to the podcast to ensure listeners discover each new podcast episode. A podcast's audience is measured based on how many subscribers it has, but more importantly by the number of listeners each individual episode of a podcast attracts via streaming and downloads combined.

▶ Examples of Popular Podcast Distribution Services (Podcatchers/Directories)

The *Apple Podcasts* mobile app comes preinstalled with iOS 14 (or later) on the iPhone and iPad but can also be downloaded and installed for free from the App Store (https://apps.apple.com/us/app/podcasts/id525463029). A similar app from Apple also comes preinstalled with the macOS Big Sur (or later) operating system for Mac computers.

The *Google Podcasts* mobile app comes preinstalled on many Android-based smartphones and tablets but can also be download and installed for free from the Google Play store (https://play.google.com/store/apps/details?id=com.google.android.apps.podcasts).

Apple Podcasts and Google Podcasts are two popular examples of "podcatcher" applications (also called podcast directories) that are readily available to anyone interested in listening to a podcast from their mobile device or computer. Countless other mobile apps, computer applications, and web browser plug-ins (extensions) also make it easy for people to find, access, and enjoy listening to podcasts via other directories or distribution services.

Why Podcasts Have Become So Popular

The fast-growing popularity of podcasts is a result of several key factors coming together in a way that makes it easy, free, and fun for people to alter their media consumption habits in favor of enjoying a podcast (as opposed to watching TV, listening to the radio, watching YouTube, reading a newspaper, or reading a magazine, for example).

Four of the key factors that have helped to increase the popularity of podcasts include:

1. Content Variety
2. Easy Accessibility
3. Cost of Podcast Listening
4. 24/7 On-Demand Access

Content Variety

As a podcast listener, the 1,750,000+ podcasts currently in existence cover every topic imaginable. Whatever your interests, chances are a collection of podcasts that directly caters to you exists.

Six of the most popular podcasting genres (topic categories) include:

1. Business
2. Comedy
3. Health
4. News and Politics
5. Society and Culture
6. True Crime

As a podcast listener, you can discover new podcast content in many ways. Word-of-mouth represents how 67 percent of podcast listeners choose what podcasts they listen to. Once you start producing your own podcast, keep this in mind! You'll definitely want to encourage your podcast audience to share details about your podcast with others.

Online promotions (via social media), hearing the podcaster as a guest on another podcast, and searching a podcast directory are other common ways for listeners

fun fact

Once a podcast attracts a listener or subscriber, the podcaster can typically count on 80 percent of their audience listening to a podcast's entire episode, or at least most of it. Thanks to the growing popularity of podcasts, a typical podcast listener subscribes to an average of six different podcasts and listens to an average of seven podcast episodes per week. This equates to the average podcast listener spending an average of six hours and 37 minutes per week listening to podcasts.

▶ Podcast Categories: A Comprehensive List

Podcast directories divide all podcasts into a wide range of categories based on subject matter. Here's a summary of Apple Podcasts' podcast categories and subcategories as of early 2020. Most other podcast directories use similar categories. As you brainstorm ideas for your own podcast, consider which category it'll nicely fit into.

▶ Arts
- Books
- Design
- Fashion and Beauty
- Food
- Performing Arts
- Visual Arts

▶ Business
- Careers
- Entrepreneurship
- Investing
- Management
- Marketing
- Nonprofit

▶ Comedy
- Comedy Interviews
- Improv
- Stand-Up

▶ Education
- Courses
- How To
- Language Learning
- Self-Improvement

▶ Fiction
- Comedy Fiction
- Drama
- Science Fiction

▶ Government

▶ Health and Fitness
- Alternative Health
- Fitness
- Medicine
- Mental Health
- Nutrition
- Sexuality

▶ History

▶ Kids and Family
- Education for Kids
- Parenting
- Pets and Animals
- Stories for Kids

▶ Leisure
- Animation and Manga
- Automotive
- Aviation
- Crafts
- Games
- Hobbies
- Home and Garden
- Video Games

▶ Music
- Music Commentary
- Music History
- Music Interviews

▶ News
- Business News

► **Podcast Categories: A Comprehensive List,** continued

- Daily News
- Entertainment News
- News Commentary
- Politics
- Sports News
- Tech News

► Religion and Spirituality
- Buddhism
- Christianity
- Hinduism
- Islam
- Judaism
- Religion
- Spirituality

► Science
- Astronomy
- Chemistry
- Earth Sciences
- Life Sciences
- Mathematics
- Natural Sciences
- Nature
- Physics
- Social Sciences

► Society and Culture
- Documentary
- Personal Journals

- Philosophy
- Places and Travel
- Relationships

► Sports
- Baseball
- Basketball
- Cricket
- Fantasy Sports
- Football
- Golf
- Hockey
- Rugby
- Running
- Soccer
- Swimming
- Tennis
- Volleyball
- Wilderness
- Wrestling

► Technology

► True Crime

► TV and Film
- After Shows
- Film History
- Film Interviews
- Film Reviews
- TV Reviews

Within each of these subject categories, you'll find hundreds of thousands of hours of original content, offered using many different show formats. These podcasts present information in unique, interesting, and specialized ways using audio.

Because the majority of podcasts cater to a niche audience (a very specialized and select group of people), it's easy to find and enjoy content that you as an audience member are

> ### ▶ Podcast Categories: A Comprehensive List, continued
>
> particularly interested in. You're never forced to sit through irrelevant or uninteresting content, or waste time consuming content presented by hosts who are boring or uninformed, or who don't appeal to you as a listener.
>
> In addition, as a podcast listener, you're able to control your listening experience by pausing, fast-forwarding, or rewinding individual podcast episodes, which you can listen to once or over and over again, with no limitations. When it comes to podcasts, there's content out there for everyone, and it's almost all free!

to find podcasts that'll appeal specifically to them. Approximately 2 percent of podcast listeners discover new podcast content using a traditional search engine (Google) search.

While the ability to access a podcast directory is built into many podcast applications (podcast listening apps), including Apple Podcasts, Google Podcasts, and Spotify, countless stand-alone, online-based podcast directories allow someone to type in a topic, keyword, or search phrase and then quickly find relevant podcast content. It's a process that works very much like using a search engine (like Google or Yahoo!) to find and access a website. Approximately 8 percent of all podcast listeners discover new podcasts to experience through the use of a podcast directory.

Easy Accessibility

Most people throughout the world now have internet access through a variety of devices and technologies, virtually all of which offer the ability to quickly find, access, and enjoy podcast content.

tip

As a podcaster, once your podcast has been published online and needs to attract an audience, you'll want to get it listed within as many of the popular podcast directories as possible. A listing of popular podcast directories, plus information on how to get your podcast listed within them (often for free), is covered within Chapter 12, "Publish Your Podcast Online."

Podcast content is typically "packaged" in a way that's easy to consume. Most podcast episodes are published on a set schedule, which might be daily, two or three times per week, weekly, or monthly. Each podcast episode then tends to be between five and 30 minutes in length (although some are longer), so a listener doesn't need to make a huge time commitment to enjoy their favorite content.

▶ Podcasts vs. Audiobooks

While a podcast and an audiobook both offer audio content that can be experienced almost anywhere using the same type of digital equipment, an audiobook tends to offer long-form programming that could take 5, 10, 20 or more hours to fully listen to, while an individual podcast episode can typically be consumed (listened to) in 30 minutes or less.

Audio dramas or storytelling podcasts, for example, tend to serialize their content over a handful of episodes, as opposed to offering it all in one long-form episode (which would make it just like an audiobook).

Since most people now carry their smartphone with them just about everywhere, they can use their mobile device to access their favorite podcasts when and where it's convenient. For example, most vehicles now link directly with an iPhone or Android-based mobile device, so podcast content that can be streamed or stored within a smartphone can easily be played through a vehicle's infotainment system and enjoyed while driving (using an iPhone's CarPlay or Android's Auto feature).

Beyond just smartphone accessibility via a specialized mobile app, podcasts are accessible from smartwatches, smart speakers, computers, and smart TVs. Research shows that 49 percent of people who listen to podcasts do so at home (as of early 2020), 22 percent of podcast listeners enjoy their favorite podcasts in a car, while 11 percent listen to podcasts at work.

Four percent of podcasts are enjoyed while listeners are working out, while another 4 percent are heard by people traveling via public transportation. Three percent of podcasts are heard by people "walking around," while 7 percent of listeners experience their favorite podcasts in "other situations."

Because podcasts can be accessed in so many ways, using a wide range of different devices that are available to us in our everyday lives, accessing and enjoying podcasts is one of the most convenient forms of media consumption available to us. For example, if you use a digital assistant that's built into your smartphone, tablet, smart speaker, smartwatch, or smart appliance, you can simply issue a command like "Hey Alexa, play the new episode of the *Man in the Window* podcast," and the latest episode will almost instantly begin playing.

Cost of Podcast Listening

In addition to easy accessibility, one of the most appealing aspects of podcasts is their price. Subscribing and listening to a podcast is almost always free, although listeners now expect to hear ads or messages from sponsors in conjunction with a podcast's content. Unlike other forms of media, like satellite radio, cable TV, a newspaper, or a magazine, there's no cost associated with subscribing to a podcast or acquiring (or streaming) individual podcast episodes. Millions of hours' worth of audio content, covering many genres, is available, on-demand, for free.

24/7 On-Demand Access

Another extremely appealing aspect of podcasts is that they're available 24/7 on an on-demand basis. Once a new episode of a podcast is published online, it can be experienced when and where the listener wants to enjoy it.

When a listener knows they'll have continuous internet access, any podcast episode can be streamed from the internet to their device (such as their smartphone, smart speaker, or computer) and listened to on-demand. In this case, the digital file that comprises each podcast episode is not stored on the device or equipment being used to hear it.

However, if someone is preparing for a long flight or trip, when a continuous internet connection may not be available, it's possible (as well as easy and free) to download episodes of a podcast and store the digital files associated with them within a smartphone, tablet, smartwatch, or computer, for example. Those downloaded and stored episodes can later be enjoyed anytime when no internet connection is available.

While a podcast listener/subscriber can learn when new episodes of their favorite podcast(s) are published online and then "tune in" at that exact time, the majority of podcast listeners appreciate the on-demand accessibility of podcast content—meaning they can start, pause, restart, stop, and replay the content when and where they wish, as often as they wish, with no limitations. It's this

fun fact

Man in the Window: The Golden State Killer is one of the world's most popular true-crime-related podcasts. Produced in 2019 by the *Los Angeles Times* and Wondery, it includes ten episodes (each between 30 and 45 minutes in length) that uncover never-before-revealed details about one of California's most notorious serial killers.

Among other places, this podcast is distributed through Apple Podcasts and the *Los Angeles Times'* own website (www.latimes.com). It's one of many true-crime-related podcasts that has captured the attention of millions of listeners around the world. As of early 2020, with more than 10 million unique listeners per month, Wondery (https://wondery.com) is reported to earn upward of $77.8 million per year from its ever-growing lineup of popular podcasts.

on-demand accessibility that sets podcasts apart from AM/FM radio programming, for example.

Moneymaking Opportunities for Podcasters

According to Statista (www.statista.com/topics/3170/podcasting), by 2022 the podcast audience within the United States alone will grow to 132 million. Also by 2022, Statista projects that podcast advertising revenue will reach $1.6 billion per year, up from the projected $650 million for 2020.

In a nutshell, podcast listeners are young, educated, and affluent, so if your niche target audience includes this group, and you're able to attract a respectable size audience to your podcast over time, there's potentially plenty of advertising and sponsorship money available, which means plenty of moneymaking potential from your podcasting efforts— that is, if you do everything right, have realistic expectations, and really focus on providing what's perceived as valuable content to your intended audience.

Keep in mind, for any podcast to generate significant and regular revenue through sponsorships and/or advertising, for example, it needs to have a sizable and loyal audience. Unfortunately, a typical podcast episode that's been live for 30 days will average only around 140 downloads, which is not enough to earn any significant advertising or sponsorship revenue.

However, if your podcast achieves more than 3,400 downloads per month, it will be ranked in the top 10 percent of all podcasts in terms of popularity. Achieving 9,000

▶ Podcast Listeners Are Young, Educated, and Affluent

More than 70 percent of consistent podcast listeners are between the ages of 18 and 54. Edison Research reported that 51 percent of the monthly podcast listeners in 2018 had an annual household income of at least $75,000, and 61 percent of podcast listeners have completed at least four years of college. This is a demographic that advertisers want to reach but that traditional advertising methods, including TV, radio, and newspapers/magazines, no longer allow them to cost-effectively reach.

Because individual podcasts tend to cater to niche audiences with specialized interests, yet also appeal to the core 18-to-54-age demographic (that's educated and affluent), advertising on podcasts is of interest to national and global businesses and brands, in addition to small to midsize businesses looking to reach highly targeted audiences.

downloads per month will place your podcast in the top 5 percent. When your podcast can boast tens of thousands or hundreds of thousands of regular listeners per month, that's when you'll be able to generate significant income from your podcasting efforts through advertising and sponsorship sales.

As you'll discover from Chapter 10, "Monetizing Your Podcast," and Chapter 11, "More Ways to Generate an Income from Your Podcast," once you build up a decent size and loyal audience for your podcast, the ability to earn a respectable income from it will follow. Realistically, building your audience to the optimal size for monetization could take months, potentially a few years, so it's important to stay focused and dedicated to your podcasting efforts. Remember, this is not a get-rich-quick scheme.

How much you can ultimately earn will be determined by a number of factors, including the size and makeup of your audience, the main topic of your podcast, your salesmanship abilities, and the quality and uniqueness of your podcast content.

From this book you'll learn that simply producing a top-quality podcast with amazing content is not enough. You then need to expertly market and promote your podcast, build an audience, and continue to cater to and expand that audience. Only then will it make sense to start pursuing any type of significant advertising and/or sponsorship revenue.

In the interim, while your podcast is establishing itself and you're actively growing its audience, some revenue-generating opportunities exist (and will be covered later) that may provide a small income. However, until your podcast audience is in the tens of thousands (or larger), don't consider quitting your current job to become a full-time podcaster.

Operating your podcast as a business, where you focus on advertising and sponsorship revenue (and other moneymaking opportunities) to support yourself and your podcast is certainly a viable option for some. Again, reaching the necessary level of success will take time. You can, however, use a podcast in many other ways that could lead to greater fame and fortune for yourself and your existing business.

Advertising and Sponsorship Options for Earning Podcast Revenue

When it comes to receiving money from companies that want to advertise or promote their brand or products/services during your podcast, a variety of options exist. *Paid advertising* means that you sell blocks of 15-, 30-, or 60-second ads that listeners will hear at various intervals during each podcast episode—just like a traditional radio ad.

Typically, advertisers pay a flat fee for traditional ads, based on a cost per thousand listeners. So if the advertiser agrees to pay $10 per thousand listeners for a 30-second ad, and your podcast has 10,000 listeners, you'd earn $100 per ad that's played during a podcast episode.

Most advertisers support podcasts that have tens of thousands or hundreds of thousands of listeners, which ensures their ad message gets heard by plenty of people. As a podcaster who is still building an audience, you have the option of incorporating commission-only or per-inquiry ads into your podcast.

Commission-only or *per-inquiry* ads mean that as the podcaster, you get paid a flat fee or sales commission each time a listener responds to an ad heard during your podcast. Advertisers only pay for results. Advertisers who utilize this type of advertising are more apt to work with podcasters with smaller or growing audiences because they only need to pay for responses or actual sales.

For a podcaster, the response rate for commission-only or per-inquiry advertising tends to be low (often less than 1 percent). So while you might make a few dollars as a result of incorporating these ads into your podcast, the revenue potential tends to be limited.

Affiliate marketing is another option that allows startup podcasters to earn money by promoting a company's products or services. In this case, the podcaster promotes a company and says something like "Use code 'podcast' when placing your order to receive 20 percent off your purchase." Each time someone uses that promotional code when

▶ Define Your Podcast's Objectives

If you set out to create a podcast with the intention of using it as a promotional or marketing tool for your existing business, you probably won't want to include any advertising or sponsorship messages from other companies within your content. Doing this will distract your audience and move their attention away from the podcast's main focus, which should be almost exclusively on your company and its products/services.

As you begin brainstorming ideas for your podcast, make sure you clearly define the overall objective of the podcast. Is it to generate money through advertising and sponsorship sales, or is it going to be used strictly as a promotional and marketing tool for your existing business? Which option you choose should then directly impact the overall approach you take to producing and promoting the podcast for its intended audience.

Without having a clear understanding of the podcast's core objective right from the start, you'll be setting the project up for failure.

placing an order, the podcaster earns a small commission. This option is open to almost all podcasters, regardless of audience size, but since the listener response rate also tends to be low, this typically does not represent a significant moneymaking opportunity.

One of the biggest revenue-generation options for a podcaster, especially once a podcast has a large audience, is to offer *sponsorships*. Instead of or in addition to incorporating traditional ads into each podcast episode, for sponsors, the podcast's host will typically make multiple announcements during the podcast stating "This podcast is sponsored by [insert company]" or "A sincere thank you goes out to our sponsor, [insert company], for making this podcast possible." The host will often then discuss or endorse the sponsor (or promote its products or services) within the podcast itself based on talking points provided by the sponsor. What a sponsor receives in exchange for their funding will vary greatly and is something as a podcaster you'll negotiate, in advance, with the sponsor.

Chapter 10, "Monetizing Your Podcast," goes into great detail about how podcast advertising and sponsorships work, how to find advertisers and sponsors, and why you might want to work with an agency that will secure sponsors or advertisers on your podcast's behalf.

If your podcast's business model will depend on earning advertising and/or sponsorship revenue in order to make money, and you're producing the podcast to be a stand-alone business venture, remember that it'll likely take months or years before your podcast builds a large enough audience to allow it to earn significant revenue from advertisers and sponsors. As you'll discover, you'll probably want to have an interim plan in place that potentially brings in some money, but that's not expected to entirely support your podcast business venture. Many of these options will also be explored throughout this book.

Use a Podcast as a Sales or Marketing Tool for Yourself or Your Business

If you have an existing company, or you're looking to promote yourself as an "expert" in your field, producing and hosting a podcast that caters to your target audience can serve as a powerful promotional and marketing tool that allows you to speak directly to your customers and potential customers in a relatively informal way and on a regular (recurring) basis.

A potential customer who listens to your podcast will get to know and trust you over time, making it easier for you to sell your company's products and services to them. You're able to include ads for your own company's products/services within your own podcast, but be sure to differentiate the podcast content from the hardcore sales-oriented ads, and use the podcast itself to discuss your company and its products using an "infotainment" format that combines sharing valuable information in an entertaining way.

When you produce a podcast with the goal of promoting your own company or its products/services, the goal isn't necessarily to generate revenue from the podcast itself. Instead, the goal of the podcast is to build an audience for your products or services, build loyalty for your brand, communicate with your existing customers/clients, and educate your target audience by providing information that's perceived by them as valuable. Many companies of all sizes and working within all sorts of industries have discovered innovative ways to utilize a podcast in order to achieve their marketing and promotional goals.

Establish Your Podcast as a Business

Once you decide you're ready to create and produce a podcast, you'll need to answer a few very important questions right at the start.

1. For you, what is the overall goal of the podcast?
2. Is the podcast being produced as a moneymaking business venture, or as a promotional/marketing tool for an existing business?
3. What will the podcast offer to its intended audience?

In Chapter 2, "Reasons to Become a Podcaster," we'll delve deeper into the many reasons why people decide to become podcasters and create their own podcast, as well as the perks, benefits, and opportunities that producing a podcast can offer.

If the goal of your podcast is for it to become a moneymaking business venture unto itself, then you'll need to set yourself up as a legitimate small-business operator and choose a podcasting business model that will allow you to grow your audience as

► Keep It All Legal

Once a podcast starts earning money, it becomes a business venture. As such, it needs to be operated as a business and it'll be required to pay taxes. Based on how you set up the podcast as a business, it can be operated as a sole proprietorship (DBA) or corporation, for example. Be sure to speak with your accountant or attorney to determine how to legally structure your podcasting business once you transform it from a hobby to a part-time or full-time moneymaking business venture. Also, be sure to file whatever copyrights and trademarks are required to protect the intellectual properties, logos, artwork, audio, and other content that's associated with your podcast.

quickly as possible so that the podcast will be able to generate revenue from ad sales and sponsorships quickly. Until that time, your podcasting business will likely be operating at a financial loss.

On the plus side, producing and distributing a podcast is very inexpensive from a financial standpoint. You won't need to invest thousands of dollars to build a fancy recording studio or broadcast facility. What you will need to invest, however, is your time—potentially a lot of time—to create, produce, edit, distribute, promote, and then manage your podcast and interact with your listeners.

Keep in mind, becoming a podcaster can be an extremely emotionally rewarding and professionally fulfilling experience, even when you're not yet making a financial fortune from your efforts. For many podcasters, they invest the time and money into producing a podcast because they have a true passion for their podcast's subject matter, and they want to share their wisdom, experience, opinions, talents, and ideas with a like-minded audience. Making money from their podcasting efforts is a secondary objective or not at all important.

Once you've decided to create and produce a podcast, develop realistic goals and expectations in terms of how quickly you'll build an audience, how much of a time commitment will be involved, how much money you'll be able to make, and what it'll take to make your podcast successful.

One of the very first things you'll want to do is determine how you'll define your own podcasting success. Establish a set of clear short-term, mid-term, and long-term goals for yourself and your podcast. One or more of your potential podcasting goals might include:

▶ Share your passion about a subject with an audience.
▶ Become a podcasting "celebrity," and build a vast audience and loyal fan base for yourself.
▶ Earn a part-time living from podcast revenue, or just enough to financially support the podcast itself.
▶ Ultimately be able to quit your full-time job and support yourself exclusively from podcast revenue.
▶ Position and promote yourself as an "expert" in your field.
▶ Seek out new customers/clients for yourself or your business.
▶ Promote your company and build awareness for your company's brand, products, and/or services.

As you'll discover, there are many reasons why people choose to become podcasters, and an equal number of goals these people hope to achieve. Chapter 2, "Reasons to Become a Podcaster," will help you better understand and define your own motivations and goals, plus assist you in determining if becoming a podcaster is the perfect fit for you, based on what you hope to achieve and in what time frame you hope to accomplish these objectives.

► Podcasting During the Covid-19 Pandemic

This book was written just before the covid-19 pandemic started in the United States and was first published in the midst of it. During this time, virtually everyone's life changed, routines were altered, and some common daily activities could no longer be experienced. As a result, those who regularly listened to their favorite podcasts while working out at the gym, commuting to work, during long airplane flights, or while on vacation, for example, discovered that their podcast listening routines also changed dramatically.

As a podcaster, finding and building an audience for your podcast as the pandemic lingers on could prove to be a challenge, as many potential listeners no longer have regular listening routines or schedules.

While your audience will likely have little difficulty finding your podcast on Apple Podcasts, Google Podcasts, or one of the many other podcast directories you will likely have it listed on, even if people subscribe and are interested in your content, don't expect them to become regular listeners of your content right away. The main reason for this is that many people are not following their regular life or work routines and have more pressing issues to contend with.

Once our lives begin to return to some level of normal in 2021 and beyond, old routines will be reestablished and new ones will be adopted. This will no doubt provide new opportunities for podcasters to grow their audiences, further proving that podcasting is more popular than ever!

The covid-19 pandemic should not stop you from launching your new podcast. It may, however, require you to adopt lower expectations for quickly building a loyal audience for it. Over time, if you handle things right, your podcast will find its audience.

2

Reasons to Become a Podcaster

For each of the podcasts that have been published and distributed online, there's a unique reason why that podcast and each of its episodes was created in the first place. The reasons why people choose to become podcasters are as unique as the podcasts themselves. This chapter explores some of the perks and benefits of becoming a podcaster, as well as a preview of the realizations many podcasters come to as they set out to produce the perfect podcast.

The first thing you need to understand about becoming a podcaster, especially when you're setting out to produce a podcast that will ultimately have advertisers/sponsors and become a revenue-generating business, is that you'll need to take on many different responsibilities and juggle those responsibilities in a way that allows you to get everything done, without cutting corners or compromising quality.

Unless you're working with a team, you'll probably need to plan, write, record, edit, produce, publish, and promote each episode of your podcast yourself. During the preproduction phase for each episode, for example, you'll need to do everything from brainstorming episode ideas, to finding and booking your podcast's guests, to writing a script, to planning the rundown of what will be included within the episode.

warning

When it comes to podcasting, when doing a cost-benefit analysis, the costs associated with becoming a podcaster are more than monetary. In addition to focusing on your financial budget, consider the cost of your time. If you need to invest 5, 10, or 20 hours per week, for example, to produce a quality podcast, will the benefits to you and/or your business outweigh the costs?

Two of the core skills every podcaster will require, especially if you're producing a podcast on your own or with just a small team, are the ability to juggle a handful of tasks simultaneously and to manage your time efficiently.

Each of the core tasks associated with podcasting requires its own set of skills and a time commitment to complete. In addition, it'll then be necessary to manage the business aspects of your podcast, which means interacting with your audience, soliciting and working with advertisers/sponsors, and handling other business-oriented tasks, like bookkeeping and paying taxes.

Depending on a bunch of factors, such as the show format of your podcast, each episode's length, how much research and preproduction is required to prepare for each episode, and the frequency you'll be producing new episodes, the overall time commitment for being a podcaster might start at just a few hours a week, but could easily wind up requiring much more.

Once you understand a potentially significant time investment is required to produce a quality podcast, it's up to you to do a cost-benefit analysis for yourself. Determine if the time commitment is worth it, based on your unique goals and objectives for the podcast.

Who Can (and Should) Become a Podcaster

The quick and easy answer to the question, Who can (and should) become a podcaster? is that *anyone* can become a podcaster and ultimately produce a successful podcast. With minimal financial commitment, and using even the most basic podcasting equipment (Chapter 7, "Set Up Your Recording Studio," focuses on the equipment that's needed), just about anyone with a core message, opinions, content, or information they want to share can become a successful podcaster.

People of all ages, from all walks of life, located all over the world, who work in countless industries, and who have a wide range of passions have become successful podcasters, and you could be next! That is, if you're able to come up with a concept for your podcast that stands out and will attract an audience, you're willing to put in the time required to produce a quality podcast, and you have the creativity and wherewithal to overcome the challenges faced by podcasters when it comes to producing and promoting their individual podcasts.

The big questions to ask yourself are:

▶ Why do you want to become a podcaster?

▶ What's your motivation to pursue this endeavor?

▶ Are you looking at podcasting to be a hobby that allows you to earn some money, a marketing tool for your existing business, or a stand-alone business venture that will hopefully lead to a full-time income?

▶ What do you want to get out of the podcasting experience?

▶ Do you have the time, creativity, motivation, and persistence required to achieve your podcasting goals, without becoming bored, frustrated, or disenchanted by the project when you discover it won't be an overnight success and that it could take months or even years to attract the massive audience you desire?

▶ How will you benefit both personally and professionally by becoming a podcaster? How might this experience enrich your life, help you expand your skill set, and make you a more well-rounded and worldly contributor to society?

Some of the Perks and Benefits of Becoming a Podcaster

For many, the process of becoming a podcaster and launching a podcast started because the podcaster had a passion or expertise related to a particular topic, and producing a podcast seemed like less work than producing videos for a YouTube channel and more fun than publishing a text-based blog or electronic newsletter.

As a result of becoming a podcaster, many have discovered a wide range of perks—some of which they'd hoped for, and some that came about unexpectedly. As with everything else related to podcasting, the perks and benefits you experience once your podcast is established will vary based on a number of factors, such as your podcast's target audience, its popularity, and the podcast's show format.

Ten Perks and Benefits Experienced by Podcasters

In addition to sharing your knowledge, talents, passion, and experience related to your podcast's subject matter, some of the common perks and benefits associated with becoming a podcaster include:

1. The ability to earn money from your podcasting efforts. How much money you're able to earn will be a direct result of your audience size and how much time and effort you put into attracting advertisers and sponsors, as well as pursuing other revenue-generating opportunities (including those discussed within Chapter 11, "More Ways to Generate Income from Your Podcast").

2. The ability to promote your existing company as well as its products/services to a highly targeted audience. This will likely help you build your existing company's brand, plus attract new customers, clients, or sales leads. At the same time, you'll build more trust with these (prospective) customers/clients as they get to know you over time as a result of listening to your podcast.

3. You could become a celebrity among your audience, among the podcasting community, and/or within your professional field. This will give you more credibility and influence.

4. You may have the opportunity to meet other experts, along with celebrities, authors, business leaders, public figures, and like-minded people who share a similar passion for your podcast's area(s) of focus. These people may be guests on your podcast, or you'll be invited to be a guest on their podcast or participate in other events with them, for example.

5. You'll receive free products and services that somehow relate to your podcast's subject matter, in hopes that you'll discuss, review, or feature those products within episodes of your podcast and share details about them (in a positive way) with your audience.

6. You'll be invited as a VIP or "celebrity" guest to participate in events that also cater to your podcast's target audience. In some cases, these could be paid appearances or high-profile speaking engagements that you'd otherwise not be able to book.

7. Through emails, text messages, and potentially calls into your podcast, or as a result of in-person meetings, you'll get to know members of your audience—people who share similar interests and passions related to your podcast's subject matter.

8. You might be invited to travel so that you can attend special events, conventions, or gatherings related to your podcast's focus.

9. As you research and produce content for each podcast episode, you'll expand your personal knowledge and expertise related to your podcast's subject matter.

10. Over time, you'll improve your public speaking skills and self-confidence, as well as enhance your creativity. You'll also likely become more experienced with time management, and in setting and achieving personal and professional goals.

> **tip** ⓘ
>
> While some of the perks and benefits to becoming a successful podcaster are money-related, don't overlook the potential perks and benefits to your personal or professional enrichment.

Share Your Message, Knowledge, Talents, Thoughts, and Expertise

After deciding that you want to become a podcaster, the next step involves deciding what your podcast will focus on and what show format it'll adopt. Based on your professional knowledge and skill set, personal interests, passions, talents, and hobbies, consider what subject matter you're qualified to produce a podcast about.

As you consider a primary subject matter for your podcast, ask yourself these important questions:

1. Do you have the knowledge, skills, experience, and/or talent that will allow you to present yourself as a credible and authoritative podcast host and producer?

2. Can you come up with an ongoing list of podcast episode topics that are relevant and that will be of direct interest to the podcast's audience? Use the Podcast Episode Idea Brainstorming Worksheet (Figure 2.1) to help you come up with topics and ideas for your initial ten episodes.

3. How will you present the content within your podcast episodes in a unique and creative way that sets it apart from other podcasts and media outlets?

4. How passionate are you about the podcast topic? Will you get bored of the topic after a few months or years?

5. Over time, how will you keep your podcast's content fresh to help retain the audience, strengthen its loyalty, and attract new listeners and subscribers?

6. Assuming the podcast becomes popular, do you personally want to become known as an "expert" related to the topic(s) the podcast covers? Will the online notoriety and fame be beneficial or detrimental to your personal and/or professional life? For example, if your podcast will cover controversial political or religious issues, will this impact how you're perceived at work? Will it cause tension and disagreements with family members and friends? Will your affiliation with the podcast tarnish your professional reputation or standing in your community?

7. With the understanding that trends and technologies continuously evolve, do you see yourself sticking with the project for the next three to five years (or longer)?

8. Are you willing and able to commit the necessary time and energy to the podcast to make it successful and to continuously create high-quality and original content that will appeal to the audience? How will this commitment impact your personal and professional life?

9. Does your podcast idea have long-term potential? Is the topic trendy right now, but likely to fizzle over time? If new listeners discover your podcast six months, a year, or three years from now, will the content still be timely and relevant?

warning

If your content will become outdated quickly and/or interest in the topic is likely to decrease dramatically in the foreseeable future, seriously consider broadening or abandoning the topic, since by the time you're able to reach the intended audience, the trendiness and audience interest in the topic might already have faded or disappeared altogether. Avoid trendy topics, unless you include those topics in a podcast with a broader appeal but that still caters to a niche audience.

Brainstorm Your Initial Podcast Episode Topics

Chapter 8, "Record Your Podcast Episodes," goes more in-depth about how to brainstorm original episode ideas for your podcast and then transform those ideas into top-quality content that'll appeal to your podcast's target audience.

Use the Podcast Episode Idea Brainstorming Worksheet within Figure 2.1 on page 27 to help you flush out at least ten podcast episode ideas. Doing this now will help to ensure that your overall podcast subject matter can be sustained over time.

Podcast Episode Idea Brainstorming Worksheet

Episode Idea/Topic	Episode Format	Guest(s) to Be Featured	Talking Point #1	Talking Point #2	Talking Point #3

FIGURE 2–1: **Podcast Episode Idea Brainstorming Worksheet**

Within the Episode Idea/Topic column of the worksheet, write a short sentence that outlines what the episode will cover. Later, you'll want to come up with a catchy and descriptive title for the episode, but for now, just focus on making sure you have the wherewithal to transform the episode idea into a compelling podcast for your audience.

▶ Podcast Episode Brainstorming Tip

Before pursuing an overall podcast topic, make sure you can come up with at least 26 awesome episode ideas. Assuming your podcast will release one new episode per week, by doing this, you'll know you have six months' worth of great episode ideas right from the start. Of course, as you proceed, you can swap out some of the original episode ideas with better ones.

Outlining your episode ideas well in advance will prevent you from running out of ideas and then scrambling to create content on a last-minute basis. It'll also give you plenty of time to find and book appropriate guests (if applicable) and perform whatever research for each episode that's required. Keep in mind, when you're forced to rush content and produce a podcast in a hurry to meet a weekly deadline, the content's quality will likely suffer if you're not prepared.

Within the Episode Format column, jot down the show format you anticipate using to present the content. Chapter 3, "Choosing Topic, Title, Format, Length, and Frequency," describes some of the more popular show formats you can choose from.

In order to keep content fresh and offer audiences different perspectives related to a topic, many podcasters rely on featuring guests. As you complete the worksheet, write down potential guests (if applicable) that you'd consider featuring within the episode. When choosing your guest(s), make sure they'll offer information or opinions, for example, that'll be perceived as useful and valuable to your audience.

warning

If you have trouble coming up with at least ten awesome episode ideas off the top of your head right now, how will you come up with 52 or 104 episode ideas over the next year or two?

Use the three right-most columns to describe the three most important talking points or topics you plan to cover during the episode. Assuming your podcast episode will be 20 minutes long, and you use 2.5 minutes to introduce the episode and 2.5 minutes to sum everything up and end the episode, will you be able to spend five minutes focused on each of the three main talking points in a way that offers valuable information or entertaining content to your audience?

Choose the Target Audience for Your Content

Once you've decided on an overall podcast topic, one of the most important things you need to research is your target audience. Specifically, who will your podcast appeal to and why? Chapter 4, "Define Your Audience," will help you carefully and accurately define and then understand your podcast's target audience.

Once you know the type of people that fit into your podcast's target audience, absolutely everything you do moving forward must cater specifically to that group. This includes when you're initially brainstorming a name for your podcast, choosing a logo, coming up with episode topics, deciding what type of show/episode format to follow, choosing guests, and selecting the background music your audience will hear. Everything related to your podcast must cater to and ultimately appeal to your target audience.

Hopefully, based on the podcast subject matter you plan to pursue, you yourself, as the podcast's host/producer, fit into your podcast's target audience. This will make many of your creative decisions moving forward a lot easier. However, if you do not consider yourself to be part of your podcast's target audience, it's absolutely essential that you put yourself in your audience's shoes when making all creative, content, and production-related decisions that pertain to your podcast and each of its episodes.

Even what you think of as being an insignificant creative decision, such as how you greet your audience at the start of each episode, will ultimately impact how your audience relates to you as the podcast's host. For example, if you start off the podcast by saying "Hi guys, welcome to [insert show name]" and the majority of your listeners are women, some people might be turned off right at the start.

When it comes to targeting your audience with your content, this goes beyond just the information you share. It also pertains to how you present the information and the vocabulary/language you use throughout each episode. Again, every single aspect of your podcast must cater specifically to its target audience, so the better you understand this group of people, and the more you get to know them, the easier this challenge will become.

How Will You Promote Your Podcast to Your Target Audience?

Knowing and understanding the wants, needs, values, opinions, habits, and lifestyle of your target audience is important when creating podcast content that is catered to a specific group. However, once you determine who comprises your podcast's audience, consider whether you have the knowledge, resources, and wherewithal to successfully market and promote your podcast to this audience on an ongoing basis.

After all, if you're unable to reach your target audience to tell them about the existence of your podcast, how will you build an audience for it? Chapter 13, "12 Ways to Promote Your Podcast," discusses some of the popular ways to share details about your podcast with its intended audience—both online and in the real world. As you'll discover, your ability to generate word-of-mouth hype for your podcast, and promote it heavily on social media,

▶ Pinpoint Your Primary and Secondary Audience

Depending on your podcast's focus, you may determine that your potential audience goes beyond a single niche group of people. In fact, you may be able to define a potentially large secondary target audience that your podcast will appeal to. If this is the case, go for it!

In some ways, appealing to more than one target audience makes growing your listenership easier. It also creates more work for you, since you'll now need to market and promote your podcast to two or more separate audiences, and when actually creating your content, make sure that you carefully craft it to appeal to the primary audience and the secondary audience.

One of the biggest mistakes you can make when defining your audience is making yourself believe that your podcast will appeal to absolutely everyone on the planet. Most of the time, this is not the case, and if you don't carefully define your audience, you'll waste valuable time and resources promoting and catering to people who have little or no interest in what you're offering.

for example, will likely play important roles when it comes to organically growing your audience.

Again, the more you know about and the better you understand your podcast's target audience, the easier it'll be to promote your podcast to this group. At the same time, if your goal is to eventually earn revenue from sponsorship and/or ad sales for your podcast, what will make your podcast appealing to potential sponsors and advertisers is your ability to reach a large and niche audience of people who trust you or your podcast's host(s). Demonstrating that you have credibility and a strong relationship with your audience will make you and your podcast more valuable to companies that choose to sponsor or advertise.

Describe Your "Perfect" Podcast

As someone who is planning to become a podcaster, have you explored the world of podcasting and begun listening to podcasts yourself? If not, stop what you're doing and start listening to a wide range of podcasts that cover a variety of subject matters, that cater to different audiences, and that follow different show formats. Discover what's possible!

Only after you've listened to and studied a bunch of different podcasts will you have the personal, firsthand experience needed to make important creative decisions about your own podcast. By listening to a wide range of podcasts, you'll discover what works and what doesn't, learn ways to cater your content to your audience, and hear firsthand how podcasters are able to capture and retain the attention of their respective listeners.

The more podcasts you listen to on an ongoing basis, the better you will understand how to present information to your audience based on what's possible using the podcasting medium. Nothing can replace the necessity to do real world research that involves listening to many different podcasts.

Keep in mind that the purpose of listening to other podcasts is not so you can copy or mimic the best ideas. Listening to other podcasts will help you discover what's possible. It's then your responsibility to use these podcasts as inspiration to help you package your own content in a unique, creative, insightful, attention-grabbing, and innovative way so it appeals to your intended audience.

Blatantly copying other people's work could lead to you infringing on someone else's copyrights, not to mention present you as a lazy and unprincipled podcaster who is not able or willing to create original content for their audience.

After coming up with a podcast subject matter or topic that you're personally comfortable with and excited about, and after you've carefully defined the audience for your content, take a few minutes to tap your creativity and envision what you believe will become the perfect podcast. Next, grab a sheet of paper and a pen. In a few sentences, describe that perfect podcast and what you envision individual episodes will sound like.

As you envision your perfect podcast, don't initially worry about budget, your technical know-how, or what production equipment will be required. In a perfect world where you're given unlimited resources, what do you envision? Focus on the show format, the scope of the content, how you'd like to present the content, production quality, frequency

► Consider the Production Requirements and Goals for Your Podcast

Once you've brainstormed what you envision to be the perfect podcast, it's time to give that concept a reality check and determine if what you want to create is logistically possible based on your know-how, production equipment, budget, and available time. Start thinking about what will be required to create what you believe will be the ultimate podcast, and consider what help and resources you'll need to make your vision a reality.

Chapter 6, "The Cost of Podcasting," will help you create a realistic production budget for your podcast, while Chapter 7, "Set Up Your Recording Studio," will help you select and gather the equipment needed to record, edit, produce, and distribute the podcast episodes.

of new episodes, and what will make your podcast unique. How and why will it attract an audience?

Define Your Podcast's Goals

Goals related to podcasting can be put into several categories. Beyond setting realistic short-term, mid-term, and long-term goals, you'll want to compile a list of goals for the podcast itself, as well as your own personal and/or professional goals as they relate to the podcast.

Think of short-term goals as those that can be created and achieved within three months. A mid-term goal should be realized within six months to a year. Goals that will likely take longer than one year to achieve should be considered long-term goals.

As you complete Figures 2.2, 2.3 (page 33), and 2.4 (page 33) and focus on the overall goals for your podcast, consider potential advertisers and sponsors you believe would be a perfect fit for your content, as well as when and how you'll approach them. Also think about who your "dream" guests would be in the months and years to come as your podcast grows.

Short-Term Podcast-Related Goals	
Short-Term Goal	**Goal Description**
Number of episodes produced and released (Include number of episodes in a specific time frame.)	
Anticipated/desired size of the audience	
Growth rate of the audience	
Potential sponsors or advertisers to work with	
Monthly revenue from sponsors/ advertisers	
Monthly revenue from other opportunities	
Specific guests to be featured	

FIGURE 2–2: **Short-Term Podcast-Related Goals**

Mid-Term Podcast-Related Goals

Mid-Term Goal	Goal Description
Number of episodes produced and released (Include number of episodes in a specific time frame.)	
Anticipated/desired size of the audience	
Growth rate of the audience	
Potential sponsors or advertisers to work with	
Monthly revenue from sponsors/advertisers	
Monthly revenue from other opportunities	
Specific guests to be featured	

FIGURE 2–3: **Mid-Term Podcast-Related Goals**

Long-Term Podcast-Related Goals

Long-Term Goal	Goal Description
Number of episodes produced and released (Include number of episodes in a specific time frame.)	
Anticipated/desired size of the audience	
Growth rate of the audience	
Potential sponsors or advertisers to work with	
Monthly revenue from sponsors/advertisers	
Monthly revenue from other opportunities	
Specific guests to be featured	

FIGURE 2–4: **Long-Term Podcast-Related Goals**

Next, think about your personal and professional goals as they relate to becoming a podcaster. As you outline these goals within Figure 2.5, consider:

▶ The level of "fame" you want to achieve
▶ How much money you'd personally like to make from your podcasting efforts
▶ How much of a time commitment you're willing to make on an ongoing basis
▶ Who you want to meet as a podcaster
▶ Places you'd like to travel
▶ What podcasting-related experiences you'd like to have
▶ What perks and benefits you want from the podcast
▶ What else you want to get out of the overall podcasting experience

Personal and Professional Goals for Your Podcast

Personal and Professional Short-Term Goals	1.
	2.
	3.
	4.
	5.
Personal and Professional Mid-Term Goals	1.
	2.
	3.
	4.
	5.
Personal and Professional Long-Term Goals	1.
	2.
	3.
	4.
	5.

FIGURE 2–5: **Personal and Professional Goals for Your Podcast**

Podcasting Isn't Always a One-Person Job

Plenty of podcasts are created, produced, and promoted by a single person. Others, however, have an entire production team behind them. This team includes one or more hosts, writers, producers, audio engineers, guest bookers (talent coordinators), ad sales peoples, office support personnel, and people in charge of promoting the podcast, for example.

Chances are, you won't need an entire team, at least initially, to create a successful podcast. All the skills that are required can be self-taught. To get your podcast up and running faster, and to avoid potential production-related mistakes, you might initially want to solicit the help and support of an experienced producer or audio engineer who understands how the recording and digital audio editing process works, or seek out one or more people who can help you with other aspects of the podcast's production that you're not yet skilled in.

Whether you plan to handle all the responsibilities yourself or delegate specific tasks to individuals on your team, here's a rundown of the jobs and responsibilities (listed in alphabetical order) a typical podcast will likely need to fill:

▶ *Advertising and Sponsorship Sales.* This is the person in charge of selling the advertising and sponsorship opportunities. Pinpointing and developing relationships with potential advertisers and sponsors will be this person's primary objective, although they might also be responsible for overseeing other revenue-generating opportunities. The responsibilities of the advertising and sponsorship salesperson are outlined within Chapter 10, "Monetizing Your Podcast."

▶ *Announcer.* In addition to the host(s), you may want to hire someone with an awesome voice to serve as the podcast's announcer, to introduce the hosts at the top of the show, for example. At the end of each podcast episode, it might be the announcer who reads the production credits, previews what'll be included in the next episode, and requests that listeners subscribe to the podcast, review it, and post comments about it online. As you'll learn from Chapter 3, "Choosing Topic, Title, Format, Length, and Frequency," you can hire a professional voice-over actor/announcer on a freelance basis.

▶ *Audience Relations and Promotions.* This is the individual or team who answers listener comments and emails, engages audience members on social media, and promotes the podcast to its target audience online and in the real world. Responsibilities might include managing the podcast's website and social media feeds, plus coordinating all other marketing and promotion efforts for the podcast on an ongoing basis.

▶ *Audio Engineer.* This is the technical person who will help the host(s) record the audio for the podcast and ensure the recording levels are suitable and that no unwanted or distracting audio (such as the sound of an air conditioner or outside traffic) is also being recorded. The responsibilities of the audio engineer are outlined within Chapter 7, "Set Up Your Recording Studio."

▶ *Executive Producer.* This is the boss and ringleader of your podcast. It's the person who oversees everything and everyone; sets and manages the podcast's budget; deals with business, bookkeeping, and legal issues pertaining to the podcast; and keeps the entire team on track. This person might also handle advertising and sponsorship sales, as well as any job(s) associated with creating, producing, distributing, promoting, and/or managing the podcast or operating the podcast business. If the podcast is being produced to promote an existing company's brand, product(s), or service(s), it'll be the executive producer who serves as the liaison between the podcast production team and the company.

▶ *Graphic Artist.* Typically hired on an as-needed and freelance basis, the graphic artist is in charge of designing the podcast's logo (cover art), website, and any other graphic elements that are needed.

▶ *Guest Booker/Talent Coordinator.* While this responsibility often falls to the host(s) or producer(s), it's the guest booker/talent coordinator's job to pinpoint the perfect guests to feature on the podcast (if applicable), initiate contact with the potential guests, gather information about them, perform preinterviews, gather talking points related to each guest for the host(s), coordinate the guest's travel (if applicable), schedule the specific date and time for each interview and confirm the interview location, and book the guests to be interviewed.

▶ *Host(s).* It's the host(s) of the podcast that your audience will hear and get to know. These people are your "on-air talent." In addition to having a calming, but authoritative and friendly voice, they need to have an outgoing personality, good vocabulary, top-notch public speaking and interviewing skills, and appeal to your target audience.

▶ *Postproduction Audio Editor.* After the audio for a podcast is recorded, this is the person responsible for mixing and editing the digital audio, adding sound effects and music, and transforming the raw audio content for each episode into a professional-sounding podcast episode. It might also be this person's job to upload the edited podcast to the various distribution services (such as Apple Podcasts, Google Podcasts, Spotify, Stitcher, TuneIn, etc.). The responsibilities of the postproduction audio editor are covered within Chapter 9, "Edit Your Podcast Like a Pro."

▶ *Producer.* The job of the producer is to assist the executive producer, plus handle any other job that's required, when it's needed. This job requires excellent time management, communication, and organizational skills, as well as the specialized skills needed to handle the specific tasks that are required of them.

▶ *Writer(s).* While not necessarily heard as hosts during the podcast episodes, a writer will be responsible for writing the scripts (if applicable) or talking points for the host(s) to use, as well as any other writing that's required to create, produce, and/or promote the podcast. This might include writing articles or content for the podcast's website or social media feeds, writing a press kit or press releases to help promote the podcast, or writing an advertising/sponsorship sales kit to be used as a sales tool.

warning

As a guest booker/talent coordinator, booking one guest per week for a prerecorded podcast won't demand much time or be too complicated. However, if your podcast is broadcast live, has multiple guests per episode, and/or airs several times per week, this job can easily become time-consuming and logistically challenging.

Gather Your Production Team

Once you've brainstormed all the details related to the creation of your podcast and determined what your production needs will be, you'll then need to carefully assess your own skill set to determine what help is required to make your podcast a reality. For example, within Chapter 15, "Interviews with Podcasting Pros," you'll read a handful of interviews with now-successful podcasters who chose to handle the majority of the jobs related to creating, producing, recording, editing, promoting, distributing, and managing their podcasts themselves.

Several of these people, however, wound up hiring or teaming up with a producer, audio engineer, audio editor, or someone with established audio recording, editing, and production skills to make launching and producing their podcasts that much easier.

In addition to determining what skills you already have right at the start, figure out what you'll need to learn or in what areas you'll need assistance. Also consider what podcast-related tasks you really enjoy and which ones you'd rather delegate to someone else. Keep in mind, you can't cut corners or simply ignore important responsibilities involved with the overall production and promotion of a podcast. If you're unwilling or unable to handle certain tasks, you'll definitely want to team up with one or more people who complement your skill set and who can handle those tasks.

Set Realistic Expectations for Success and Growth

Once again, it's important to emphasize that producing a podcast is not a get-rich-quick scheme that will start generating revenue right away or that will allow you to immediately attract a large audience that'll result in you becoming famous. Even if you team up with a bunch of extremely talented people and have a true passion for the subject matter your podcast will cover, ongoing dedication and patience are essential.

As you get started, make sure all your expectations are realistic. This includes expectations related to what's possible from a production standpoint, an audience growth standpoint, an advertising/sponsorship sales standpoint, and what you personally will get out of the podcasting experience.

> ## ► Jason Rich's Featured App of the Week: A Podcast Example from This Book's Author
>
> During the covid-19 pandemic, with so much extra time on my hands, I decided to launch a podcast. I chose the subject matter for the podcast by tapping my more than ten years' experience writing about the Apple iPhone, Android smartphones, and other consumer electronics.
>
> I decided to create a podcast that would help non-tech-savvy people better understand what their smartphone could do by showcasing cutting-edge and useful mobile apps. Thus, the concept for *Jason Rich's Featured App of the Week* (www.FeaturedAppPodcast.com) was born. The target audience for the podcast is the tens of millions of adult smartphone users who own the latest smartphone model, but don't know about everything it can do, and who are not yet comfortable using this technology in their everyday lives. These are the people who typically attend my personal enrichment lectures that (prior to COVID-19) I regularly presented aboard cruise ships around the world.
>
> After writing a few sample scripts and planning the content for the podcast, I visited UpWork. com and hired a freelance graphic designer to create a logo for the podcast. This wound up costing $50. To give the podcast an added level of professionalism, I hired the folks at Radio Voice Imaging (https://radiovoiceimaging.com), and for less than $100, had an intro and outro for the podcast recorded and produced. The background music and sound effects used in each episode are free of copyright and licensing fees.
>
> Next, I began recording the first few episodes, as well as an introductory episode for the podcast. I invested in a $100 USB microphone that connected directly to the Mac and used Audacity as

► **Jason Rich's Featured App of the Week:
A Podcast Example from This Book's Author,** continued

the recording software. Once the concept for the podcast proved itself to be viable, I later invested about $1,300 and purchase the Rode Caster Pro Production Console bundle (www.rode.com/rodecasterpro), which included an easy-to-use digital mixing board, two professional-quality microphones, headphones, and just about everything else need to dramatically enhance the audio quality of the podcast (while still using the Mac and the free Audacity recording and editing software).

With the first few episodes recorded, the next big decision was choosing an online hosting service for the podcast. For this I turned to Buzzsprout (www.buzzsprout.com). This company offers low-cost hosting, with a bunch of really great features ideal for first-time podcasters. For example, the service makes it easy to get a podcast quickly listed with virtually all of the popular podcast directories, including Apple Podcasts and Google Podcasts. Plus the service's Magic Mastering feature makes postproduction much easier for people with no audio editing or production background.

Initially, writing, recording, and doing all of the postproduction work myself on each five- to 10-minute long episode took upwards of six hours. With practice and experience, this has been reduced to about three hours per episode.

After publishing the first few episodes, attention shifted to promoting the podcast and building an audience. In addition to relying on my established social media presence (on Facebook, Twitter, Instagram, and LinkedIn) and my own website traffic (www.jasonrich.com), I chose to do some paid online advertising on Facebook and Instagram. I also used paid advertising on the Overcast podcast directory (https://overcast.fm/ads). Although the Overcast advertising cost around $200 per month (for three months), this proved to be the quickest way to gain subscribers and listeners early on. However, since the podcast was not created specifically as a revenue-generating tool, spending thousands of dollars to quickly build an audience for the podcast didn't make financial sense in this particular situation.

Paid advertising was used to build an initial audience, which I would then grow using many of the free, more grassroots promotional efforts described later in this books. The ultimate goal is to begin promoting the podcast during the enrichment lectures I will again be presenting aboard cruise ships once the covid-19 pandemic is under control. This will allow me to reach at least 5,000 potential listeners per month for free.

Starting in the next chapter, the process for actually creating your podcast will begin. It's during this phase that you'll make some important creative and business decisions, analyze your concept, pinpoint your target audience, research your competition, and take steps to ensure that your overall podcast idea or concept is actually viable.

Choosing Topic, Title, Format, Length, and Frequency

O ut of the millions of podcasts already available
to listeners, where and how will yours fit into
the mix? What will set it apart? Why *should*
people listen? Why *will* people actually want to listen?
The preplanning and research you do prior to launching
your podcast is as important as each episode's content

and production quality. After deciding that podcasting is the right move for you, next focus on the overall subject matter you plan to cover.

The overall subject matter refers to the podcast's broad focus or scope. The individual podcast episodes will allow you to narrow that scope or focus to one topic or area of interest that can be covered within a specific time frame (which is the length of your typical podcast episode).

Fine-Tune Your Subject Matter

As a producer and/or host, determining and then truly understanding the subject matter and scope of your podcast is important. Once you select the general subject matter, focus in on your personal area(s) of interest, experience, and expertise. Figure out what areas of that subject you're best able to cover. In other words, start by selecting a broad topic, such as music, and then narrow it down a bit so that the podcast's scope will better cater to a niche audience that you understand, can identify, and know how to ultimately reach. Music as a podcast subject is too broad, but '80s pop music, for example, is more niche-oriented.

While you are determining the scope of what your podcast will cover, create a detailed list of specific subtopics or areas that you definitely plan to include. Also, create a list of the topics or areas related to the podcast's focus you plan to stay clear of. Make sure the overall scope of your podcast remains broad enough so it'll appeal to a large enough niche audience, yet isn't so broad that over time the podcast will lose focus or cause listeners to lose interest.

Keeping the overall scope of your podcast in mind, make sure you'll be able to brainstorm an ongoing lineup of episode topics that won't get boring or repetitive, and that'll directly appeal to your target audience.

> **warning** ⚠
>
> If after you've determined the scope of your podcast, you can't immediately come up with at least 26 or 52 attention-grabbing, interesting, and relevant episode ideas, your podcast concept still needs some fine-tuning. Before you start producing episode number one, map out what your podcast will cover over its first six months, and figure out how you'll present that content.

Compose a Nicely Crafted Podcast Description

Now that you have a clear understanding of what your podcast will be about, carefully craft a one-sentence description of it, as well as a separate one-paragraph description. In a clear, concise, and attention-grabbing way, these two descriptions should make it obvious what the podcast is called, what it's all about, what the scope of its content is, who it'll appeal to, and why someone should start listening.

After reading the podcast's one-sentence or single-paragraph description, someone who has never heard of your podcast, but who is interested in the subject matter, should want to drop everything they're doing, find your podcast online, and start listening to it right away.

Crafting the perfect podcast description is not something you'll be able to do in just a few minutes. It'll take time to write, edit, rewrite, and fine-tune until you're confident that the vocabulary, tone, and information conveyed is absolutely perfect and targeted to the right audience. Needless to say, it should contain no spelling or grammatical errors, and within mere seconds, it should help people understand what sets your podcast apart from all others.

Moving forward, your podcast description will be used in several important ways. For example, either the one-sentence or one-paragraph description will be included within all podcast directory listings. It'll also be used when promoting your podcast on social media, and as part of all other marketing and promotional efforts online and in the real world.

Be sure to memorize your podcast description so that you can recite it in an energetic and attention-getting way when you're having discussions with potential listeners, you're speaking in front of an audience, or you're a guest on someone else's podcast. In just a few seconds, you need a clear, easy-to-understand way to explain and promote your podcast.

Choose an Appropriate Podcast Category

You already know that all podcast directories divide up podcasts into categories and subcategories. Now that you have a clear concept of what your podcast will cover, determine which podcast category and subcategories it fits perfectly into.

Based on how and where you plan to distribute your podcast, each distribution service or directory has its own podcast category and subcategory listings. Here's how to find this listing for some of the popular podcast directories:

▶ *Apple Podcasts*—https://podcasts.apple.com/lr/genre/podcasts/id26

▶ *Google Podcasts*—https://podcasts.google.com (Click on the All Categories pull-down menu option.)

▶ *Spotify*—https://open.spotify.com/view/topic-grid (Only supported on the Chrome, Firefbox, Edge, or Opera web browsers, as well as the Spotify desktop app. The directory is also available onfrom the Spotify mobile app.)

▶ *Stitcher*—www.stitcher.com/stitcher-listen

▶ *TuneIn*—https://tunein.com/podcasts

A more extensive list of podcast directories, complete with details about how to get your podcast listed within each of them, can be found at: https://www.buzzsprout.com/.

Research Your Competition

You may think you have the perfect idea for a new podcast—one that's unique, totally original, and that'll definitely appeal to a specific target audience. That's great, but are you 100 percent sure? The only way to be certain is to do some research!

Before you invest the time, money, and resources to start producing your podcast, visit several of the popular podcast directories as a listener and start exploring. Within the search field, enter keywords and search phrases that relate to your podcast's focus or subject matter and see what competition pops up in the search results. Next, within the various podcast directories, click on what you believe will be your podcast's subject category, and then start listening to some of the existing podcasts you find listed.

Figure out what similar podcasts exist, what approach each is taking, the scope of each podcast, and the target audience of each. Once you discover what's already out there, ask yourself what you'll do differently. What will make your podcast stand out? Why will people want to listen to your new, unestablished podcast, compared to what's already available?

If you discover there's already a lot of competition in your podcast category that's also targeting your intended audience, and you can't come up with legitimate reasons why potential audience members will want to listen to your podcast (in addition to or instead of the competition), you need to go back to the drawing board and rethink your concept, your content, your approach, and who your audience will be.

As you're doing your initial research and then moving forward once you become an active podcaster, you always want to set aside time in your schedule to listen to the latest podcast episodes from your competition so you hear firsthand what they're doing and how they're doing it. Failure to understand your competition and know what they're doing is as big of a mistake as not understanding your target audience or catering every aspect of your podcast to those people.

Select Your Podcast's Title

The title you choose for your podcast becomes its identity. This is one of the most important decisions you'll make as you're setting up and establishing your podcast. Selecting your podcast's title is not a decision you should make lightly.

▶ Don't Be Egotistical When Naming Your Podcast

Unless you already have a large and well-established following, don't consider naming your podcast after yourself. Oprah is one of the most famous women on the planet, so it makes sense that her former talk show was named after her. If you name your podcast after yourself, such as *The John Doe Show*, if people don't have any idea who you are or what you represent, why would they bother wanting to invest that extra few seconds to read your podcast's description to determine what it's really all about or figure out who you are?

You're much better off coming up with a descriptive title for your podcast, and then adding a subtitle that includes your name as the host. For example, a more descriptive title might be, *Let's Talk Politics With Right-Wing Conservative John Doe*. Unless you're already a celebrity, simply naming a podcast after yourself is egotistical and uninformative. It won't capture the attention of perspective listeners.

If you look at a list of the most popular podcasts, those podcast titles that contain someone's name are all hosted by a well-known celebrity or public figure, such as *The Joe Rogan Experience*, *The Rachel Maddow Show*, *Rumble With Michael Moore*, or *Conan O'Brien Needs a Friend*. Podcasts based on already-successful TV or radio shows utilize the name of the existing program as the podcast's title. For example, there's *This American Life*, *Dateline NBC*, *Fresh Air*, *On the Media*, and *TED Radio Hour*.

Virtually all of the other most popular podcast titles are descriptive. For example, when you see the podcast titles: *My Favorite Murder*, *True Crime Garage*, *Stuff You Should Know*, *Planet Money*, *Criminal*, *Fantasy Football Today Podcast*, *Handel on the Law*, and *Comedy Bang Bang: The Podcast*, you immediately have a pretty good idea of what they're each about.

Another approach is to come up with a word or phrase that's unique, but not at all descriptive. This approach, however, can be tricky, because it relies on the title piquing someone's interest enough for them to take the extra time needed to read the podcast's description. Examples of this approach include: *The Daily*, *Radiolab*, *In the Dark*, *The Moth*, *Morning Joe*, *99% Invisible*, and *Snap Judgment*.

Consider the following tips when brainstorming a title for your podcast. The podcast's title should be:

- ► Easy to pronounce and clearly say aloud
- ► Short and to the point
- ► Memorable
- ► Easy to spell
- ► Descriptive
- ► Unique
- ► Original and not violate someone else's copyrights or trademarks
- ► Appealing to your target audience

People utilizing the internet have a very short attention span. As someone is browsing a podcast directory, for example, if your podcast's title doesn't capture their attention immediately, they won't invest the additional few seconds needed to read the podcast's description or take a look at its ratings and reviews.

A podcast's title can be accompanied by a descriptive subtitle. If you choose to utilize a subtitle, make sure it adds something to the title that helps convey useful information to potential listeners. What's an important piece of information that you want potential audience members to know about your podcast right away, but that the title itself does not convey? This is the information you want to include in your podcast's subtitle.

Once you know what your podcast will be about and who it'll be targeted to, come up with a list of at least 25 potential podcast titles. Next, follow these steps to help you select the perfect podcast title:

1. Put yourself in your potential audience member's shoes, and then narrow down your list to ten.
2. Gather together a group of people who fit into your target audience. These might be friends, family members, or people you've met on social media, for example. Present them with your tentative list of podcast titles and ask them each to choose their top three. Based on the results, narrow down your list to five potential podcast titles.
3. Check out the various podcast directories and see if any podcasts already exist that have the same or a very similar title. If so, remove that title from your list.
4. Conduct some research online. Make sure that none of your proposed podcast titles violates anyone else's copyright or trademark. You may want to consult with a lawyer. However, you can research copyrights and trademarks yourself by visiting these websites:

> ▶ U.S. Copyright Office—www.copyright.gov/rrc
>
> ▶ U.S. Patent and Trademark Office—https://www.uspto.gov/trademarks/search
>
> ▶ LegalZoom.com—www.legalzoom.com. This is an independent, for-profit company that can help a business or organization complete the copyright or trademark application process for an additional fee over and above the filing fees charged by the U.S. government.

5. Based on the remaining three to five potential podcast titles that you really like, think about the logo and podcast cover art that will accompany it, and then narrow down your selection to a final title that you absolutely love, that your audience will relate to, and that you'll be proud of.

▶ Register the Dotcom for Your Podcast Name

As soon as you've selected your podcast's title, visit a website domain name registrar and make sure that the website domain name for your podcast's exact title is available with the dotcom extension. Popular domain name registrars include: GoDaddy (www.godaddy.com), Wix (www.wix.com), Domain.com (www.domain.com), Bluehost (www.bluehost.com), HostGator (www.hostgator.com), and Namecheap (www.namecheap.com).

Using the search field for any domain name registrar, enter your podcast title (with no spaces) and include the website extension ".com" at the end. Within seconds, you'll be able to determine if your desired website domain name is available. If so, register it. If not, seriously consider choosing a different title for your podcast.

Hundreds of different website domain name extensions are available, including: ".com," ".net," ".org," ".info," ".club," ".website," and ".biz." A more comprehensive listing can be found at: www.namecheap.com/domains/domain-name-search. While you might also want to register your website with one or more of these additional extensions, it's absolutely essential that you acquire the ".com" extension for your podcast name. In other words, "YourPodcastTitle.com."

Web surfers are accustomed to entering ".com" at the end of the website they're looking for. Even if you tell them your website is "YourPodcastTitle.org," or they see it listed in print, for example, the majority of people will still enter "YourPodcastTitle.com" into their web browser. Thus, if you don't control this domain name, your potential listeners could be directed to someone else's website.

When you register your podcast's domain name (e.g., www.YourPodcastTitle.com), consider the most common misspellings or typos that people might make when entering the domain

▶ Register the Dotcom for Your Podcast Name, continued

name into their web browser, and register those domain names as well. Otherwise, once your podcast becomes successful, your competition will figure out the common misspellings and typos for your domain name, register those domain names for themselves, and direct those people who enter your domain name incorrectly to your competition's podcast or website.

The cost of registering a domain name with a .com extension should be between $10 and $20 per year, depending on which domain registrar you use. You'll often receive a discount if you register the domain name for two or more years at a time and/or register multiple domain names at once.

After you've registered and acquired the domain name for your podcast's title, contact the domain name registrar, your web hosting service, or your email service provider, and set up email accounts that end with "@YourPodcastTitle.com."

For example, you'll want a separate email address for each of your podcast's hosts and co-hosts, as well as the producer(s) and talent bookers on your team. You might also want to set up email addresses like "Feedback@YourPodcastTitle.com" or "Advertising@YourPodcastTitle.com" to handle specific types of email correspondence.

Maintaining even a simple web page for your podcast is an absolute must. Meanwhile, having personalized email addresses that include your podcast's title/domain name gives your podcast an added level of professional credibility, as opposed to using a free email address from Gmail, Yahoo Mail, Microsoft, or Apple (iCloud), for example.

Every Podcast Episode Also Needs a Catchy Title

As you'll discover when you begin publishing new podcast episodes on a continuous and hopefully regularly scheduled basis, in addition to the podcast itself having a title, each individual episode should be numbered and have its own title.

The episode numbers should be sequential, starting with Episode #1. If you choose to produce a group of episodes and then take a seasonal break, you might consider labeling each episode by season number and episode number, along with a title. This is what's done with TV series, for example. Thus, a sample podcast episode might be labeled and listed as "[Podcast Title], [Season Number]/[Episode Number], [Episode Title]."

Of utmost importance, each episode title needs to be descriptive and offer a preview of what your audience can expect from that specific episode. In addition to attention-grabbing episode titles, each individual episode can often have a text-based description. Depending on which podcast distribution service you use and which podcast directories you focus on getting your podcast listed on, each episode description can be anywhere from one sentence to several paragraphs in length.

Keeping the short attention span of your potential audience in mind, always keep your episode descriptions concise, yet describe the content in a way that'll be enticing. Be sure to check out the episode descriptions for a handful of different podcasts to see what's possible and to provide some inspiration.

At the end of each episode description, consider including your podcast's website address and any other contact information that's relevant, like where potential listeners can go for more information. If your podcast is designed to promote your brand, company, product, or service, provide the appropriate website links within the podcast episode descriptions. This information can and should also be included within the episode's show notes (which will be explained later).

Another useful link you can provide is to a specific web page for your podcast that includes a preview of the next (upcoming) episode(s) as well as a detailed episode listing and upcoming schedule.

tip

If you want to produce 8, 10, or 12 episodes, and then take a several-week break before releasing new podcast episodes, consider developing a seasonal schedule for your podcast. Season one might go weekly, from January to March or January to July, for example. Then, after a break, you'd continue with season two, which might go from April through July or August through December. As long as your audience understands your production schedule, they'll know when they should be looking out for and excited to hear new episodes.

Decide How You'll Present Your Content

Think of a podcast as being a radio show that's distributed via the internet. Understand that every show follows a specific format. Once you choose your podcast's subject matter, scope, and target audience, select a show format that allows you to present your content in the best way possible. The podcast format you adopt determines how you'll organize and ultimately deliver your content to your audience.

Some podcast formats work better when each episode is prerecorded and edited, and postproduction elements (including sound effects or background music) are mixed into each episode. Other formats are better suited to a livestreaming format. By adopting a live format, it's easier to solicit and incorporate real-time participation from your audience.

Once an episode streams live, the recording can then be offered for future listeners to stream or download.

Hosting a live podcast requires more skill, since you'll need to be able to improvise, think on your feet, adapt to whatever happens, and at times, be forced to keep your content on topic if callers, guests, or a co-host go off topic, argue, or get distracted. When streaming live, you need to speak clearly and without using "ums," for example. "Ums" can, however, easily be edited out of a prerecorded podcast.

Eight of the most popular podcast formats include:

1. *Audio Theater Format.* This is when a group of "actors" present a radio-style, fictional drama, often with sound effects and music mixed in. This style of podcast might focus on an original story or play, or present a reimagined version of an existing story (assuming it does not violate any copyrights). Audio dramas might break up a several-hour performance into a series of separate episodes that are 15 to 30 minutes each in length. Thus, a two-hour audio-based story can be told over four or eight episodes, for example.

2. *Conversational-Style Format With Two or Three Co-Hosts.* This format allows two co-hosts to discuss the episode's topic, and potentially answer questions or respond to feedback from audience members who submit questions via email or through social media, or call the show at a predetermined time when it's being recorded or streamed live. The approach you can take might be similar to a talk radio show, commentary show, or opinion show, but the main focus is on two or more co-hosts conversing and sharing their thoughts, knowledge, or opinions.

3. *Hybrid Format.* As a podcaster, you have the ability to combine any of these show formats to create one that works perfectly for your approach to presenting your content to your podcast's target audience. Think beyond the potential restrictions offered by other formats and create something that's unique, that's creative, and that keeps your audience's attention.

4. *Interview Format.* This format involves one or two hosts, for example, interviewing one special guest at a time during each podcast episode. The episode takes on a question-and-answer or discussion format. The great thing about a Q&A style interview podcast is that all the host needs to do is prepare an introduction and conclusion, as well as a series of questions for their guest. The guest then does most of the talking.

5. *Nonfiction Storytelling Format.* These podcasts tend to focus on retelling what happened during real-life events. They can include first-person accounts or recount something based on research, for example. Autobiographical, biographical, and

travel-related podcasts where the host shares their experiences (or describes the experiences of others in an authoritative way), as well as true-crime-related podcasts often utilize this format.

6. *Panel-Discussion Format Featuring Host(s) and Special Guests.* This podcast format involves one or more hosts and/or special guests who gather together to discuss a specific topic. Each person shares their own thoughts, ideas, experiences, and knowledge. Panel members might debate each other, openly disagree, or even engage in friendly arguments. If you adopt a panel-discussion show format, make sure one host serves as the ringleader, keeps everyone on topic, and ensures others don't talk at exactly the same time or constantly interrupt each other. These mistakes can't be edited out of a recorded podcast and will make your podcast difficult for the audience to listen to and understand.

7. *Repurposed Content Format.* If you have content, such as recordings of public speaking engagements, classes you've taught, text from articles you've written, audio from press conferences, or audio from other events you've been a part of, consider repurposing this content into a series of podcast episodes where a host (or voice-over announcer) strings the pieces of content together in a cohesive style.

▶ Multiple People Can Offer Multiple Viewpoints

When your podcast features two or more co-hosts, or it includes appearances by several special guests, this allows you to cover a specific topic while sharing multiple viewpoints or perspectives. For the audience, this is often more entertaining and engaging than listening to a solo host engage in a one-directional, noninteractive monologue.

For the host(s), it's important to prepare for each podcast by researching the guests and having a list of interview questions compiled in advance that'll allow for more information to be covered while staying on topic. If the interview will last 30 minutes, for example, have at least ten questions prepared. Then be ready to improvise with follow-up questions related to how a guest answers your particular questions. If the guest tries to dodge a question, you may need to rephrase it one or two times to get them to open up.

Another benefit to inviting guests to come on your podcast is that if they're a published author, celebrity, or public figure, for example, they'll already have followers and fans that will likely tune into your podcast to hear that guest be interviewed. Be sure to ask your guest to promote their appearance on your podcast in advance to their following on social media, for example.

8. *Solo Host Monologue Format.* This popular podcast format features a single host sharing their thoughts, knowledge, experience, and/or opinions about a subject matter as they speak into a microphone directly to their audience. One challenge is keeping your audience's attention if you're not a dynamic speaker. Another challenge is that unless you're well prepared, it's easy to go off topic, get distracted, or become repetitive when trying to fill each 15- to 60-minute episode. On the plus side, the host becomes the center of attention during the podcast.

warning

From episode to episode, a podcast can successfully change show formats once in a while in order to better present specific information or content, but listeners will typically appreciate and often expect consistency in your approach and podcast show format.

Select Your Host(s) and Co-Host(s)

As you're brainstorming ideas for your new podcast, think about your ideal host(s). Will you be the main host or a co-host? Who else do you have in mind to take on the hosting duties? Eight of the key qualities that make the perfect podcast host include someone:

1. With an outgoing personality and great sense of humor.
2. With a pleasing-sounding voice.
3. With public speaking skills. (This includes having a good vocabulary. The host should speak at a normal pace with minimal "ums" and be understood by the listeners.)
4. Who is knowledgeable on the subject(s) your podcast covers. The host needs to be believable and promote a sense of authority on the subject matter.
5. Who relates to and appeals to your podcast's audience.
6. With interviewing skills (if your podcast will feature guests or take calls from listeners).
7. Who can stay on topic and not constantly go off on tangents that'll make the podcast's content hard to follow or understand.
8. Who has excellent chemistry with their co-host(s), if applicable. (Having good chemistry does not mean the co-hosts need to agree on everything. It simply means that they work well together in a way that's enjoyable for the audience to listen to.)

If the host will simply be reading a prepared script, and you want someone who sounds professional, consider hiring or teaming up with an experienced voice-over announcer.

You can find one through management agencies or online services that handle voice-over talent. As a producer, you can determine the type of voice you're looking for and then listen to demos.

If your plan is to host your own podcast, but you have no previous hosting or voice-over work experience, consider working with a vocal coach or experienced producer who can get you up to speed and help you practice and fine-tune your hosting and speaking skills. Before recording and publishing your first podcast episode, practice your hosting skills by recording several sample episodes and carefully evaluating how you sound.

For example, if you're reading from a script or teleprompter, does your voice sound natural? Speaking too quickly or too slowly, mumbling, inserting too many "ums" when speaking, and/or having too much or too little emotion in your voice are all common mistakes made by inexperienced hosts. All these problems can be fixed with practice.

A skilled producer will be able to fix minor issues within a voice-over track if a podcast is prerecorded (as opposed to streamed live). Issues like speech speed, pitch, the removal of unwanted pauses, and/or the removal of "ums" is a relatively easy process when using audio editing (postproduction) software.

tip

If you're looking to cast a professional voice-over actor or announcer as a host, as a co-host, or to create specific segments (or ads) for your podcast, consider visiting one or more of these services to help you find and hire the perfect announcer, host, or co-host:

- The Voice Realm— https://www. thevoicerealm.com
- Voice123—https:// voice123.com
- Voice Casting Hub— https://voicecastinghub. com
- VoiceJungle—www. voicejungle.com
- Voiceovers.com— https://voiceovers.com

If you're an expert in your field who is sharing what's perceived as valuable information within your podcast, your audience will likely be somewhat forgiving if your "on-air" presence is not up to par with a professional radio host. However, if your podcast follows more of a storytelling format, for example, and your audience expects quality equivalent to what they'd hear listening to a radio show, audiobook, or professional speaker, you may need to practice and fine-tune your hosting skills.

Meanwhile, to give your podcast an additional professional production element, consider hiring a professional announcer or radio jingle production company to create and record an intro and outro for your podcast.

▶ A Professionally Produced Intro and Outro Will Give Your Podcast Added Production Value

Investing a small amount of money to have a professional production company prerecord a highly produced intro and outro for your podcast is often a great investment. For example, use a professional voice-over person to announce the name of the podcast and introduce the host(s) with some attention-grabbing excitement and fanfare.

A pre-produced intro might sound like something you'd hear on FM radio and include voice effects, sound effects, and royalty-free music to capture your audience's attention at the very top of each podcast episode. A voice-only intro does not include voice effects, sound effects, or music, but features a professional announcer presenting your pre-written intro or outro (typically up to 15 seconds in length).

A company like Radio Voice Imaging (https://radiovoiceimaging.com), for example, will pre-produce a "sweeper" (intro or outro) that's up to 15 seconds in length, for $15. A package of ten sweepers is priced at $125. You can use a single sweeper as a general introduction to your podcast, or have a separate sweeper pre-produced for each podcast episode that includes the podcast name, introduces the host(s), and previews each separate episode's topic or theme.

The sweeper production company you work with will take your script, and with your direction, produce the content to appeal specifically to your target audience. To find other freelance production companies that can create attention-grabbing, professional-sounding sweepers for your podcast, using any internet search engine (such as Google or Yahoo!), enter the search phrase "sweeper radio production."

Some of the search results you'll discover will likely include: Push Button Productions (www.pushbuttonproductions.com), Longtrain Productions (www.longtrainproductions.com), and Audiobag (www.audiobag.com).

Many podcasters use announcers or an outside production company to produce ads or sponsorship messages to be heard during each episode. This helps to set that content apart from the main podcast, so your audience does not get confused about what content is part of the podcast's independent or unbiased content and what's paid or sponsored content.

One of the most powerful types of podcast ads is one where the host takes a handful of talking points from the advertiser and then ad-libs the advertisement, so it sounds like the host is sharing their personal thoughts, opinions, or review of a product or service in a way that leverages their credibility with the audience. These ads are not scripted word-for-word and tend to generate better responses from listeners, especially when the host is well-spoken and presents the ad in a conversational and believable way.

While you're not typically obligated to differentiate between your main content and paid or sponsored content that's presented in the form of an ad, advertorial, or message, to maintain the trust of your audience and produce a podcast that's perceived as ethical, it's best to be open, honest, and fully transparent with your audience when presenting information or content that's coming from an advertiser or sponsor.

Leave the Audience Wanting More

Each episode of your podcast will be a specific length. Depending on the format of your podcast, your target audience, and the information or content you plan to share, an episode length can be anywhere from 15 minutes to an hour or longer. Keeping in mind that your audience probably has a short attention span, keeping each episode of your podcast to between 15 and 30 minutes long will make it easier to keep their attention.

However, if you have a special guest and you're able to take live calls during an episode, or you have a panel discussion with multiple hosts and guests, you'll likely have little trouble filling a 30- to 60-minute episode with plenty of good content.

Choosing a longer podcast length gets tricky when you're a solo host sharing information directly with an audience with no guests or calls from audience members to break things up. It's very difficult for even a professional broadcaster to perform a monologue and keep an audience attentive and interested for more than a few minutes at a time, even if you have great information to share.

When choosing how long an episode of your podcast should be, always take your own ego out of the decision. Don't assume that people will enjoy listening to you speak for an unlimited amount of time, and that producing an extra-long podcast episode is doing your audience a favor. Instead, focus on the information you plan to share and

tip

Just like every other decision you make pertaining to the production of your podcast, episode length should be based on the makeup and expectations of your audience, as well as the information/content you plan to share and the show format your podcast will utilize. Especially if you're producing a prerecorded podcast, you have a lot of flexibility during postproduction to edit out repetitive, boring, or irrelevant content.

the show format you're using. Determine the ideal length for including all your planned content, without becoming boring or repetitive, based on your target audience and what their expectations are for your podcast.

Whatever average length you determine works best for your podcast, for the most part, be consistent. If your audience expects each episode to be 25 minutes long (which tends to be an optimal length for many types of podcasts), stick with that length from episode to episode. Of course, you're welcome to throw in an occasional "bonus double-length" episode once in a while if the content of that episode warrants it. It's always important to meet or exceed your audience's expectations based on the time commitment they expect to make listening to your podcast.

If you have 45 minutes' worth of really great and expertly produced content that covers a particular subject, for example, but your podcast episodes are typically 15 minutes long, seriously consider breaking up that content into three separate episodes and promoting each episode as part of a multipart series.

Set a Production Schedule That Won't Cause You to Overextend Yourself or Resources

When you are first planning your podcast, you may have a ton of awesome episode ideas and believe you can sustain producing and releasing new episodes multiple times per week. Don't be fooled! Creating just one amazing, well-produced, and expertly crafted podcast episode per week is likely going to be a time-consuming challenge. Don't take on more than you, your available resources, your schedule, and your budget can handle.

Each episode of your podcast will need to be planned, researched, written, recorded, edited, and uploaded to a podcast hosting service. You may also need to book guests and handle a wide range of other preproduction, production, and postproduction tasks in conjunction with each episode. Each of these steps or tasks takes time and cannot be rushed. Keep in mind, outsourcing some of these tasks will cost money, while handling them yourself will require an abundance of your time.

Consider starting with a one-episode-per-week schedule, for example, and make sure this is something

warning

As soon as your podcast's content and/or production quality loses its consistency from episode to episode, you'll also start losing subscribers and listeners. As a podcaster, do not promise or commit to more than you can handle! This also applies to your new episode release schedule.

you can handle for the first several months. Over time, you can occasionally include a bonus episode every few weeks. Also, before publishing your very first episode, prerecord the first three or four episodes, if possible, so that you have some scheduling flexibility moving forward.

One of the biggest mistakes you can make is promising your audience three, five, or seven new episodes per week, and then disappointing them when you determine you're only able to produce one or two episodes per week. Another way you can easily disappoint your audience is by promising five to seven episodes per week, and then to maintain that schedule, you produce really low-quality, poorly produced content for each episode. As soon as you adopt this approach, you can bet your audience size will quickly begin to shrink.

tip

Chapter 7, "Set Up Your Recording Studio," and Chapter 8, "Record Your Podcast Episodes," focus more on how to achieve the highest possible audio production quality, even if you're working with a tight budget.

By committing to a specific number of new episodes per week, you're promising your audience quality content that (you guessed it) will consistently meet or exceed their expectations. Whatever content and production quality you introduce to your audience starting with your podcast's very first episode must stay consistent or improve from episode to episode moving forward.

When focusing on meeting or exceeding your audience's expectations, you have a bunch of things to consider related to each new podcast episode. First, focus on the quality of the content or information. Are you presenting something new, unique, interesting, entertaining, and that your audience will perceive as valuable?

If applicable, consider the quality of your guests. Does the guest have a talent, area of expertise, or message that your audience will appreciate and enjoy? Will their presence on your podcast fit into your podcast's format and overall focus?

Also, always consider your podcast's production quality and do not compromise it. This includes the quality and clarity of the audio, music, sound effects, voice-overs, and all other elements. Again, production quality must remain consistent from episode to episode (and throughout each episode), or better yet, improve over time.

Keep in mind, as long as you're using a good quality microphone to capture your audio, you can use low-cost (and in some cases free) audio editing and postproduction software to make each episode sound amazing, if you're willing to invest the time.

Define Your Audience

Producing a podcast that doesn't attract an audience is an absolutely pointless endeavor. In order to attract an audience and then grow it over time, you'll need to develop a thorough understanding of exactly who you're trying to reach and why. As a podcaster, figure out what your podcast will offer to its intended audience and determine (in advance) why they'll perceive it as valuable. Then, decide how you'll expertly convey your content. Only by understanding your target audience will you be able to effectively promote it specifically to the people who'd most want to hear and ultimately subscribe to it.

A *target audience* is a group of people (i.e., your potential audience) who have one or more things in common, including an interest in the subject matter or focus of your podcast. As you'll discover, you can define a target audience in many ways. The more succinctly you define your podcast's target audience, the easier it'll be to produce and then promote it effectively.

In addition to the primary target audience for your podcast, it's likely that it'll also appeal to a secondary group of people. It'll become necessary to learn about and cater to this audience as well to further grow your podcast's audience while maintaining its core focus.

Simply defining the intended target audience for your podcast isn't enough. You need to invest time and effort to get to know this audience, who they are, where their interests lie, and their media consumption habits, for example. Moving forward, every decision you make pertaining to anything having to do with your podcast needs to focus on and address the wants and needs of your audience. When it comes to promoting your podcast so you can grow its audience, you'll ultimately need to become a niche marketing expert.

How to Define Your Target Audience

As a startup podcaster, it's easy to trick yourself into believing that your podcast will appeal to absolutely everyone, from all walks of life, and from all over the world. In most cases, however, this is *not* the case! Even if by some chance it is the case, catering to this massive audience in terms of creating content that'll appeal to everyone on an ongoing basis will be a nearly impossible task.

By carefully defining the target audience for your podcast, you'll have a much easier time creating your content and then marketing and promoting that content to people who will want to hear it. The question is, How do you define a target audience?

For starters, your podcast's target audience is comprised of people with an interest, fascination, or passion for the subject matter your podcast is about. Your audience will include people *willing* and *able* to invest the time to listen to your podcast episodes and who have the equipment and technical know-how to find and access it.

You can define a target audience in many ways beyond just their interest in your podcast's subject matter. The group of people you'll target can be grouped together and defined by any number of factors, including:

► Is Your Audience *Willing* and *Able*?

People who are *willing* to listen to your podcast are those with an interest in its subject matter and who will allocate time each week, for example, to enjoy it. People who are *able* to subscribe to and listen to your podcast are those with the right equipment (such as an internet-connected smartphone, tablet, computer, smart speaker, smartwatch, or smart TV) and the technical ability to use this equipment to find and access your podcast episodes.

The people in your podcast's target audience must be both willing and able to experience it. If a potential listener is willing, but does not have the right equipment, technical knowledge, or understanding of how podcasts work in general, those people likely won't become listeners.

Likewise, someone who is willing might have the right equipment, but have no clue how podcasts function, so they're not able to listen. For this segment of your potential audience, consider offering step-by-step directions on your podcast's website and social media feeds that explain exactly how to find and download or stream your podcast episodes. To reach this group, you'll likely need to take extra steps to educate people about podcasts in general.

- ► Age
- ► Education level
- ► Exercise/fitness habits
- ► Fashion preferences
- ► Favorite entertainment genre (e.g., Sci-Fi, Romance, Comedy, Horror, True Crime, Biography, History, or Mystery)
- ► Favorite TV shows, movies, books, music, actors, musicians, authors, etc.
- ► Gender
- ► Height
- ► Hobbies
- ► How they like to relax
- ► Income
- ► Marital status
- ► Media consumption habits
- ► Medical conditions, allergies, physical limitations
- ► Occupation
- ► Opinions/beliefs
- ► Overall intelligence or knowledge about a subject matter
- ► Personal goals or objectives

- ▶ Political affiliation
- ▶ Religion
- ▶ Social media habits
- ▶ Sexual orientation
- ▶ Type of vehicle they drive
- ▶ Weight
- ▶ Where they like to go on vacation
- ▶ Where they live

The more specific you are when defining your target audience, the better. For example, if your podcast is all about art collecting, your target audience might include people with an interest and knowledge about a specific genre of art who are college educated, have a $50K or higher annual income, live in a single-family home, drive a higher-end car, and have memberships to several museums.

Professionals who study demographic data to determine the target audience for various media outlets, products, and services, for example, combine *demographic data* with *location data* and *psychographic data* to develop a thorough understanding of a specific group.

Three services that can help you study and analyze demographic data are: Facebook IQ Audience Insights (www.facebook.com/business/insights/tools/audience-insights), Google Trends (https://trends.google.com/trends), and Synthesio (https://resources.synthesio.com).

When it comes to analyzing and determining a target audience, location data refers to information about the group's location or geography. Are you trying to reach people in a specific neighborhood (or neighborhood type), city, state, or country? A company called Claritas (https://claritas360.claritas.com/mybestsegments) offers a tool called MyBestSegments that can help determine and study a target audience's location and geography-related data.

Psychographic data relates to people's opinions, thought processes, and interests, for example. When analyzed in conjunction with demographic data and location data, it becomes easier to understand all aspects of an audience, including their preferences and behaviors.

Describe Your Podcast's Audience

Based on the previous list provided, think about who the core demographic is for your podcast. Mix and match the various criteria as appropriate so that when you're done, you have a very clear and precise description of your (niche) target audience. Start by listing at least 15 things about your intended audience that they all have in common. Use the questionnaire in Figure 4.1 on page 63 to help you get started.

Target Audience Questionnaire

The target audience for my podcast is primarily:

Between the ages of _____ and _____.

Gender: ❑ Male   ❑ Female   ❑ Other

Education Level:

   ❑ High School Graduate   ❑ College Graduate   ❑ Advanced Degree

Regularly Utilizes:

   ❑ Facebook   ❑ Instagram   ❑ Twitter   ❑ LinkedIn   ❑ Snapchat   ❑ TikTok

Earns at least $_____ per year.

Favorite Hobbies: _____

Political Beliefs or Affiliations: _____

Religious Beliefs or Affiliation: _____

What specific websites, podcasts, magazines, newspapers, TV shows, radio shows, etc. does your target audience currently utilize that cover similar content to what your podcast will offer? _____

_____

_____

_____

List at least five additional criteria that define your audience:

1. _____

2. _____

3. _____

4. _____

5. _____

FIGURE 4–1: **Target Audience Questionnaire**

▶ Don't Get Too General (or Specific)

If you decide your podcast will be about dogs, for example, you'll likely come to the obvious conclusion that your target audience is comprised of dog lovers—people from all walks of life, both male and female, from around the world, and of all ages—who are dog owners.

"Dogs" is a pretty broad topic, and stating that your podcast's audience is "dog enthusiasts" is also very broad. Instead, consider focusing your podcast on just one breed of dog, such as Yorkshire terriers, and focus on a niche audience comprised of Yorkshire terrier owners and enthusiasts. You'll discover a large niche audience exists that'd be interested in a podcast all about owning, raising, breeding, and training Yorkshire terriers, and you'll find plenty of related topics to cover.

However, if you were to produce a podcast specifically for Yorkshire terrier show dog owners that only covers the competitive aspect of preparing for and participating in dog shows, that niche audience is likely too small and specific, which will make it difficult to grow your audience.

Determine the Size of Your Potential Audience

Now that you know who comprises your target audience, it's necessary to perform some research (online or elsewhere) to determine the potential size of your audience and how you'll reach them. If the audience is too specific (niche) and you can't effectively reach your intended audience, your podcast's actual audience will be too small and have trouble growing. If the target audience is too large and broad, you may initially get people to listen, but if the content doesn't nicely fit their area(s) of interest, you'll wind up losing them quickly.

Promoting your podcast to grow its audience will require a significant and ongoing time commitment, and potentially a financial investment as well. Based on the resources you spend, you ideally want to get someone to listen regularly, subscribe to your podcast, plus hopefully share details about it through word-of-mouth (online and in the real world) with the people they know.

If you initially attract people to listen to your podcast, but after hearing a portion of one episode, they skip the rest and go elsewhere for similar content, you've done something wrong. For example, maybe you don't understand who the target audience is for your podcast and you're creating content for the wrong people, or your promotional efforts for the podcast are not reaching the appropriate people. Either way, figure out where the disconnect is and refocus those efforts.

One of the easiest ways to determine the potential audience size for your podcast is to research the size of similar podcasts targeting the same audience. A wide range of research tools are available that allow you to learn more about specific demographic audiences. For example, a company called Podtrac (http://analytics.podtrac.com/podcast-measurement) offers tools for measuring and predicting podcast audience sizes.

Pinpoint a Secondary Audience for Your Podcast

Once you've done your homework to pinpoint and then learn everything you can about your podcast's primary target audience, repeat these steps to determine if your podcast will also appeal to a slightly different, secondary target audience.

If applicable, take the steps required to carefully define this niche audience as well. Moving forward, as you make all podcast-related decisions, consider the wants and needs of your target audience *and* your podcast's secondary audience.

How Will You Reach Your Audience?

Knowing and truly understanding your target audience will allow you to make educated decisions when deciding what topics to cover and how you'll cover them. It'll also make it easier to handle production-related decisions, such as the selection of background music, since you'll know how you need the podcast to sound so that it'll appeal to a specific audience. These are all decisions that'll help you attract, keep, and grow your podcast's audience.

From a promotional standpoint, you'll need to adopt a multifaceted approach—online and in the real world—to educate your target audience about your podcast's existence, and then encourage those people to listen. As you'll discover, one of the great things about paid online advertising and free (and paid) social media marketing is that you can reach a very targeted audience with your promotional message.

The number-one most powerful and cost-effective way to promote your podcast and expand its audience is through word-of-mouth. Encourage your listeners, subscribers, and social media followers (online friends) to share details about the podcast with their (online) friends and family, and to rate/review it on the podcast directories and distribution services where your podcast is available. They should also be encouraged to post comments about the podcast.

The more you know about your target audience's interests, media consumption habits, and social media habits, for example, the more effectively you'll be able to promote your podcast to that group of people. Chapter 13, "12 Ways to Promote Your Podcast," offers details about numerous ways to promote your podcast to a niche target audience in a cost-effective way.

Figure Out What Your Podcast Will Offer Its Audience

As you're doing the preliminary brainstorming and planning for your podcast, and later when planning individual episodes, compose a written list that details everything your podcast (and each individual episode) will offer to its intended audience.

Answer questions like:

- ► Why should people listen and subscribe?
- ► What's in it for them?
- ► How will they benefit?
- ► How will your podcast improve the lives of your audience members, solve their problems, help them overcome obstacles, and/or make them happier, wealthier, or healthier, for example?
- ► What sets your podcast apart from others?
- ► Why will listeners perceive your content as valuable?
- ► Why will your show format be appealing to the audience?
- ► What information or content is being offered that's not available elsewhere?

Once you determine why people should listen, you can compose more compelling podcast and episode descriptions, plus know exactly what to say when discussing or promoting your podcast to potential listeners who are within your target audience.

Ways to Build a Loyal Audience

Getting people to listen to one episode of your podcast is a big enough challenge. However, once they start listening, your goal as a podcaster is to transform each listener into a loyal subscriber. Some ways to do this are:

- ► Cater your content to your audience.
- ► Encourage audience participation through submitting comments or questions via text message, email, or posts on social media. If your podcast is streamed live, you can also take calls from listeners.
- ► Request feedback from your audience and encourage people to suggest future episode topics or recommend guests.

- ▶ Create an online (moderated) community using social media, allowing your audience to interact with the podcast's producers, writers, hosts, and guests, as well as with each other. At the very least, stay active on social media.
- ▶ Incorporate contests with prizes into your podcast.
- ▶ Always promote the next episode of your podcast within the current episode. (Include a preview, if possible.) Get your audience excited about what's coming up next.
- ▶ Offer transcripts and detailed show notes, along with website links to companies, services, products, or associations you mention throughout each episode.
- ▶ Instead of or in addition to a dedicated Facebook page for your podcast, consider producing a regularly published, free electronic newsletter or blog that your listeners can subscribe to. Use this as a promotional tool and as an informal way to connect with your audience. What's featured within the newsletter or blog can delve deeper into topics discussed within podcast episodes, or cover related topics that are not specifically included within the podcast, but that the audience will also be interested in.

The more you interact with your audience, either directly within your podcast, using social media, or through your podcast's website, for example, the better you'll get to know the people listening. This will allow you to better cater to their wants and needs, and to better address your target audience. If done correctly, the result will be more loyal listeners!

▶ Consider Paying Established Social Media Influencers to Promote Your Podcast

There are social media influencers on YouTube, TikTok, Instagram, and countless other social media services that have extremely loyal and highly targeted audiences that sometimes reach into the tens of millions. One way to quickly build awareness for your podcast is to pay one or more of these influencers (who already reach your target audience) to promote your podcast. This can be done in a variety of creative ways. However, the more popular the social media influencer is, the more you'll have to pay them to promote your podcast.

When you access the online profile for any social media influencer, if they're interested in doing paid promotions, they'll typically list a "business contact" email address. Use this email address to reach out to them to discuss how you might work together, your budget, and the creative ideas you have that would allow you to tap their existing following to boost your podcast audience.

By catering to the wants and needs of your target audience and encouraging members of your audience to use word-of-mouth and social media to help you promote the podcast, you'll see your audience grow organically over time.

As you'll discover from Chapter 13, "12 Ways to Promote Your Podcast," you also can use your own resources to speed up the audience growth process. Some of these activities, such as targeted online advertising, paid social media marketing, or utilizing a public relations campaign, will require a financial investment, but if done correctly, will help you attract and grow your podcast's audience much faster.

Brand Your Podcast

Establishing a brand for your podcast is a way to differentiate it from the competition, and at the same time, better target it to your audience. Branding is all about creating a unique, attention-grabbing, memorable, and consistent audio and visual image that's distinguishable.

At this point, you should have completed a handful of podcast planning and brainstorming tasks, including:

- ▶ Choosing a title for your podcast.
- ▶ Creating a detailed description for it.
- ▶ Knowing the type and scope of the content you want to present.
- ▶ Determining the show format you'll use to present your content, as well as selecting your podcast's host(s).
- ▶ Pinpointing your podcast's target audience and learning as much as possible about that niche group.
- ▶ Brainstorming topics to cover for the first few months of episodes.
- ▶ Figuring out the types of guests (if applicable) you'd like to feature within your podcast.

With all the information you now have on hand about your new podcast, it's time to start creating its brand. Your podcast's brand will include audio and visual content that will help differentiate your podcast and make it identifiable to your audience.

For the podcast itself, this will include:

- ▶ Creating a logo (cover art).
- ▶ Properly utilizing the podcast's text-based description(s).
- ▶ Choosing appropriate intro/outro music for the podcast as a whole (to be used within all episodes).
- ▶ Writing and producing slogans and promos (including sweepers, show IDs, stingers, and other audio elements).
- ▶ Generally staying consistent with your podcast's format from episode to episode.

The brand you create for your podcast should be synergistic across all aspects of the podcast itself, as well as the content created for the podcast's website and social media feeds. All the branding decisions you make and adopt should cater to and appeal to your target audience. The color scheme, fonts, and typestyles used in your podcast's logo/cover art should coordinate with the visuals used throughout the podcast's website, for example.

Keep Branding Consistent

If you're creating a podcast as a sales, promotional, or marketing tool for an existing company, or using it to showcase and promote an individual, the brand for the podcast should adopt the already established branding created for the company, product, service, or individual. Stay consistent, on message, and targeted to the audience you know you're trying to reach.

What exactly is a *brand*? According to Wikipedia, "A brand is a name, term, design, symbol, or any other feature that identifies one seller's goods or services as distinct from those of other sellers. Brands are used in business, marketing, and advertising for recognition. Name brands are sometimes distinguished from generic or store brands." The concept of a brand also applies to podcasts and everything you'll be doing to promote and market your podcast to build its audience.

Companies, products, services, groups, events, associations/organizations, and individuals can all have a brand. How your podcast sounds (and all audio elements used within it), as well as the text and graphics used to identify and describe your podcast, all contribute to and support its (hopefully unique) brand.

Creating a brand that people (in this case your podcast's target audience) appreciate, like, and most important, trust takes time, planning, a lot of thought, and proper implementation. It'll likely take your audience listening to your podcast episodes over a period of weeks or months before they truly trust you (your hosts) and your content. As a podcaster, you'll want to carefully think about the brand and identity you create for your podcast, focusing on the relationship you hope to build with your audience.

Focus on the Audio and Visual Aspects of Your Podcast's Brand

The audio aspect of your podcast's brand includes *everything* your audience hears. The visual aspect of your podcast's brand relates to *everything* your audience sees. All audio and visual elements must fit perfectly together to promote your podcast's unique brand. Again, every audio and visual element used must also appeal to your target audience.

warning

A brand's positive reputation (in this case, your podcast and host's brand and reputation) will take weeks, months, or even years to establish, based on your content and target audience. This includes the trust people have associated with your podcast's content and its host(s).

However, a single mistake that somehow alienates or offends your audience (or if your host gets caught doing something that goes against the established brand) could easily tarnish or destroy your brand's positive reputation almost instantly. Once this happens, it's often very difficult (and sometimes impossible) to repair a tarnished brand and reputation, and then regain the trust of an audience. Protect the brand you create!

► Create a Slogan or Catchphrase

If you listen to almost any radio show on an AM, FM, or satellite radio station, one thing you'll hear every few minutes is the show's name, host's name, and radio station/network's name or call letters. This is conveyed using the same slogan(s), catchphrase, and/or jingle (including audio sweepers and stingers) that are heard over and over again throughout each broadcast. After creating a slogan or catchphrase for your podcast, use it often so it becomes an integral part of your identifiable brand.

In addition to or instead of a slogan, some of the world's most famous broadcasters have a unique tagline when opening or closing each of their broadcasts. This too can be a useful branding tool for your podcast and host(s).

For example, back in the day, newscaster Walter Cronkite ended each edition of *CBS Evening News* by saying, "And that's the way it is." For decades, radio personality Casey Kasem ended every episode of *American Top 40* by saying, "Keep your feet on the ground, and keep reaching for the stars. And keep your radio tuned right where it is." Most popular sportscasters also have their unique catchphrases that help differentiate them from their competition and make them more identifiable. Viewers of *The Tonight Show Starring Johnny Carson* would tune in nightly to hear Ed McMahon say, "Here's Johnny!" while fans of the original *Star Trek* series came to expect Mr. Spock to say, "Live long and prosper."

The right catchphrase can help define a podcast host and establish a brand for their podcast. You don't need a catchphrase, but if you brainstorm a catchphrase that works and that appeals to your audience, use it.

Just as many businesses and corporate brands have slogans, so can a podcast. For example, Nike's slogan is "Just Do It." Apple has spent billions on marketing and advertising telling people to "Think different," while L'Oréal cosmetics wants people to spend a little bit extra for their products by boosting their potential customers' self-esteem with the slogan "Because you're worth it." Allstate wants its customers to feel safe, so it uses the slogan "You're in good hands with Allstate." Millions of people visit the Disneyland theme park every year because it's known as "The happiest place on Earth."

If you opt to use a slogan to help market and promote your podcast, make it simple, easy to remember, attention-getting, and descriptive. You want your audience to instantly associate your slogan with your podcast and have positive thoughts going through their mind when this happens.

▶ **Create a Slogan or Catchphrase,** continued

Of course, your podcast does not need a catchphrase or a slogan starting on day one. It's something that might organically be created and used over time. It should not be forced. However, understand that once you come up with the right slogan or catchphrase, it can become an extremely valuable part of your podcast's overall brand.

The slogan you adopt for your podcast can be spoken by your host(s) during each episode, and in some cases, it might fit perfectly as the subtitle for the podcast itself.

Podcasters as well as business operators often make many common mistakes in creating and maintaining a brand. The biggest mistake is inconsistency in the brand's identity. Every episode of your podcast as well as all its podcast directory listings, web page content, and social media content should utilize the same name, logo (cover art), slogan, and color scheme. As for the audio content, the production quality and overall sound should stay consistent. For example, if you use a different podcast logo (cover art) as part of your podcast's listing within each podcast directory, and the podcast's website uses another logo design too, this goes against building an identifiable brand and it will confuse your audience.

tip

The brand you establish and ultimately promote for your podcast should identify and exhibit the core philosophy, beliefs, and goals of the podcast, its hosts, its producers, and its sponsors.

Unprofessional-looking visuals and low-quality (or inconsistent) audio production are two other common mistakes made by podcasters. It's also important to keep your branding straightforward and simple, so it's easy to understand and remember. Since you're trying to build trust with your (prospective) audience, the branding also needs to be believable. Don't make grandiose statements, claims, or inferences that are untrue, embellished, or misleading. For example, describing your host as "The world's leading expert on [insert podcast subject]" when they're not is a misrepresentation that listeners will ultimately resent.

Creating a Logo and Cover Artwork

Every podcast needs a logo or cover artwork associated with it. This is a visual that gets displayed as part of a podcast's listing within every podcast directory. It's also seen on the screen when someone is listening to a podcast's episode using a podcast player application on their smartphone, tablet, computer, smartwatch, or smart TV, for example.

Just like a company or product logo, your podcast's logo (cover art) is a visual that should quickly identify your podcast. It can include an original graphic design, photography, or other visual elements, but most important, it should appeal to your target audience, be unique, be easily identifiable, and be memorable.

Some podcast logos/cover artwork designs include a photo of the host(s) as well as the podcast's title. Others showcase a unique graphic design or a text-based message that utilizes a specific and identifiable typestyle/font.

The logo or cover artwork for your podcast is something that needs to look professional. In other words, if you do not have a graphic arts background, and you're not particularly creative when it comes to creating art designed to appeal to a specific audience, seriously consider hiring a professional logo designer or graphic artist to help you brainstorm and create the perfect logo and/or cover artwork.

When hiring a freelance logo designer or graphic artist, find someone willing to work on a flat-fee basis (as opposed to by the hour). Also, when creating a freelance contract, make sure you stipulate how many different logo/cover art design options will be created initially for you to consider, and then how many revisions to the selected design will be included in the flat-fee price.

Be sure to have a detailed discussion with the graphic artist during which you clearly describe your podcast and your target audience, as well as provide some initial design ideas that you may already have. Assuming you have some idea about what you want your podcast's logo/cover art to look like, review the portfolios of at least five to ten different freelance graphic artists and choose to work with someone who has an artistic style that fits what you're looking to have created.

tip

As you're brainstorming a logo or cover artwork design for your podcast, study what works. Visit a popular podcast directory, access a listing of the current most popular podcasts, and check out the logo or artwork associated with each of them. For example, start your research by visiting The Stitcher List— Top Shows listing (https://www.stitcher.com). From this listing, you'll discover the most popular podcasts, their respective ranking for the current week, their logo or cover artwork, their title, their genre/category, and their respective rank change from the previous week.

During your negotiations with the freelance graphic designer, in addition to settling on a flat-rate price for the work to be done (which should be listed in the contract), the written contract (or freelance agreement) should include:

▶ A written description of the project itself, as well as your expectations.

▶ The deadline for the project. For example, you may have a deadline for the initial concepts, and then another for the final logo/cover artwork to be completed.

▶ A statement that ensures the artwork being created will be 100 percent original and not violate anyone else's trademarks or copyrights.

▶ A statement that indicates that you (the client) will have full ownership of the logo design or artwork, which you can then obtain a copyright or trademark for in your name. The artist will retain no legal rights to the design or work whatsoever.

▶ The rate that will apply if additional revision or work needs to be done beyond what's initially agreed to. This hourly or per-revision rate should be pre-negotiated.

▶ That the final artwork should be supplied to you in electronic form (as a digital file in the industry standard file format you want).

▶ That the artist will provide a list of the exact fonts, typestyles, and colors used within the logo or cover artwork.

You do not need to hire a lawyer to draft a contract between you and the freelance artist, but you do want to create something in writing that both parties date and sign, so that you properly convey your expectations and both parties have the same understanding of what the project will entail.

The cost of a professionally designed logo or cover artwork will range from $50 to several hundred dollars, depending on the complexity of your needs, the qualifications of the freelance graphic artist you hire, and where you hire them from. While you can typically expect to pay top dollar if you hire someone from a well-established advertising, marketing, or graphic arts agency, you can often save a fortune by hiring a freelancer from an online service, such as:

▶ 99designs—www.99designs.com

▶ DesignCrowd—www.designcrowd.com

▶ Fiverr—www.fiverr.com

▶ Freelancer.com—https://www.freelancer.com

▶ Upwork—www.upwork.com

If you're on a tight budget, another option for finding a skilled, freelance graphic artist is to contact a local graphic arts school's internship department. You'll likely discover a wide selection of up-and-coming graphic artists looking to expand their professional portfolios.

Online services and software packages designed to help amateur artists create their own logos are also available, but the end results are seldom as professional-looking as what you'd wind up with if you hire an experienced graphic designer. Since your podcast's logo/cover artwork will be used in so many ways as a marketing, promotional, and branding tool, this is something you want to invest the time and money into so you get it right.

Every podcast directory will have specific electronic file guideline requirements for uploading a logo or cover art. Make sure the graphic artist you hire provides the file format(s) you need to meet the requirements of the podcast directories and/or hosting services you plan to work with. Keep in mind, you'll want to use the same artwork within your podcast's own website and social media feeds.

Choosing the Perfect Music

As a podcaster, the main way you'll be providing content to your audience is using audio. Whether it's through spoken words, music, sound effects, singing, or some other content that your audience listens to, the quality of the content itself and the quality of the audio production are equally important. Once again, consistency in quality is key.

How your podcast sounds and what your audience hears both contribute to its overall brand and directly impact whether your target audience will appreciate and enjoy your content.

Some things you can do to develop the audible brand for your content include:

▶ Producing attention-grabbing stingers and sweepers that identify your podcast's title and potentially the host's name. These short, highly produced elements might feature a professional announcer along with vocal and sound effects.

▶ Utilizing memorable and appropriate intro/outro music. If you have the budget, hire a professional musician to compose and record something original. Otherwise, acquire the rights to royalty-free music. Remember, in most cases and without written permission, you can't simply use your favorite song from your favorite band/recording artist or use any music that violates other people's copyrights within your podcast.

The intro and outro music you use should be 30, 60, or 90 seconds long. Ideally it should be instrumental, so the host(s) and/or announcer can easily talk over the music. The genre, volume, and tempo of the music, for example, should also be appropriate to your content and appeal to your audience. The music should complement whatever the host(s) or announcer says, and not be overbearing or distracting. This also applies to any background or transitional music heard throughout each episode.

warning

The music you choose to play at the top of each podcast episode can help lure someone in, grab their attention, and set the tone for the whole episode. It can just as easily distract someone or cause them to exit out of your podcast immediately.

Finding and selecting the perfect intro/outro and/or background music probably won't be an easy decision, because it will play a huge role in defining your podcast's brand and audience appeal. Keeping in mind that the attention span of your audience will be very short, a new listener might listen to just 15 to 30 seconds of a podcast episode before deciding whether they should stick to it and listen to the whole thing or find something else to listen to.

Likewise, appropriate background music can be used behind your podcast's main content to set the tone and pace of the episode and to help retain your audience's attention. When mixing background music into your podcast episodes, pay attention to the volume, tempo, and overall appropriateness of the music.

If the selected music is too loud or incompatible, for example, your audience won't be able to hear what's being said or discussed, and they'll quickly lose interest or believe that your podcast offers unprofessional, low-quality production. Using music with lyrics (singing), as opposed to instrumental music, can also easily become distracting to your audience. It could also be a potential copyright violation.

Understand that you'll likely want to add any background music during postproduction, not while recording the spoken audio for your podcast episodes. You'll learn more about adding background music to your podcast within Chapter 9, "Edit Your Podcast Like a Pro."

Remember, you also need the legal rights to use whatever music you select to include within your podcast. Again, unless you are a musician with access to a recording studio (or you know someone who is), you'll probably need to rely on royalty-free music from a production music library.

Instead of hiring a musician to write and record original music for your podcast (which can be costly), for a low and flat fee, you can acquire the rights to use music from a royalty-free production library. This is professionally produced music that's already been composed and recorded, and that's ready to be mixed into your podcast.

Instead of paying a per-use royalty each time the music is used (based on the size of the audience and other factors), seek out royalty-free music, so you pay a predetermined flat fee for the use of the selected music or track. In some cases, production music is offered copyright-free and there is no charge whatsoever to use it, but more often than not, you'll be required to pay a small fee for each music track you want to use.

The easiest way to find royalty-free production music that you like is to launch your favorite web browser, and within the search field, type "royalty-free podcast production music." You'll discover hundreds of stock music catalogs you can browse through and preview online. Remember, in most cases, you will need to pay a one-time licensing fee to use each music track.

A few of the online-based, royalty-free music catalogs you'll find include:

- AudioJungle— https://audiojungle.net/category/all
- Epidemic Sound—www.epidemicsound.com
- Melody Loops—www.melodyloops.com
- Music Vine—www.musicvine.com
- PremiumBeat by Shutterstock— www.premiumbeat.com
- Soundsnap—www.soundsnap.com
- Soundstripe—www.soundstripe.com
- Storyblocks—www.storyblocks.com

After visiting any one of these online-based services, select the Browse Music (or equivalent) option, and then choose a genre or music tempo to start previewing tracks that are available. For example, you'll discover instrumental music genres like: Acoustic, Ambient, Blues, Classical, Corporate, Country, Easy Listening, Indie Pop, Latin, New Age, News, Piano/Solo Instrumental, Pop, R and B, Rock, Trailer, or World. Start with a genre that fits your content and your podcast's brand.

You'll typically be able to preview one music track at a time. You'll see the track's title, duration, beats-per-minute (BPM), length, and whether the music seamlessly loops. After listening to dozens, perhaps hundreds, of tracks, choose ones that fit your podcast perfectly for its intro and/or outro. This is also music you might play leading up to a commercial break during an episode.

tip

An online service called Free Music Archive (www. freemusicarchive.org) offers a vast collection of copyright-free music tracks for use within online media projects that are created by musicians and recording artists around the world who have chosen to share their work through this open-source community. Be sure you understand what legal rights and permissions are being granted by Free Music Archive, based on how you plan to use the music. This is all explained on the service's website. Visit https://www. freemusicarchive.org/ License_Guide for more information.

When you find the perfect track, purchase the royalty-free rights and then download the digital music file. You can then incorporate and mix in the music during the production or postproduction phase of your podcast's recording process. If it's not offered for free, the cost per track could be anywhere from less than $10 to several hundred dollars.

With just a little bit of research, you'll find thousands of music tracks you could potentially use within your podcast. The benefit to recording your own original music is that it'll be exclusive to your podcast and you'll own its copyright. Thus, you can use the music whenever, wherever, and as often as you'd like. Original music helps to define and establish your podcast's brand more easily.

tip

Some of the online-based music production libraries use a monthly subscription model. As long as you continue paying the subscription fee (typically between $20 and $50 per month), you're able to use as many music tracks from the collection as you'd like within your podcast.

The drawback to using free music, or paying for royalty-free music, is that the same tracks are available to all podcasters, TV producers, radio producers, and movie producers, for example, so there's no exclusivity. You also may be limited to where, when, or how individual music tracks can be used. With creative postproduction when editing your podcast episodes, you can utilize music from a royalty-free production library, for example, in ways that will make the podcast sound more unique, but you still won't own the exclusive right to use the selected music.

To avoid getting sued for copyright infringement as a result of including music within your podcast that you did not have permission to use, consider brushing up on the copyright laws related to podcasting and music use.

The Ari's Take blog (www.aristake.com/how-to-get-music-in-podcasts-and-make-moneylegally) offers some useful information. Another excellent resource for legal information pertaining to the use of music in podcasts can be found on the ASCAP website (www.ascap.com/help/ascap-licensing).

Leverage Your Brand

The unique brand you create for your podcast can later be leveraged in many ways when it comes to marketing and promoting your podcast, creating content for your audience outside of the podcast, and developing additional revenue streams. For example, your podcast's unique logo, cover art, slogan, or catchphrase could be printed on merchandise (such as T-shirts, hoodies, stickers, and coffee mugs) and sold to your listeners and fans.

As you'll read later in Chapter 11, "More Ways to Generate Income from Your Podcast," you can leverage your podcast's brand and reputation to earn more money. For example, if you grow a large and loyal audience, sponsors and advertisers will be willing to pay you more. You could also potentially charge guests a premium to appear on your podcast to promote themselves and/or their company, plus earn more from paid public speaking engagements. Opportunities for podcasts to be transformed into TV series, movies, books, or documentaries also exist. With a well-established and identifiable brand, combined with a large and loyal audience, the additional moneymaking opportunities are virtually limitless.

The Cost
of Podcasting

As with any type of business venture, both startup costs and then ongoing costs are associated with podcasting. These costs relate to launching, producing, maintaining, and promoting a podcast. On the plus side, thanks to ongoing advances in technology, these costs tend to be very low, which means fewer barriers to entry exist.

The Production Equipment You'll Likely Require

The largest one-time expense associated with launching a podcast involves acquiring the right recording and production equipment. To save money, do some research and only purchase what you need to get started. You can always upgrade your equipment later. The exact collection of studio and recording equipment you'll need will vary greatly, based on the type of podcast you'll be recording and the format of your show.

At the core of your home, work, or remote recording studio will likely be a Windows PC or Mac computer (either a desktop or a notebook computer). You do *not* need one of the latest, most cutting-edge, fully equipped computers to produce an audio podcast. The computer will, however, need a large capacity hard drive for digital audio file storage.

Instead of purchasing a brand-new computer or paying to upgrade the internal hard drive of your existing computer, for less than a hundred dollars, you have the option of linking a 1TB or 2TB external hard drive to your computer, which will provide the additional storage space you'll need for your digital audio files. From a technical standpoint, investing in an SSD (Solid State Drive) from a popular manufacturer offers a faster read/write speed, but often at a slightly higher cost.

Companies like Seagate (www.seagate.com) and Western Digital (www.westerndigital.com) offer a selection of external hard drive options. You can purchase an external hard drive from any consumer electronics retail store, but you can often save money by shopping online.

> **warning** ⚠
>
> If you'll be producing a video-based podcast with episodes more than five minutes long that'll need to be edited, a powerful computer with a fast processor, a decent amount of RAM, a powerful graphics card, and a massive hard drive (for digital video file storage) will be needed. The technical requirements for recording and editing just audio on a computer, however, are a lot lower.

One-Time Expenses

In addition to a computer, perhaps your largest upfront cost will relate to purchasing one or more microphones. As a podcaster, capturing the highest quality audio possible is essential, so invest in the best quality microphone(s) you can afford.

Depending on the show format of your podcast and where you'll be recording, you may need to acquire two or more microphones. Specific types of microphones are designed to capture and record specific types of audio in specific situations. Choosing the right type of microphone(s) for your needs is important. Within Chapter 7, "Set Up Your Recording Studio," you'll learn how to select the appropriate type of microphone(s) for your podcasting needs.

Initially, you might get away with investing between just $100 and $300 on a decent-quality microphone that connects directly to your computer via its USB port. However, as your audience grows and your podcast starts generating more revenue, you'll likely want to upgrade your microphone(s) to achieve higher-quality audio recordings.

A professional-level microphone will cost at least $300, depending on the microphone type and manufacturer. (You can easily, however, spend thousands on a single microphone, but for a podcaster, this typically isn't necessary.) Keep in mind, a separate audio interface that links the microphone(s) to the computer or digital audio recorder and that converts the analog audio to digital audio will also likely be necessary, especially if you'll be recording with a higher-end microphone or multiple microphones simultaneously.

While some microphones can connect directly to your computer via its USB port, allowing you to control the recording levels for a microphone using the recording software running on your computer, if you'll be recording with two or more microphones simultaneously, or want additional control over the microphones during the recording process, you'll likely need to purchase an audio interface or multichannel mixing board. This device connects between your computer and microphone(s). The price for a basic audio interface will vary greatly based on its quality and capabilities, but for a startup podcaster, plan on spending at least $100 to $300 for an audio interface with multiple microphone or audio inputs.

> **tip**
>
> Along with your selected microphone(s), additional equipment that may be required includes a microphone stand, a microphone pop screen (also referred to as a pop filter or wind screen), compatible cables, and an audio interface.

If you'll be recording your podcast while on the go, or recording on-location interviews, for example, and need to be very mobile, instead of using your computer as your primary recording studio, you may want and need to invest in a high-end, portable digital audio recorder from a company like Tascam (www.tascam.com), Sony (www.sony.com), Marantz (www.marantz.com), or Olympus (www.olympus.com). Once you record your raw audio, those digital files can then be transferred to your computer for editing, mixing, and other related postproduction tasks.

Another "must have" piece of equipment needed by all podcasters are good stereo headphones (ideally with noise-canceling capabilities). After all, it's necessary to hear and

▶ Your Smartphone or Tablet Can Serve as a Digital Audio Recorder

By connecting a high-quality microphone and using an appropriate audio recording mobile app with your iPhone, iPad, or Android-based smartphone or tablet, this equipment can also be used to capture high-quality audio on location. Companies like Shure (www.shure.com) offer versatile as well as specialty microphones that will connect directly to the USB-C or Lightning port of your mobile device. Ultra-portable audio interfaces for use with mobile devices (such as a smartphone or tablet) are also available. These allow you to connect virtually any professional-quality microphone to your mobile device to capture high-quality recordings while on the go.

To find appropriate audio recording mobile apps, if you're an iPhone/iPad user, visit the App Store. Android smartphone or tablet users should visit the Google Play store. Within the search field, enter the search phrase "audio recording" or "podcast recording." Be sure to check out mobile apps like Anchor, Ferrite Recording Studio, PodRecord, Podcast Studio, and/or Mobile Podcaster. Specialty apps for recording phone calls (interviews) via your smartphone are also available.

monitor what you're recording, and then be able to focus only on that recorded content during the postproduction phase when you're editing your audio for each episode. As with any type of equipment, headphone prices range from around $50 to several hundred dollars.

When purchasing headphones, focus on sound quality, comfort, noise-canceling capabilities, mobility, whether the headphones are wireless or wired, and price. Keep in mind, higher-end headphones from a premium name brand, like Bose, will typically cost more than similar quality headphones from a lesser known or not as prestigious brand, even though the functionality may be similar. It's best to try out headphones firsthand before making a purchase.

Some of the popular headphone manufacturers that offer headphones used by podcasters include: Audio-Technica (www.audio-technica.com), Beats (www.beatsbydre.com), Bose (www.bose.com), Sony (www.sony.com/electronics/headphones), Skullcandy (www.skullcandy.com), Panasonic (https://shop.panasonic.com/audio-and-video/headphones), Harman Kardon (www.harmankardon.com), and Sennheiser (https://en-us.sennheiser.com).

Also, depending on your audio recording needs (based on your podcast's show format, for example), it may become necessary to build a soundproof recording booth or studio in your home or office to achieve the audio quality you're striving for (and to avoid recording unwanted ambient sounds). Soundproofing requires you to purchase and install soundproofing materials for your walls and ceilings, for example.

Building a small soundproof recording booth for one or two people is not too expensive, but creating a full, room-size soundproof recording studio can get costly. Many types of soundproofing options and materials are available. If you have a large production budget, a WhisperRoom sound booth (www.whisperroom.com), for example, starts in price at $3,900. However, individual panels of soundproofing foam that can easily be mounted on walls or ceilings will cost as little as $50 per panel.

Using the search phrase "build a sound booth" or "build a vocal booth" on YouTube, you'll discover a collection of how-to videos that explain how to build a one- or two-person soundproof recording booth for just a few hundred dollars. Meanwhile, using any search engine (such as Google or Yahoo!), enter the search phrase "soundproofing foam" to find companies selling soundproofing materials.

Aside from the physical recording and audio production equipment you'll likely need, specialized software to handle the recording, audio editing, mixing, and other postproduction tasks associated with creating a podcast is also required. This required software ranges in price from free to several hundred dollars.

One of the most widely used audio recording and editing applications (aka audio work-station applications) for Windows PCs and Macs is called Audacity (www.audacityteam.org). This is open-source software that's available for free, yet it offers the same features, functions, and capabilities provided by professional audio recording and editing applications that cost hundreds of dollars. As you're first getting started, if you'll be recording and editing your podcast episodes on a computer, consider using this software. Other options are discussed in Chapter 8, "Record Your Podcast Episodes," and Chapter 9, "Edit Your Podcast Like a Pro."

Ongoing Production-Related Expenses

Some of the other production-related expenses you might have as you begin creating episodes of your podcast will be optional and will vary based on your show format, target audience, and goals. First and foremost, you want to focus on production quality. Make sure you're creating content that will meet or exceed your audience's expectations in terms of production quality, what you'll be covering during each episode, and the approach you'll take to present your content.

That being said, some of the production-related expenses you might need to incur (and that should potentially be budgeted for) include:

▶ Hiring a professional and experienced producer, recording engineer, and/or audio editor. These tasks might be handled by one person or delegated to several people.

Depending on your own level of experience and knowledge of the topic your podcast will be covering, prerecording each episode might take two to three times longer than each episode's actual length. Then, you could easily spend another three to five hours editing each 15- to 30-minute episode, which includes handling postproduction tasks, like cleaning up the vocal (voice-over) tracks, mixing in music and sound effects, and then uploading the edited episodes to your chosen podcast hosting service.

▶ Hiring an announcer to record your podcast's introduction, closing credits, and/or ads (and sponsorship messages).

▶ Hiring a host and/or co-host.

▶ Hiring writers and/or a guest booker, depending on your skills and experience.

▶ Hiring a production company to record and produce audio stingers, IDs, and other audio elements used in each episode to help brand your podcast.

▶ Licensing fees associated with music and sound effects to be used within your podcast, including intro, outro, and background music.

▶ Hiring a graphic artist/logo designer to create a logo or cover artwork for your podcast. You may then want to acquire a copyright and/or trademark for that original artwork.

▶ Paying an ongoing fee to your podcast hosting service. (In some cases, this is free, but most companies charge. For example, the Basic podcast hosting services from SoundCloud are free, but a $12 to $16 monthly fee applies for the company's Pro Unlimited hosting and distribution services.

Some startup podcasters choose to hire a full-service podcast production company to handle almost all of a podcast's production and postproduction needs. An example of one such company is Podcast Buddy, which you'll learn more about from Chapter 9, "Edit Your Podcast Like a Pro." To find others, simply enter the search phrase "podcast production companies" into any internet search engine (such as Google).

Additional Podcasting Expenses

Producing an awesome podcast is only the first step toward building an audience and potentially generating revenue from your efforts. The biggest podcast-related time and financial expense outside of production-related activities will be spent promoting your podcast. This is something that needs to be done on an ongoing basis.

As you'll learn from Chapter 13, "12 Ways to Promote Your Podcast," generating word-of-mouth publicity via your audience is free, as is promoting your podcast using social media (Facebook, Instagram, Twitter, etc.). Depending on your goals and budget, however, you may need to pay for online advertising and real-world advertising.

Another ongoing expense will be the cost of creating, maintaining, and hosting a website for your podcast, which is optional, but highly recommended. You'll also have fees associated with your high-speed internet service, which is a necessity for all podcasters. If you want custom email addresses for your hosts and producers (e.g., username@ YourPodcastName.com), there will be a monthly or annual fee associated with this, as well as an annual fee to register one or more domain name addresses (URLs) for your podcast's website (and email service).

Based on your technical know-how, you may need to hire (and pay for) a social media expert to help manage your podcast's online promotional activities and interactions with your audience. It may also be necessary to hire a website designer to help create, publish, and then update the podcast's website. Of course, you can learn to do these activities on your own, but each needs to be done correctly and consistently, which requires a potentially significant time commitment.

Once you decide to include advertising or solicit sponsorships for your podcast in order to generate revenue, you may want or need to hire someone (or an agency) with experience to solicit and sell those ads or sponsorships, plus manage those relationships and produce the ads. You'll learn more about your options from Chapter 10, "Monetizing Your Podcast," but keep in mind, you'll likely need to pay someone to handle these tasks and/or pay a commission to an agency that helps coordinate ad placement or sponsorships.

During the planning stages of your podcast, once you know what your podcast's objectives and production requirements will be, you'll better be able to determine your upfront and ongoing costs. Since a lot will depend on your goals for the podcast, the frequency you'll be releasing new episodes, and your show format, it's important to iron out these details before trying to determine your startup and ongoing operating budget.

Production Budget Forecasting Worksheet

Based on the potential expenses outlined in this chapter, use the worksheet in Figure 6.1 on page 88 to help create a realistic startup and ongoing production budget for your podcast.

Podcast Budget Worksheet

Expense Description	Upfront Cost ($)	Ongoing Monthly (or Per Episode) Cost ($)	Notes
Advertising and sponsorship sales			
Audio editing and production software			
Audio engineer/editor salary			
Audio interface			
Audio stinger/promo production			
Cables (for computer and audio equipment)			
Computer			
External hard drive			
Guest booker salary			
Headphones			
Host salary			
Internet service			
Legal services			
Logo/cover artwork design			
Microphone accessories			
Microphone(s)			
Office expenses (printer, phone service, letterhead, business cards, office supplies, etc.)			
Ongoing advertising and promotion expenses			

FIGURE 6–1: **Podcast Budget Worksheet**

Podcast Budget Worksheet

Expense Description	Upfront Cost ($)	Ongoing Monthly (or Per Episode) Cost ($)	Notes
Podcast hosting service fees			
Portable digital audio recorder			
Producer salary			
Soundproofing supplies and equipment			
Website creation, management, and hosting fees (including email accounts)			
Writer salary			
Additional advertising/ marketing/PR expenses			
Additional equipment acquisition			
Additional salary for staff and freelancers			
	Total: $	Total: $	

FIGURE 6–1: **Podcast Budget Worksheet,** continued

Set Up Your Recording Studio

Among the biggest attractions to becoming a podcaster are the low startup costs. If you already have a computer, you can use free recording/postproduction software (such as Audacity). You'll then require only a small collection of additional recording equipment to get started. Plus, while working with a professional audio engineer and/or production company would definitely be beneficial, you'll likely be able to handle all the key production tasks yourself with a small amount of training and a bit of practice.

Analyze Your Podcast to Determine Your Needs

Before investing any money in recording or production equipment, understand that no perfect "home studio" or "remote" recording solution fits the needs of every podcaster. Next, keep in mind that whatever your needs turn out to be, low-cost, mid-priced, and high-cost solutions are always available to you.

Once you brainstorm the overall concept for your podcast and determine what the show format will be, think about where you'll be doing your recording. Will you be recording at home or at work, will you be doing most of your recording on location, or do you have the budget to record in a professional studio?

▶ The Pro Studio Recording Option

Choosing to record your podcast in a professional recording studio has a handful of benefits. First, you'll likely have access to state-of-the-art equipment, so your podcast's production quality will be top-notch. Second, the studio will likely include a skilled and experienced audio engineer to handle the equipment for you and perform many of the production and postproduction tasks required for your podcast.

When seeking out a professional studio to work with, make it clear you'll be producing a podcast (as opposed to music), and describe the format and needs of your show. In addition to the recording, how much postproduction will the studio you hire be responsible for? How quick of a turnaround will you require?

Based on the frequency you'll be recording and editing new episodes, negotiate a discount. Recording studios can be very flexible with their pricing, especially if you become a regular customer and you're willing to work during hours when the studio isn't otherwise busy.

A less expensive option is to seek out an audio engineer/producer who has their own home recording studio. While the equipment won't likely be as elaborate as what you'd find in a professional recording studio, chances are what a home studio offers will be more than sufficient for your podcast production needs. In this case, the skills and experience of the audio engineer/producer are what should be of utmost importance to you as a podcaster.

If you choose to handle your own recording and postproduction, after determining where you'll be doing your recording, think about how many people you'll need to record at the same time during each episode.

In general, to achieve the highest quality recordings, each host and guest should always use their own microphone. Thus, if you'll be using two or more microphones during a typical recording session, you'll also need an audio interface which the microphones connect to. This interface then connects directly to your computer (the hub of your home recording studio) and allows you to control those microphones.

You'll also need to choose recording software, plus utilize a handful of related equipment and accessories, such as microphone cables, microphone stands, pop filters for the microphones, and headphones.

By using your computer (either a Windows PC or Mac) as the hub of your home recording studio, as recordings are made, the raw digital audio files will be stored directly on your computer's hard drive (or on a connected hard drive). You can then edit these files and handle your postproduction needs on that same computer.

In addition to your recording and production equipment, you'll need to carefully analyze the space where you'll be recording. Does that space need to be soundproofed to eliminate unwanted ambient noise?

As you'll discover shortly, even if your recording space does have some ambient noise that you can't eliminate prior to recording, the microphone you choose may have the ability to cancel out or not capture some of this noise. Plus, the postproduction (editing) software you use will have tools and digital filters for eliminating some or all of the unwanted sound.

If your podcast requires you to record on location, chances are you won't want to lug around your computer, microphones, an interface, and all the related equipment. In this situation, you have a wide range of recording options, which include connecting a professional-quality microphone to your smartphone or tablet and using that as your digital recorder, or investing in a stand-alone, multitrack digital recorder that allows you to simultaneously record two or more microphones on separate tracks.

Again, first figure out your podcast's needs, and then work with an audio engineer to help you select the ideal recording and production equipment to meet those needs and your budget. If you don't have an audio engineer to help make these decisions, you'll need to do your own research to find the best equipment at the best prices.

Gathering the Required Equipment

After defining the ongoing needs for your podcast, make sure your Windows PC or Mac will be able to serve as the hub for your recording studio. In other words, it needs to have plenty of available hard drive storage space, include a decent processor, and meet the technical requirements of the software you'll be using.

To determine the system requirements for Audacity and then download the free software, visit one of these web pages:

- ▶ Windows PC—www.audacityteam.org/download/windows
- ▶ Mac—https://www.audacityteam.org/download/mac

Once you know the recording and postproduction software you've chosen will run on your computer, focus on the rest of the recording and production equipment you'll need. Based on your available budget, you can go with lower-end, inexpensive equipment (such as microphones), but your production quality could be compromised somewhat. While some podcasters can get away with using $50 microphones that plug directly into their computer via USB, this is not typically the best solution if your goal is to offer professional-quality audio and radio-quality production.

If you don't have the funds to buy higher-end microphones and equipment new, consider seeking out used (or manufacturer refurbished) equipment. Besides eBay, Amazon Marketplace, and Craigslist (where you can buy all sorts of used goods online, including recording and audio production equipment), a handful of companies specialize in buying and selling used audio and recording equipment, including:

- ▶ Adorama—www.adorama.com/l/Used/Audio
- ▶ Audiogon—www.audiogon.com
- ▶ B&H Photo Video—www.bhphotovideo.com/c/browse/Pro-Audio/ci/2875
- ▶ Guitar Center—www.guitarcenter.com/Used/Recording-Gear.gc
- ▶ Sweetwater—www.sweetwater.com/used/categories/studio-recording
- ▶ Equipment manufacturers—Visit the equipment manufacturer's website to see if they sell online directly to customers, and if they offer manufacturer refurbished equipment at a discount.

While you'll often receive much more personalized customer service and advice from an in-person salesperson working at a retail store that specializes in recording and studio production equipment, you'll typically save money by shopping online from reputable companies, such as Adorama (800-223-2500, www.adorama.com) and B&H Photo Video (800-606-6969, www.bhphotovideo.com). Both of these companies offer free phone-based sales assistance from knowledgeable people.

Again, before purchasing any recording or audio production equipment, after defining your needs, do some online research to determine what's available and at what price point. The list of companies in Figure 7.1 on page 95 will help you get started with your research:

Breakdown of Audio Equipment Companies

Company	Website	Type of Equipment Offered
Audio-Technica	www.audio-technica.com	Microphones and related accessories
Blue	www.bluedesigns.com	Mid-priced microphones, headphones, and other podcasting equipment
Focusrite	www.focusrite.com	Audio interfaces and (also offers podcasting/home studio recording equipment bundles.)
Rode Microphones	www.rode.com	Microphones, microphone accessories, and audio interfaces
Shure	www.shure.com	Microphones, microphone accessories, headphones, and podcasting-related production/recording equipment
Tascam	www.tascam.com	Digital audio interfaces, portable multitrack audio recorders, microphones, headphones, and other podcasting equipment
Zoom	https://zoomcorp.com/en/us/	Audio interfaces and multitrack recorders

FIGURE 7–1: **Breakdown of Audio Equipment Companies**

Choosing Your Microphone(s)

In addition to going with the general rule that every person who is being recorded should be speaking into their own microphone, as a podcaster, it's important to invest in the right type(s) of microphones based on what you'll be recording and where you'll be doing your recording.

For the best control over your audio, acquire the best quality microphones you can afford and utilize an audio interface between the microphone(s) and your computer (or mobile device). Alternatively, invest in the appropriate types of microphones that connect directly to your computer (or mobile device) via its USB port.

Audio interfaces are available from a wide range of companies and with different numbers of microphone/instrument inputs. If you'll typically be recording two co-hosts or one host and one guest, an interface with two microphone inputs will be fine. However, if you'll be recording four or more people (for panel discussions, for example), you'll need an interface with at least four separate microphone inputs.

The least expensive option for recording one host is to acquire a microphone that connects to a computer via its USB port. However, to enhance the audio quality, audio interfaces that offer just one microphone input are available and allow for higher-quality microphones to be used in conjunction with your computer and recording/postproduction software.

Microphone Selection and Recording Advice from a Pro

To help you choose the right microphone(s) to meet your podcasting needs, Soren Pedersen, senior product specialist at Shure, offers plenty of expert advice in this in-depth and exclusive interview. In addition to his full-time work with Shure, Pedersen is an accomplished and experienced audio engineer who works with several professional recording studios in the Chicago area. He refers to himself as a "certified mic nerd."

Since 1925, Shure (www.shure.com) has been one of the audio industry's pioneers in the research, development, manufacturing, and distribution of microphones. The company's equipment is used within most of the top recording studios around the world, as well as by some of the world's best-known performers, musicians, broadcasters, and podcasters. In addition to offering midrange to the highest-quality microphones, the company offers

tip

If you opt to use your smartphone or tablet as a digital recorder, don't rely on the microphones built into your mobile device. Instead, invest in an external microphone that connects directly to your mobile device via its USB-C or Lightning port, for example.

Another option is to purchase the portable Tascam iXZ Mic/Instrument Interface ($50, https://tascam.com/us/product/ixz/top) or a similar interface from another manufacturer. The iXZ device allows you to connect any professional-quality microphone (with an XLR jack) to your iPhone or iPad to achieve superior recording quality while on the go.

microphone accessories, audio interfaces, headphones, and other equipment designed specifically for use by podcasters.

Over the past few years, and in late 2020, Shure has introduced a range of mid-priced microphone and recording products specifically for podcasters. These are part of the company's Motiv product line. However, some of the world's best-known podcasters rely on other Shure microphone products, which are also widely used by performers, musicians, and broadcast professionals.

"Two of Shure's microphones that have become bestsellers amongst podcasters are among our older and well-established products. The Shure SM58 [www.shure.com] retails for around $99 and is probably the bestselling and most widely used dynamic vocal microphone in the world. It's a true workhorse that features the familiar ice cream cone shape. This microphone is designed to record both spoken word and singing, which makes it ideal for podcasters," said Pedersen.

For podcasters on a higher budget, Pedersen strongly recommends Shure's $399 SM7B vocal microphone [https://www.shure.com/en-US/products/microphones/sm7b]. It's designed for in-studio use and is a global favorite among professional broadcasters and podcasters alike. "This microphone has become the aspirational microphone of choice amongst podcasters, because it's designed to capture vocals and record the clarity, quality, and radio quality that many podcasters strive to achieve," said Pedersen.

While the SM58 is a handheld microphone that can be used with a wide range of microphone stands in almost any recording situation, the SM7B is meant to be mounted on a microphone stand either from the floor or using a boom-style (bendable) arm that attaches to a table.

"The SM58 is really good at picking up the audio that's directly in front of it, as opposed to what's surrounding it or to the sides. In a podcast studio, this focuses the recording on the speaker's voice and much less so on capturing the environment they're in. This microphone's recording quality will be brighter than the SM7B, for example. It's a great starter podcast microphone. The SM7B is a step up in terms of offering broadcast-quality fidelity," explained Pedersen.

Regardless of which microphone you choose, select a dynamic vocal microphone that offers internal pop protection and an internal shock mount (both of which are built into the SM58 and SM7B). Since dynamic vocal microphones are designed to be positioned very close to someone's mouth as they're speaking, these microphones pick up the vocal pops that occur when the speaker uses words with a strong *P* sound, for example. While it's easy to add an optional pop filter between a microphone and the speaker, having some pop protection built into the microphone itself will allow you to capture clearer spoken audio.

Beyond the microphone itself, podcasters will typically require a suitable microphone stand and a microphone cable. The cable will connect the microphone either directly to a computer or to an audio interface (which connects to the computer) when recording. "The audio interface transforms the analog audio signal captured by the microphone and converts it into a digital signal that can be captured and stored on a computer," added Pedersen.

"There are many audio interfaces out there. Lately, I've been seeing a lot of podcasters use a Focusrite 2i2 audio interface [https://focusrite.com/en] with Shure micro-phones, for example. This is a two-channel interface that's priced around $100. In my opinion, there's no clear answer in regard to whether it's better to use a microphone with an interface or a microphone that plugs directly into the USB port of a computer when recording a podcast. It all depends on the rest of your recording setup and your skill level using that equipment.

> **tip**
>
> When using a more sensitive condenser microphone, a pop filter is definitely required when recording vocals. A pop filter can (and should) also be used with many dynamic vocal microphones, although these are less apt to pick up and record those strong *P* sounds that often occur when people are speaking.

"If you choose a poor-quality audio interface and/or a low-quality microphone, this will negatively impact your recording quality. Likewise, if you use a low-quality USB microphone that does a poor job converting the analog sound to digital, this too will negatively impact your audio quality. The right audio interface will enhance the audio quality captured by a microphone," said Pedersen.

Even when using a handheld microphone to record a podcast, Pedersen advocates for using a microphone stand. "I recommend using a boom arm-style mic stand that clamps to the side of a table or desk. It allows the person to fully adjust the position of the microphone in front of their mouth while maintaining good body posture and staying comfortable. You don't want to be thinking about the microphone while you're recording your podcast. You want to be focused on what you're saying and your message," added Pedersen.

"When positioning your microphone, make sure you're sitting up nice and straight or standing. Slumping over will actually affect your vocal tone and breathing. A well-positioned boom arm mic stand also helps prevent you from accidentally touching or bumping the microphone while recording," he added.

As for choosing appropriate microphone cables, Pedersen stated that there are many cable qualities to choose from, but for the average podcaster, cable quality doesn't really matter. Pedersen explained, "Better quality cables are more durable and offer better shielding when a longer cable length is needed. For the podcaster, these are rarely considerations, so pretty much any compatible microphone cable will work fine."

Assuming the podcaster is starting off with a good quality microphone, using their recording/postproduction software, according to Pedersen, they'll typically want to do a little bit of EQ adjustment to the vocal tracks. He also recommends using the software's High Pass (Low Roll-Off) feature while processing voice tracks. Doing this will help remove unwanted ambient noise and unwanted frequencies, making the person's voice typically sound a bit better.

"From an audio processing point of view, there are no real rules for processing audio tracks using postproduction software. Some podcasts strive for a more shiny, higher production value, while others try to sound more natural. Whatever sound you're trying to achieve, make sure it aligns with your content. I highly recommend listening to a bunch of podcasts, choose a few that you think sound really good, and then strive to emulate that production quality and methodology," said Pedersen.

In addition to recommending the use of one microphone per person when recording a podcast, Pedersen stressed that the position of each microphone is important. Each microphone should be directly in front of the speaker's mouth. When two or more microphones are being used, they should be pointed directly away from each other.

"You can't compensate digitally for being physically far away from the microphone. If you're using a USB microphone, keep in mind that your computer is not designed to handle more than one microphone at a time. Thus, if you'll be using two or more microphones at the same time, definitely use an audio interface as part of your setup. If you're recording a podcast with two people, using two Shure SM58 microphones and the Focusrite 2i2 audio interface, for example, will cost around $300 and provide a great recording solution for a home studio podcast recording setup," explained Pedersen.

In general, Pedersen does not recommend trying to record more than four people at once for a podcast, using four separate microphones and an audio interface. This becomes trickier from a technical standpoint. From a content standpoint, it's difficult for the host(s) to prevent everyone from talking over each other or interrupting each other, which makes the content harder for your audience to understand.

The benefit to using an audio interface is that during the recording process you have more control over input levels. Then, when two or more voice tracks have been recorded, during the editing and postproduction phases, you have much more control over the processing of the separate audio tracks. "During the recording process, make sure you isolate what each microphone is picking up as much as possible. Then during the editing and postproduction phase, cut the audio from vocal tracks altogether for the people who are not currently speaking," said Pedersen.

For someone without an audio engineering background, Pedersen explained that when two people are being recorded (either co-hosts or a host and a guest, for example), those people should be positioned face-to-face so that the front of their microphones are pointing in opposite directions. This will prevent audio from bleeding in between audio tracks as they're being recorded.

"As for recording levels, as you're looking at the recording meter displayed by your recording software, as someone is speaking, the vocals should just barely touch the yellow part of a meter. As long as you're seeing just a little bit of yellow on your meter, you're in a good place. You want to leave a little headroom, so if during a conversation, someone raises their voice slightly to make a point or laugh, for example, this won't cause distortion in the audio signal. Basically, if you see red in the meter while recording, that's bad," stated Pedersen.

Keep in mind that almost every piece of recording software, including Audacity, has podcasting presets that can be selected prior to recording. When offered, be sure to take advantage of them, especially if you don't have an audio engineering background and you're still learning to use your recording software. He added, "If you use the podcasting preset built into the software, you set up the microphones correctly, and you watch your recording levels and manually adjust them when needed, you'll typically wind up with a great quality recording."

Once you've gathered all the recording equipment needed as a podcaster, get to know your recording space. "Very few people have the luxury of recording their podcast in a professional recording studio or a fully soundproofed room. Instead, you need to acquaint

▶ Pay Attention to Recording Levels

When it comes to audio editing, you can always digitally boost the audio levels during editing or postproduction, but you cannot undistort audio that's been incorrectly recorded. The Shure Motiv microphones, which are designed for podcasters, offer built-in digital signal processing to help prevent problems while recording audio. These microphones also utilize technology that adds some processing to what's being recorded during the recording process, so when you play back that audio, it already sounds like it's been processed. The Motiv microphones come with free recording software that's designed for use by podcasters as opposed to highly experienced audio engineers.

yourself with your recording space and learn how to work within it to avoid capturing unwanted ambient sounds," said Pedersen.

"Walk into a room and clap. If you hear an echo or reverberation, you need to add some type of soundproofing to that space before recording, or choose a different space to record. Next, pay attention to ambient noise from nearby traffic, air conditioner sounds, pet sounds, or the sounds of people in nearby rooms, for example. Figure out how to eliminate these sounds, either during the recording phase or digitally during the postproduction phase.

"Using the right microphone will also help eliminate unwanted environment audio during the recording process. Again, Shure is a world leader in dynamic voice microphones that help to eliminate these unwanted sounds and make someone's voice sound warmer. If you use a condenser microphone, you'll need to do a lot more to soundproof the room and then digitally process the audio after its recorded.

"As an audio engineer, anytime I walk into a new space where I will be recording, I close my eyes and 'view' the space with just my ears for at least 30 seconds. During this process, I pay attention to every sound I hear. I then determine what's causing each sound, and figure out what needs to be done to eliminate it," explained Pedersen. "Utilizing acoustic foam in a recording space will always help eliminate unwanted sounds. However, you do not need to cover every inch of the room with the foam for it to work effectively.

"Again, recording voices with a good quality dynamic microphone will eliminate a lot of the unwanted ambient noise for you. Make sure you read the directions for using your chosen microphone, so you know exactly how to position it in front of the speaker's mouth," he added.

Next, as you're recording, make sure everyone maintains the same distance from their microphone throughout the recording process. "If someone moves closer and then farther away or changes their angle, this will negatively impact the recording. Always experiment with a sample recording before recording an entire podcast episode. Listen to the sample recording carefully and make sure it sounds perfect. You can always experiment with different microphone recording techniques to see what works best for you," added Pedersen.

For podcasters who are experts in their field or in regard to their podcast's subject matter, but who don't want to get involved at all with editing and production, Pedersen recommends working with a professional podcast production company or producer who, for a fee, will handle all aspects of the production and postproduction for you.

"It's very easy for anyone to record a podcast. Editing and handling the postproduction, and achieving the results you desire, is a bit more difficult. This requires developing a specific skill set and practice, unless you outsource this part of the job. Maintaining a professional-sounding podcast is absolutely essential if you plan to monetize it. If you don't have the resources to hire a full-service podcast production company, seek out a freelance audio producer or audio consultant to give you the guidance you need," said Pedersen. "Working with a professional podcast production company or an experienced producer/editor can save you up to 80 percent of the time required to create an awesome podcast."

Record
Your Podcast
Episodes

You've already done a lot of brainstorming and research to come up with a concept for your podcast and its scope. You should have also pinpointed and defined your target audience, and based on your show format, gathered the production equipment you'll need to record and edit each episode of your podcast.

The next steps are planning your production schedule, finalizing your initial group of episode topics, planning each episode, booking your guest(s), writing your scripts, gathering your production elements, and actually recording (then editing) your individual episodes. During your brainstorming process, as you defined the scope and subject matter for your podcast as a whole, hopefully you've already come up with a collection of individual episode ideas. It's now time to really flush out those ideas.

Since you'll likely be recording individual episodes on a regular schedule, it's a good idea to plan that schedule early on and get yourself into a routine. For example, every Monday, hold a meeting with your entire production team. Plan the exact schedule for the week and delegate preproduction responsibilities as needed.

Keep in mind, you'll want to handle some tasks, like inviting and booking guests, several weeks before you're scheduled to record. This gives you time to research your guests, create a list of interview questions, and then promote that guest in the weeks leading up to their appearance.

Use the Podcast Episode Planning Checklist in Figure 8.1 to help you create your weekly preproduction, production (recording), and postproduction schedule. The preproduction

---

Podcast Episode Planning Checklist

This checklist will help ensure you handle all the necessary preproduction tasks associated with recording and producing each episode of your podcast. The order you complete these tasks will vary, and not all of them will apply to your show format or topic.

Choose an episode topic.

❑ Flush out the topic, ensuring you'll have enough interesting content to fill an entire episode without being repetitive or going too far off topic to fill time. For a 30-minute episode, you'll likely want to clearly define the main topic (the scope of the episode), and then brainstorm at least three to five main talking points that are directly relevant.

❑ Do whatever topic-specific research is required so you, your host(s), and your producers are prepared.

❑ Find and book your guest(s), do research on them, determine how you'll introduce them based on their credentials, and compose open-ended interview questions in advance. Asking open-ended interview questions

---

FIGURE 8–1: **Podcast Episode Planning Checklist**

Podcast Episode Planning Checklist

encourages your guest(s) to share their knowledge and opinions, plus provide more than a "yes," "no," or one-word answer. Of course, while you're actually recording your interviews, you'll need to listen closely to your guest's answers, so you can ask relevant and insightful follow-up questions as needed.

❏ Create a minute-by-minute rundown for the episode. (How to do this will be explained shortly.)

❏ Write the script. Depending on your show format and your abilities as a host, you may not want to write out a word-for-word script for each entire episode, especially if you're able to speak extemporaneously on the topic. It is a good idea, however, to script your show's intro and outro, so you remember to include all the pertinent information that needs to be conveyed to the audience (including reminding them to subscribe to the podcast, review it, and share details about it with their friends).

❏ Gather the production elements you'll want to add to the episode, such as intro and outro music and prerecorded elements (including ads).

❏ Set a production schedule for the week, including time to record the episode with your host(s), guest, and/or panel, and time to handle all postproduction and editing tasks.

❏ Record the episode. As a novice podcaster, plan to record each episode multiple times and then edit together the best takes to create the final episode. Using this strategy, recording a 30-minute episode might take you two to three hours.

❏ Edit the episode and handle postproduction tasks. This will likely take at least one to five hours per 30-minute episode, depending on your audio production experience and skills, as well as the complexity of the production elements you add to each episode.

❏ Create episode-specific materials, such as the episode title and description, as well as show notes, transcripts, and web links you want to share with your audience.

❏ Upload the episode to your podcast hosting service.

❏ Start promoting the episode.

When everything is done related to your newest episode, keep up your promotional efforts, but return to step one and begin work on your next episode.

FIGURE 8–1: **Podcast Episode Planning Checklist,** continued

tasks include what needs to be done before you start recording your podcast episodes (or streaming live). The production tasks are those related to actually recording each episode. Postproduction includes everything that needs to be done between when the episode gets recorded and the final edited version is uploaded and published on the internet via your podcast hosting service.

Keep in mind, postproduction does *not* include everything involved with promoting the podcast and each new episode on an ongoing basis. Be sure to read Chapter 13, "12 Ways to Promote Your Podcast," to develop a strategy for promoting your podcast and building its audience using tools available to you online and in the real world.

Planning Each Episode's Minute-By-Minute Rundown

If you know your podcast's topic well and you're considered one of the world's leading experts on that topic, you probably won't want to script out each entire episode of your podcast word-for-word, especially if you're a really good (and experienced) public speaker and can talk extemporaneously using just bullet point notes, for example.

Even without a script, it's definitely a good strategy to preplan each podcast episode and create a minute-by-minute episode rundown. Figure 8.2 on page 107 includes a sample rundown for a 30-minute podcast episode. The first digit of the timecode represents minutes and the second digit represents seconds.

During postproduction, while you're listening back to your recorded content and editing the audio to remove unwanted pauses, "ums," and repetitive statements, for example, you might discover that certain sections of the podcast (referred to as blocks) run long. In this case, put yourself in your audience's shoes and determine if the additional content is extremely worthwhile.

Will extending the length of the episode serve your audience well, or cause them to get bored or lose interest? You might be very proud of the content you've created, but if it doesn't cater to your audience's wants and needs while keeping their attention and avoiding unnecessary repetition, consider making cuts.

You're always better presenting a shorter length episode that's literally jam-packed with amazing content than stretching out an episode's length and offering just average content. If you can't fill a 30-minute episode with awesome content, produce a 20-minute episode instead. Likewise, instead of offering a one-hour (or longer) episode, consider breaking it up into two or more shorter episodes. Always keep your audience wanting more by the end of an episode, not wishing it would hurry up and end.

Sample 30-Minute Podcast Episode Rundown	
0:00—0:15	Pre-Roll Commercial
0:16—0:45	Introduction with Music and Announcer
0:46—2:00	Host(s) Introduce Themselves and Discuss the Episode's Topic or Focus
2:01—9:00	Talking Point #1 Related to the Topic
9:01—10:01	Mid-Roll Commercial / Sponsor Message
10:02—15:00	Talking Point #2 Related to Topic
15:01—16:01	Mid-Roll Commercial / Sponsor Message
16:02—26:00	Interview Guest
26:01—28:30	Wrap Up
	Tease Next Episode
	Remind Audience to Subscribe, Review the Podcast, Post Comments, and Send in Emails with Questions or Feedback
	Thank Advertisers, Sponsors, and Audience
	Promote Podcast's Website and Social Media
28:31—28:59	Closing Credits with Music and Announcer
29:00—30:00	End-Roll Commercial / Sponsor Message

FIGURE 8–2: **Sample 30-Minute Podcast Episode Rundown**

While it's designed to create rundowns for TV shows and radio programs, the Shoflo software can be used for creating show episode rundowns for a podcast. For more information, visit: https://shoflo.tv.

Scripting Tips and Techniques

Some people are experts at reading a word-for-word script (from paper or a teleprompter) and making it seem like they're speaking extemporaneously. They're able to read aloud using a conversational style (speech pattern), and speak at a natural pace without awkward stumbles or pauses. This is a skill that typically takes time and a lot of practice to master. If you're able to do this, writing a word-for-word script for each of your podcast episodes is definitely an option.

Most podcasters, however, perform much better working from notes that list bulleted talking points they want to cover. You need to figure out what works best for you, and if you'll be working as a host in conjunction with a co-host, what allows you two to have the best on-air chemistry that'll be appealing to your audience.

One benefit to working from a pre-written, word-for-word script is that you can edit out all the ancillary information and repetition before you start recording. If you'll be working from notes or written out talking points, you may be more apt to repeat yourself, babble too much, forget to mention important information, or have trouble keeping to an episode's prepared rundown. When you're prerecording your podcast, this can all be edited out during postproduction, but it becomes a challenge determining what content to keep and what to delete. You then need to edit the remaining parts together in a cohesive way.

Becoming a great podcast host takes practice, plenty of preparation, and confidence, along with top-notch public speaking skills. As a beginner, you'll be better off hosting a prerecorded podcast, so you (or your producer/editor) can edit out awkward pauses, "ums," and other elements of the voice-over tracks to make the podcast sound more professional. Especially as you're recording the first several episodes of your podcast, consider participating in several recorded "rehearsals" before recording the actual episode. After each rehearsal, listen back to the recording with your production team and figure out how to make it better.

Whether you plan to write out your scripts word-for-word or work from notes, make sure you're using

tip

Try to listen to other podcasts or shows your potential guest has appeared on to give you an idea of what to expect. However, when they're a guest on your podcast, try to go beyond what the guest has done during previous appearances or interviews elsewhere.

Use your interview skills to draw out interesting stories or anecdotes, and ask more probing questions that'll elicit answers that'll get your audience's attention. Also, think about creative ways you can have fun with the guest during their appearance on your podcast. Anytime you and your guest are having fun, this will become obvious to your audience and make your podcast more enjoyable to listen to.

vocabulary that your audience will understand and that the tone and emotion you convey in your voice is appropriate to the subject matter. Your audience should always be able to hear the passion in your voice about whatever you're talking about. This is something that's hard to fake. If you're uninterested, bored, or unhappy with what you're discussing during an episode of your podcast, this will quickly become obvious (in a negative way) to your audience.

Keep practicing your hosting, interviewing, speaking, and listening skills until you're able to record podcast episodes that are fun, engaging, interesting, and entertaining to listen to. If necessary, consider taking some public speaking classes, or figure out ways to overcome your self-consciousness or fears, so your true personality comes through to your audience.

Remember, being prepared and knowledgeable about the subject matter you'll be discussing during each episode of your podcast will help to boost your confidence. Taking the time to practice public speaking and then rehearsing before each recording session or live broadcast will also help you fine-tune your hosting skills.

Tips for Booking Guests

If your podcast show format will include having guests, you'll need to take on a handful of additional responsibilities. First off, you'll need to come up with a potential list of guests that your audience will be interested in, who have something insightful or entertaining to share, and who would be interested in appearing on your show.

Before confirming a guest, consider what they'll bring to your podcast. How will you utilize them, and how will they be perceived by your audience? One way to determine the types of guests your listeners would want to hear on your podcast is to ask them for suggestions.

As for making contact with potential guests, try visiting their websites and looking for contact information. You can also make contact with people through social media, or work with their publicist, for example. By attending conventions and conferences related to your podcast's subject matter, you're more apt to meet potential guests in person. Or, if you discover a potential guest is making an in-person appearance somewhere, consider attending that event so you can introduce yourself.

Some services and publications you can subscribe to as a podcaster that will make finding and booking guests easier include:

▶ *Help a Reporter Out* (www.helpareporter.com). Send out a request for guests with specific credentials or areas of expertise, and those people can then contact you directly.

► *Interview Guests Directory* (www.interviewguestsdirectory.com). This service offers a massive database of entertainers, experts, authors, and public figures who are looking to be booked as a guest on podcasts, radio shows, and television shows. As a podcaster, access to this directory (which has more than 50 topic categories) is free, and you'll discover information about thousands of potential guests.

► *Podcast Guests Directory* (www.podcastguests.com). This service matches experts, public figures, authors, and other would-be guests with podcasters looking to book guests on their show. As a podcaster, access the free online directory, select a subject category, and then see a listing of relevant guests (including their contact information).

Once you've compiled a potential guest list, you'll need to research how to get in touch with each potential guest—whether directly or through a publicist or employer. Then, it's necessary to invite the guest onto your show (which is typically done via email or telephone). Assuming they agree, you'll need to choose a date and time to record their appearance.

The next step is to do research about each of your guests. Keep in mind, most people who will agree to be a guest on your podcast will want to promote something, such as their product, company, service, book, TV show, radio show, or own podcast. You'll need to allow them to do this. At the same time, however, to keep your audience interested and to ensure your podcast episode doesn't wind up sounding like an infomercial, you'll need to ask insightful questions, solicit interesting information from the guest, and keep them on subject.

Becoming a good interviewer is a skill set unto itself that you'll need to develop and fine-tune over

tip

When inviting a guest to appear on your podcast, ask them to initially commit to a 15- to 30-minute interview (in person or by phone), and give them multiple date options and times to choose from, if possible. Be as flexible as you can with scheduling, and for high-profile guests, try to book them as far in advance as possible, since they'll rarely accept last-minute invitations.

time. What you'll discover is that one of the keys to being a good interviewer is to go into the interview fully prepared, having done your research. In addition to being ready with a selection of insightful questions that will elicit an interesting conversation with your guest, as the interviewer, you'll need to listen. Pay attention to what your guest is saying, and be prepared to ask relevant follow-up questions or take the conversation in a different direction if that direction is something your audience will be interested in and want to hear.

If you're prerecording your interviews, you're able to extend the interview as long as necessary and then edit it down to the desired length while taking out any repetition or unrelated content. Keeping your guest's busy schedule in mind, it's a good idea to schedule them for 15 to 30 minutes. You'll likely have a more difficult time getting a potential guest to commit to an hour or more of their time, especially if your podcast doesn't yet have a massive audience that the guest wants to reach.

By booking your guests weeks in advance, this gives you time to promote them on your podcast and build demand. You can also ask your guest to promote their appearance on your podcast to their own audiences on social media and elsewhere, which can easily help to increase your audience size.

Knowing that your guest will likely want to promote something, find out what that is in advance, and work it into your introduction. Then allow them to do their promotion during the interview in between answering your questions. End the interview by reminding your audience about whatever it is your guest wants to promote. The guest will often appreciate you mentioning their website or social media feeds as well.

warning

If you broadcast your podcast live, as opposed to prerecording it, when booking a guest always have a "Plan B" ready to go if the guest doesn't show up, is late, or has difficulties calling into your show. As you become a veteran podcaster, you'll develop relationships with some of your more frequent guests, and you'll know whom you can rely on. It's also good to cultivate relationships with guests you can call upon on a last-minute basis when needed.

A sample introduction for a book author might be "I'd like to welcome to our show a very special guest. He is the author of [insert book title]. This new book is all about [describe book in a sentence or two], and it's now available from bookstores everywhere. [Insert guest's name], welcome to [insert your podcast's title]. First off, I read your book and found it intriguing. Can you tell me what inspired you to write it?"

As the author's interview comes to an end, conclude the interview by saying something like "[Insert author's name], thanks so much for joining me here on [insert your podcast's title]. I'd like to remind our audience that the title of your new book is [insert book title]. It's published by [insert publisher name], and it's now available from bookstores everywhere. You can discover more about our guest by visiting their website at [insert guest's website address], or by following them on social media at [insert Facebook username, Twitter username, and/or Instagram username]. [Insert guest's name], again, thanks for being such a great guest. I hope you'll come back again soon!"

Recording Your Podcast Episodes

The trick to producing a professional-sounding podcast is to start with recorded vocals that offer the highest production quality possible. This means the vocals should be recorded using a good quality microphone that makes the host's voice sound great, without simultaneously recording ancillary and unwanted background noise.

Unwanted background noise might include the sound of an air conditioner, outside traffic, people talking in another room, the sound of someone touching or repositioning the microphone while speaking, wind noises captured by the microphone, popping sounds when the host pronounces words with the letter *P*, heavy breathing by the host, or anything else that gets recorded and detracts from the clarity of the intended voice(s) being recorded.

The easiest way to avoid recording unwanted sounds is to gather the right recording equipment and use it properly, based on the type of audio you plan to include within your podcast. Sound effects, background music, ambient sounds that you want heard, and other audio assets you intend to include within the podcast should be added during postproduction to keep the actual voice-over recording process as simple as possible.

Ideally, when recording vocals, the hosts should be within a sound booth or soundproofed recording studio, especially if you'll be recording with a lower-quality microphone that picks up everything nearby, as opposed to just the person who is positioned directly in front of that microphone.

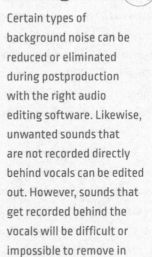

warning

Certain types of background noise can be reduced or eliminated during postproduction with the right audio editing software. Likewise, unwanted sounds that are not recorded directly behind vocals can be edited out. However, sounds that get recorded behind the vocals will be difficult or impossible to remove in postproduction.

Each time you start recording a podcast episode, record 30 to 60 seconds of spoken audio and then listen back to that recording (using headphones) to ensure the microphones and recording equipment are set up correctly and that you're not accidentally recording unwanted sounds in the background.

Overview of Recording Applications

Again, depending on your approach to recording your podcast and the number of people you need to be recording simultaneously, you can utilize a few different equipment configurations. For example, if you need to record just one person speaking into a single microphone, you can connect the microphone directly to your computer (or digital recorder) and use your recording software to monitor and control the recording levels.

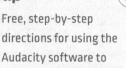

tip

Free, step-by-step directions for using the Audacity software to record a podcast can be found at: https:// www.buzzsprout.com/ blog/audacity-podcast- tutorial or https:// theaudacitytopodcast. com/tap060-how-to- record-and-edit-a- podcast-with-audacity.

When two or more microphones will be used simultaneously during the recording process (or you have audio coming in from multiple inputs), you'll definitely want to use a separate audio interface that connects between the microphones and your computer (or digital recorder). The mixing console will allow you to monitor and separately adjust each microphone or audio input, plus potentially record each on a separate digital track.

Beyond utilizing the highest quality microphones you can afford, using feature-packed recording software will give you added functions during the recording process. In many cases, the recording software and postproduction software you use will be one and the same.

As mentioned previously, Audacity (www.audacityteam.org) is a powerful Windows PC and Mac application for recording audio and handling multitrack postproduction tasks.

Other audio recording, audio production, and digital audio workstation (DAW) applications you might look into using include:

▶ *Adobe Audition* (www.adobe.com/audition). Available for Windows PCs and Macs, this software transforms your computer into a professional audio workstation for recording and editing multitrack recordings. Priced at $20.99 per month/ per user, the software offers a collection of tools designed to clean up audio and help users create professional-quality audio productions. For specific information on how to use Adobe Audition to record, edit, and export audio podcasts, visit: https://helpx.adobe.com/audition/how-to/create-podcast.html.

▶ *Alitu: The Podcast Maker* (www.alitu.com). Designed for amateurs with no recording experience whatsoever, this application helps podcasters record their show, clean up audio files, add music and sound effects, and gather all the digital files and assets required to produce, upload, and distribute each podcast episode. All the tools are offered for $28 per month, or $280 per year.

▶ *Apple GarageBand* (www.apple.com/mac/garageband). Designed to record and mix music, this digital audio workstation (DAW) software can also be used to record and edit vocal/voice-over tracks. It's a free application available from Apple for the Mac, iPhone, and iPad.

▶ *Apple Logic Pro* (www.apple.com/logic-pro). This is a pro-level, multitrack audio recording and editing application from Apple. It's available for the Mac and can be purchased outright for $199.99.

▶ *Hindenburg Journalist Pro* (www.hindenburg.com). Available for Windows PCs and Macs, this too is professional-level software designed specifically to serve as a multitrack editor for audio producers (and podcasters). In addition to utilizing microphones to record audio, this software offers tools for recording interviews via Skype or FaceTime. The software can be purchased outright for between $95 and $500 per user, depending on the version and the functionality that's required. For podcasters, Journalist Pro, for example, can also be rented for three ($40), six ($75), or 12 ($120) months at a time. The purchase price for Journalist Pro is $375.

▶ *Zencastr* (www.zencastr.com). Designed specifically for podcasters who rely on conducting remote interviews, this software includes tools for recording Voice over Internet Protocol (phone) interviews either directly through Zencastr or using a third-party service, such as Skype. This is cloud-based software that works with most popular web browsers. No software installation is necessary. The Hobbyist version of the application is free, but use of the postproduction tools costs extra. The Professional version costs $20 per month/per user and includes postproduction tools that can be used on up to ten hours of audio per month.

Most of the fee-based audio recording and production applications offer a free 7-, 14-, or 30-day trial, allowing you to utilize a full working version of the software before making a purchase.

In addition to these Windows PC/Mac computer applications, if you want to use your smartphone or tablet to record audio for your podcast, or fully produce your podcast while on the go, be sure to visit the App Store (iOS) or Google Play store (Android) to discover a wide range of podcasting apps. Within the search field, enter the keyword "podcasting" to find mobile apps like: Anchor, Ferrite Recording Studio, and Spreaker Studio.

Tips for Recording in a (Home) Studio

Anytime you're recording two or more people in a single location, make sure each person has their own microphone and that the sound levels and settings for each are adjusted appropriately. In certain situations, you could get away with a host passing a microphone back and forth between themselves and the person they're interviewing, but if the microphone is not positioned in front of someone's mouth each time they're speaking, you'll wind up with varying recording levels based on the distance someone is from the microphone.

Microphones that can be placed between two or more people and that are designed to pick up all audio exist, but these microphones will capture all the sound in the room, not just the voices of the people speaking. Based on the number of people being recorded and the recording situation, make sure you're using the right type of microphone(s).

12 Tips for Recording a Podcast from a Home Studio

To achieve the best recording results working from a home studio, follow these tips:

1. Use the right equipment for the task at hand. For example, to record voice-overs or vocals, use a directional microphone that's designed to pick up only the audio that's directly in front of it. Don't use the microphone that's built into your computer, smartphone, or tablet. Invest in a microphone designed for the type of recording you'll be doing. Refer back to Chapter 7, "Set Up Your Recording Studio," for tips on selecting the best type of microphone(s) to use based on the recording situation and environment.

2. Make sure the host(s) and guest(s) warm up their voices before recording. Have everyone drink some room temperature water and make sure their body is acclimated to room temperature (especially if someone has just come inside after being outside in the cold). Using your favorite search engine (such as Google or Yahoo!), enter the search term "vocal exercises" for quick and easy ways to warm up your vocal cords before recording.

3. Make sure your recording area is quiet. Turn off the air conditioner/fan, close the windows, and remove anything that generates unwanted sounds. If you're using a sensitive microphone to record, even the ticking of a nearby clock could accidentally be recorded.

4. Use a microphone stand and adjust the microphone so that it's at the perfect height and distance for the person it'll be recording. Be sure to use a pop filter between the microphone and the speaker's mouth. From the audio software (or mixing board), separately adjust the audio levels for each microphone that's being used. Based on the microphone you purchase, make sure you know exactly how to set up and use it. Positioning the microphone correctly and adjusting the recording levels for it (via your recording/audio production software or audio interface) is essential for achieving professional-quality results.

5. At the start of each recording, hit the record button, but stay silent for about 10 to 15 seconds. This allows you to create a noise profile that will later be used

by your audio production software to remove unwanted ambient (background) noise.

6. Once you start recording, make sure the volume levels and microphone adjustments remain consistent throughout the entire recording session. It's also important for the people being recorded to remain in the same position and at a consistent distance from their microphone. Each person's microphone should be recorded as a separate audio track using your audio recording/production software.

7. Practice breathing while you're being recorded and speaking. Train yourself to inhale or exhale in between sentences, for example. Breath sounds that are recorded in between words or sentences can be edited out. Heavy breaths taken while you're speaking will garble your speech pattern and can't typically be edited out during postproduction.

8. Before recording an entire podcast episode, set everything up and record a 30-second to one-minute test. Play back the test recording while wearing headphones and make sure everything sounds perfect. If necessary, make adjustments to the audio input levels related to the microphone(s), reposition the microphones, or better situate the people being recorded so that they're sitting upright (or standing) and relatively still in front of the microphone while speaking.

9. During the recording of each episode, allow one person to speak at a time, without interrupting or speaking at the same time as others. When multiple people are recorded speaking simultaneously, for example, it becomes very hard to edit that audio during postproduction. Depending on the audio software being used during the recording process, if you're using multiple microphones to record multiple people, mute the microphones for the people who are not speaking. However, make sure you unmute each person's microphone before they begin speaking each time, or you'll wind up cutting off the beginning of words or sentences.

10. Drink room temperature water before and during the recording process. Avoid anything carbonated. Especially for long recording sessions, it's important to keep your vocal cords hydrated so you'll sound your best while being recorded. A dry voice will often sound raspy, for example.

11. Consider standing up when you're recording to help make your voice sound clearer, more powerful, and more confident. If you'll be reading from a printed script or notes, place them on a music stand and be careful you don't record the sound of papers being shuffled.

12. Record your voice-overs as a WAV or AIFF digital audio file at a high resolution (such as 24-bit, 48kHz). After the files are edited and produced, you'll export the audio file into an MP3 format at a bit rate between 96Kbps and 192Kbps. If your audio includes music, for example, stick to a higher bit rate within this range.

Tips for Recording "On Location"

Anytime you're recording on location (not in a soundproof studio), you'll have a few extra challenges to contend with, including the sound of wind, ambient noise, and sounds generated as a result of excessive motion (handling the microphone or moving around while speaking into the microphone).

The biggest problem you will likely encounter when recording in a public place is the sound of vehicles, random people, and ambient music. Capturing the audio from a car alarm, fire trucks passing by, airplanes flying overhead, or music that's continuously playing in the background all have the potential to ruin a recording or make it very difficult to edit.

If you must record your podcast in an open area (as opposed to within a soundproofed environment), eliminate as much ambient or unwanted noise as possible. Do not attempt to record with music playing in the background. Also, be sure to use a directional microphone for each person being recorded, and adjust the levels appropriately to the recording environment.

If you're using a single microphone to record and an interview with a guest, for example, have the host stand as close to the guest as possible, and have the host move the microphone back and forth between themselves and the guest, based on who is speaking. Using a windscreen on the microphone head will help reduce unwanted noises from being recorded. However, if you're using a poor-quality microphone and/or its levels are not set properly, you'll likely record the unwanted sound of the host touching and handling the microphone each time it's moved.

Tips for Recording Phone Interviews

There are many ways to record a phone interview (or even a group conference call with multiple people at different locations) and wind up with good quality audio. One option is to use a third-party mobile app on your smartphone to record phone calls. You can find these optional apps within the App Store (iOS) or Google Play store (Android). Specialized podcast recording applications for computers that allow Voice over Internet Protocol (internet-based) phone calls (via Skype, for example) to be recorded with ease are also available.

If you're in a studio, specialized equipment can be connected to a landline telephone or smartphone that will allow the guest to be recorded on one audio track (when using multitrack audio recording software) while the host speaks into a microphone and listens to the guest on the telephone using headphones.

Based on how heavily your podcast will rely on phone interviews with guests, you'll want to find a solution that works best for you and that fits within your production budget. To discover a wide range of solutions for recording phone interviews based on the equipment at your disposal, enter the search phrases "how to record phone interviews for a podcast" or "ways to record Skype calls" within any search engine (such as Google or Yahoo!). You'll also discover informative how-to videos for recording phone interviews on YouTube using these same search phrases.

As you're recording a phone interview, if you plan to edit it later during postproduction, it's particularly important that the people being recorded (the host

► Episode Zero: Make a Positive First Impression with a Podcast Trailer

Sure, you can jump right into your podcast and publish Episode #1, but if you want to establish a positive first impression with your audience, offer a taste of what to expect from your podcast, introduce your host(s), and provide listeners with an overview of your podcast's goals, consider producing and publishing an introductory "Episode Zero" or trailer.

This episode should be no more than two minutes long and provide your audience with an introduction to the podcast in a way that'll entice them to immediately subscribe and start listening to your actual episodes.

Production quality is of utmost importance, as is the content of this Episode Zero trailer, as it'll allow your podcast and its host(s) to make a positive first impression with the audience. Put some thought into how you want to present your podcast before recording this episode/trailer, as it could become your podcast's most powerful promotional tool.

In addition to publishing Episode Zero as part of your actual podcast, this same content can be published on your podcast's website and social media feeds. In fact, you should consider adapting your podcast's Episode Zero into an Audiogram, which is a promotional tool you'll learn more about in the next chapter.

and the guest, for example) do not talk over each other (at the same time) during the interview.

Ideally, to make editing easier later, you want the host to ask their question and then the guest to pause for a second before responding. Depending on how you plan to edit the interview, you might also encourage the guest to repeat the host's question as they're answering it. For example, the host could ask the guest "What's your favorite color?" The guest might respond "That's a great question. My favorite color is blue, because . . ."

Putting It All Together During Postproduction

As you'll quickly discover, recording top-quality audio during the recording phase of a podcast episode's production is only the first step. The next phase is postproduction, where the audio gets edited and production elements (such as sound effects and background music) are mixed in. Depending on the audio production software you're using, you'll likely have a broad range of tools available that'll allow you to enhance the quality of the recorded audio, edit out unwanted sounds, equalize and normalize the recording, add effects to the recording, and mix in other elements to create a podcast episode that sounds amazing and highly professional. Editing each episode of your podcast is the focus of the next chapter.

Edit Your Podcast Like a Pro

Hopefully by now you've discovered that a handful of equally important elements go into every successful podcast. One of those is properly editing your audio to create fully produced, professional-sounding podcast episodes that adhere to your podcast's brand and cater to your target audience.

Podcast editing and postproduction are skill sets unto themselves that you'll need to master, or hire someone to handle on your behalf. *Podcast editing* refers to taking your raw voice recordings, digitally cleaning them up, and shortening them (when necessary), and then making those audio tracks, which feature your hosts, announcer, and guests (when applicable), as clear sounding as possible using the digital editing tools at your disposal.

Postproduction then takes advantage of additional digital editing tools and audio elements to incorporate intro and outro music, background music, ads, sound effects, vocal effects, and other content into your podcast episodes to create fully produced, professional-sounding productions.

In some cases, podcast editing and postproduction are handled at the same time, by the same person. However, these tasks can also be handled one after the other, before the final fully produced digital file for each episode gets uploaded to a podcast hosting service and ultimately published online.

Choosing Your Audio Editing and Postproduction Software

The features and functions you'll need to record, edit, and handle postproduction using your computer (or a tablet) are similar, regardless of your podcast's format or length. The most widely used free option for audio workstation software is Audacity. iPhone, iPad, or Mac users can also use GarageBand, which is available for free from Apple.

Priced between $20.99 and $31.49 per month is the subscription-based Adobe Audition software for Windows PC or Mac (www.adobe.com/products/audition.html). For Mac users, Apple offers a professional-level audio workstation application called Logic Pro for $199.99 (www.apple.com/logic-pro).

Regardless of which application you use, there will be a learning curve associated with using the software to record and edit your podcast, so plan accordingly. Take advantage of workshops, classes, free tutorials available from the software's publisher, and free how-to videos on YouTube to learn the basics for using your chosen audio workstation software. Before you start publishing podcast episodes, invest whatever time is necessary to record and edit a handful of practice episodes to make sure you're doing everything correctly.

The more time you spend working with your chosen audio workstation software, the better acquainted you'll become with that application, and the more efficient you'll be at recording and editing your podcast episodes. Initially, it might take you four to six hours (or longer) to record and edit a single 30-minute episode. However, as you gain experience, you'll likely be able to produce half-hour podcast episodes, for example, in 90 minutes to two hours each (possibly less) without compromising sound quality or production value.

The best way to discover what's possible when it comes to recording and editing podcast episodes is simply to start listening to a handful of different podcasts. As you listen, pay attention to recording quality and the way music and audio effects are used throughout each episode.

Defining Your Podcast's Unique Sound and Format

If you're the host of your podcast, it should showcase who you are as a person and capture your personality, while allowing you to share whatever content relates to the subject matter or focus of each episode. Ultimately, you (as the host/producer) will be one of the major factors that sets your podcast apart from the competition, so take full advantage of what makes you unique.

Many first-time podcasters who have no previous public speaking or broadcast experience are extremely self-conscious when it comes to how they sound and are picky about the aspects of their personality they choose to share with listeners. Most podcasters, at least initially, hate how they sound. As a result, they use features and functions of their audio workstation software to digitally alter their voice and edit out audio that would otherwise showcase who they are as individuals.

While you should use these editing tools to remove "ums" or awkward pauses, for example, focus on leaving all other aspects of your vocal recordings that make you sound like you. Keep the sound of your podcast authentic and real. Use "crutches" like sound effects, audio enhancements, and background music only when needed.

Over time, focus on developing a unique sound and format for your podcast that your audience will instantly recognize after just a few seconds of listening to each episode.

Create an Episode Template

Back in Chapter 8, "Record Your Podcast Episodes," you learned how to create a Podcast Episode Rundown for each episode of your podcast in advance of recording it. Now, as you begin producing an ongoing series of episodes, develop a production template for yourself using your audio workstation software.

An audio production template will preload and place your intro/outro music, as well as other elements of your podcast, for example, that are included in each episode. Doing this will help you save time during the editing and postproduction process.

Podcast Editing Tips and Tricks

You may have spent years or decades becoming an expert on the subject matter of your podcast, and because of your passion for that topic, you've decided to host and produce a podcast. Well, professional audio engineers have also spent years, perhaps decades, learning and fine-tuning their skills and pursuing their passion for creating great audio programming.

As a podcaster, you don't need to drop everything and attend an audio production school full-time to pursue a degree in audio engineering or production. If you plan to edit and produce your own podcast, you will, however, need to develop and practice some core audio production skills and become proficient using your selected audio workstation software. If you don't have the inclination or wherewithal to obtain this skill set, hire an audio engineer or producer to work with you on your podcast. Do not compromise the production quality of your podcast!

The following is a list of useful podcasting editing tips that'll help you enhance the audio quality of your podcast episodes:

- ▶ As you're recording your podcast, jot down notes and timecodes that relate to content you want to definitely keep, edit, or remove during the editing process. This will help you find and work on those parts of the recording later.
- ▶ Experiment with your audio workstation software and its tools. As you're learning to use various tools, like Normalize or EQ, figure out what sounds good, but rely on the Undo feature if you apply a tool that makes your recording sound worse or unauthentic. Don't overuse audio altering tools, and don't use tools that aren't needed just because they're available to you.
- ▶ Virtually all audio workstation applications have built-in shortcuts to speed up your workflow. Learn the shortcuts and practice using them. They'll ultimately save you a lot of time.
- ▶ When combining voice-over tracks with music and other audio elements during the postproduction process, be careful of the sampling rate that's being used. Make sure that when applied to music, it does not negatively alter the voice-over track(s) or vice versa. Instead of using the copy-and-paste function to add content into your production, use the import function, and then stick with an industry-standard sample rate. For a .wav audio file, for example, this will likely be 44.1kHz/16bps.
- ▶ Using audio workstation software, your audio tracks will be displayed as visual waveforms. Over time, you'll learn how to quickly identify aspects of a waveform that need to be adjusted or edited, even before you listen to the audio. Don't rely

on just your eyes, however. Always listen carefully to your audio after you make an alteration, edit, or cut. Anytime you need to make a finite edit, zoom in or expand the waveform for that audio. Ideally, listen back to all audio using noise-reduction headphones to block out all other sound than what's actually within the audio file you're listening to.

▶ Listen back to your podcast at a louder than normal volume to ensure you don't miss anything. However, make sure the final mix is saved at a volume (level) that's appropriate for your audience.

▶ Keep the voice-over tracks sounding authentic. Resist the urge to delete all breath sounds, and don't use the editing and audio enhancement tools to overly adjust the timing of the spoken audio. Remember that human speech has a natural rhythm. Study the natural rhythms of your host's and guest's voices, and keep them authentic.

▶ Every podcast producer needs to develop their own workflow habits when it comes to producing episodes of their podcast. That being said, a good strategy for editing and postproduction is to take a four-step approach. First, listen to the raw audio from start to finish. Second, go in and make the major edits and cuts. Third, listen back again and fine-tune, focusing on the smaller cuts and edits. Fourth, after the editing and postproduction are done, take a break to clear your head, and then go back and listen to the entire podcast using headphones (at normal playback speed) at least twice from start to finish.

▶ Don't rush the editing and postproduction process. Assuming you follow a production schedule to release new episodes on a regular basis, allocate plenty of time to handle these essential tasks so that you're never working under a tight deadline and rushing.

▶ Bad editing will be distracting to your listeners. Anytime you cut out something, for example, make sure the audio still sounds natural, especially when music is involved. Make sure you do not accidentally clip the beginning or ending of words, and that you've done whatever possible using the tools at your disposal to remove unwanted background noises.

▶ When using the Normalize, EQ, and related tools, listen for cadence or tone changes that don't sound natural. Make sure all audio elements of your podcast are presented at the appropriate levels and volume. Background music, for example, should be heard but not be distracting or overwhelming, especially when someone is speaking.

▶ Make sure that the voices people hear during your podcast episodes are mixed at an appropriate level, no one is shouting, and people are not constantly speaking over each other. These types of problems make a podcast difficult to listen to and will likely turn off your audience.

▶ Ensure all your levels are consistent. Adding too much audio enhancement or effect on a track will impact how it sounds. Avoid abrupt starts and stops, EQ problems, or overly compressing the audio.

▶ Stay consistent with the length of your episodes. Edit out the fluff and repetition. If your audience expects episodes to be around 25 to 30 minutes long, stick to that length, but go with a shorter length if you don't have enough really good content to fill the full 30 minutes. Leave the audience wanting more, not counting the minutes for the podcast to end because they're bored.

Podcast Editing Advice from Travis Brown, President of Podcast Buddy

If you ask any successful business leader, CEO, or entrepreneur for tips that'll help you achieve success, you'll likely be told to find yourself a mentor or role model. The same advice also applies to podcasters. The best way to master the art of becoming an amazing podcaster is to seek out advice, guidance, and training from someone with experience and a proven track record.

Meet Travis Brown. When it comes to learning what you need to know about podcasting—including how to edit and produce podcast episodes that'll capture the attention of your target audience—he's the perfect mentor and role model. Having produced more than 1,500 podcast episodes and helping others launch more than 50 separate podcasts, Brown has discovered what works, how to avoid common podcasting mistakes, and how to make every episode of your podcast sound awesome.

In this exclusive interview, Brown shares advice to up-and-coming podcasters. He offers tips and strategies for recording, editing, producing, and promoting your podcast episodes. As the president and founder of Podcast Buddy (www.podcastbuddy.co), podcasters can hire his company to handle all their editing, postproduction, distribution, and podcast promotional needs.

As a client of Podcast Buddy or participant in the "Shortcut to Podcasting" course, you'll gain access to Travis Brown as a personal mentor. While it's always a good idea to meet and work with your mentor in-person or virtually (via phone calls or video calls), this interview offers a taste of the wisdom you can gain from an experienced podcaster.

"In my early 20s, I was part of a band that recorded records and toured around the country. Throughout that process, I learned audio engineering so I could record my own band and my friends' bands. Once the band had taken its course, I continued to record my own music and record music for other musicians as a professional audio engineer," said Brown.

In recent years, it has become harder for music studios to earn money recording musicians and bands, since people can now easily use their own computers and recording equipment to create professional-quality results from home. Seeing this trend, Brown decided to pivot into something else that was related to music production, but quickly growing. He started recording and producing podcasts for friends, and later for paying clients.

"Five years ago, I started listening to podcasts," explained Brown. "I determined that I could use my extensive experience in audio and music production to produce podcasts. A friend of mine who was a business professional approached me and asked for help starting his own podcast. He needed an audio engineer and producer. I agreed to produce his podcast. Five years later, his podcast has had hundreds of thousands of downloads, and as a result of his podcast's success, his business now generates a high six-figure income annually."

tip

If you plan to handle all your own production-related efforts, Podcast Buddy offers an in-depth, video-based course called "Shortcut to Podcasting" (www.podcastbuddy.co) that teaches participants how to edit and produce their own podcasts. The company also offers Pod Decks ($19 each, www.poddecks.com), which are innovative idea-generation, creativity, and interview tools for helping podcasters create more compelling content, regardless of a podcast's subject matter.

While working on that original podcast, word-of-mouth quickly spread about Brown's talent as a recording engineer and podcast producer. This led to him launching his own company, called Podcast Buddy, which now caters to more than 30 clients.

"I help potential podcasters create and produce their podcast and podcast episodes. I also help businesses grow their podcast and expand their overall online presence, using a podcast to funnel new leads into their business," said Brown.

"The perfect customer for Podcast Buddy is a small-business owner, business/professional coach, or entrepreneur who is wearing lots of hats, who has something to promote or sell, but who doesn't have the bandwidth to spend time learning how to launch, record, edit, produce, distribute, and promote a podcast. We provide a back-end solution to individuals and companies that want to produce a podcast, but don't want to invest the time and energy learning the skills needed to do it," he explained.

Podcast Buddy's services include helping companies come up with an idea for their podcast, launch their podcast, and then produce, publish, and promote each episode. "Part of our service includes promoting each new podcast episode in unique and proven ways on behalf of our clients. We offer a full back-end service," said Brown. While Podcast Buddy can help a company hire a professional host for a podcast, whenever someone wants to host their own podcast (which is something he strongly recommends), he teaches them how to simply record just the voice track for their podcast episodes from virtually anywhere using inexpensive equipment.

Podcast Buddy then takes the raw audio recording and affordably produces it into an episode, complete with music and other audio elements. All the editing, postproduction, distribution, and promotion for a podcast is done on behalf of their clients.

When selecting technology to record any podcast, there are two main considerations—budget and the recording environment. Based on these two factors, Podcast Buddy will recommend the perfect recording equipment to utilize. The recording environment where the audio for a podcast will actually be recorded will determine what type of microphone someone needs to use.

"A condenser microphone is a more sensitive microphone that is typically used in studios. It allows for very crisp audio to be recorded in the right environments, so it provides very high-fidelity output," said Brown. "A dynamic microphone is a lower-sensitivity microphone that doesn't pick up as much ambient sound in a recording environment. It's a great option for most non-studio recording environments, but during the editing phase of putting a podcast episode together, the recordings will often require a bit of extra tweaking to make them sound awesome.

"For most podcasters, I recommend they invest in the highest quality dynamic microphone they can afford. One of my personal favorites is the Rode Pod microphone paired with the Rode Podcaster Pro, which is a mixer interface. This equipment combo is priced around $600. One of many less expensive options is an Audio-Technica ATR2100-USB microphone [https://www.audio-technica.com/en-us/atr2100-usb], which is priced around $80. It plugs directly into a computer for recording audio," explained Brown.

When asked whether a podcaster is better off recording their content using an appropriate type of microphone directly connected to their computer, or whether a digital audio recorder should be used, Brown stated, "Both options can generate equal quality digital recordings. If someone is going to interview guests on location, I recommend using a digital audio recorder for the convenience and portability. If you're going to be recording phone interviews or 'in studio' guests, a microphone connected directly to your computer will work just fine. If you'll be recording multiple hosts and/or multiple guests at the same time, you have multiple options, but I find using a multitrack digital audio recorder to be the easiest and most convenient to use, especially if you won't be doing your own editing and postproduction."

When using a computer as a recording tool, in addition to utilizing the right type of microphone, you'll also need to use recording software. In regard to this, Brown stated, "All digital audio workstations are almost exactly the same in terms of what they can do. Professionally, I use Apple's Logic Pro X for recording, editing, and postproduction, but for simply recording audio that'll be edited and produced by someone else, the free Audacity software works great.

"For podcast recording, you don't need software with a lot of bells and whistles. You just need the ability to record a few separate audio tracks at the same time. For up-and-coming podcasters who will be recording

tip

To learn more about Rode's microphones and related podcast recording equipment, visit www. rode.com. Also be sure to look into the microphone and recording options offered by Shure, which you learned about from the interview with Soren Pedersen, senior product specialist at Shure, featured in Chapter 7, "Set Up Your Recording Studio."

their own audio, I recommend choosing one recording option and then sticking to it. Learn everything you can about that recording option, since they all function just a little bit differently, but ultimately, they all do pretty much the same thing," said Brown.

Looking back at his podcast production career thus far, when asked which of the podcasts he personally likes the best, he was excited to talk about a podcast called *Stretch* (www.stretchpodcast.com). The host is Alison Kuhlow.

Brown explained, "Alison wanted to create a podcast that had more of a journalistic vibe to it, as opposed to following a traditional question-and-answer interview format. We produced her show by having her go out and interview people. She then goes back and listens to that audio and crafts and records her own narrative in between the questions. This allowed the podcast to take on more of a storytelling element, which helps it to stand out. The format creates a tremendous amount of value for her listeners."

Brown is a big fan of podcasts that do not include a lot of fluff. "What I coach my clients, I encourage them to forgo a lot of small talk, especially at the start of each episode. I believe a podcaster should get right to the meat of that episode. When someone listens to a podcast, they're often attracted to it because of a number of factors. For example, they may already be a subscriber or fan. However, for new listeners, chances are they're interested in the overall subject matter of your podcast or the topic a specific episode will be covering. In this case, their attention might have been piqued by the episode's title or description.

"Instead of starting a podcast with an advertisement or a bunch of small talk, I highly recommend getting right into what the meat of the episode is. If the episode promises five tips for producing a great podcast, I would start the podcast by saying something like 'You want five tips for creating a great podcast, well, let's start right off with tip number one . . .' Don't waste your listener's time.

"There's a saying for songwriters and musicians that goes, 'Don't bore us, get us to the chorus,' because the chorus is often the most exciting and memorable part of the song. You want to get to the chorus right away, so the listener will continue listening to the rest of the song. The same rule applies to podcasting. Launch each episode with important information or content, and then if necessary, add a touch of small talk later on in the program," said Brown.

One of the things that Podcast Buddy offers its clients is a 72-hour turnaround time. Once a podcaster records and submits the audio track, the team at Podcast Buddy listens to every second of the audio. Show notes are then produced, and the full audio production and postproduction efforts immediately begin.

To keep things affordable for up-and-coming podcasters, clients can pay for Podcast Buddy's services on a per-episode basis. The base rate is $150 per episode, which can be up to one hour long. This includes all the mixing and mastering, the show notes creation, and uploading the final production to the preselected podcast hosting service. The company also offers a plan where a podcaster can create up to four episodes (up to one hour each) for a flat fee of $500 per month.

In addition to fully producing each podcast episode, Podcast Buddy produces what it calls a promotional "Audiogram" for each episode. This Audiogram production service can also be purchased on an a la carte basis for podcasters who produce their own podcasts, but who are looking to utilize this unique and proven promotional tool.

"To create an Audiogram, we pull out the juiciest 60 seconds of a podcast episode. We then create an animated image, and display a text-based transcription of what's being said. We produce Audiograms in three different formats, suitable for posting on Instagram Stories, Facebook Stories, Facebook pages, and Twitter. Based on our research, we have found that using Audiograms to promote podcast episodes via social media, as opposed to static posts, podcasters attract about five times more traffic to their podcast," he said.

Brown believes that more people are likely to watch and listen to something that contains captions. When people view social media posts from their phones, for example, they typically don't have the audio turned on. When an image in a post starts moving, it catches the viewer's eye. When the transcript appears, viewers start reading along. This engages the viewer more. Once someone's attention has been grabbed, they're more apt to turn on the audio to experience the full content within that Audiogram.

"Audiograms offer a powerful tool podcasters can use to promote their new episodes and create excitement for them. By providing 60 seconds' worth of the episode's best content, the potential audience is more inclined to seek out and listen to the entire episode," said Brown. "The concept is somewhat similar to watching a trailer for a blockbuster movie. When Podcast Buddy produces each Audiogram, we create the graphic and animation, and mix it with the 60 seconds of audio from the podcast episode it's promoting. We do all of the production on behalf of the client."

After producing thousands of individual podcast episodes for many different podcasters, Brown has developed his own proven approach to production. "From a scientific standpoint, the first thing I do is listen to the raw voice recording(s), and then apply EQ [Equalization] to the voice-over tracks. This mainly consists of removing unwanted audio frequencies to make the voice tracks sound as pleasant as possible. After all, if a podcast sounds bad, people stop listening.

"Next, I apply compression and limiting to make sure all of the audio is uniform. For example, when someone is excited, their voice might get a little louder, and when they're relaxed, their voice might sound a bit calmer or softer. Overall, however, the audio track needs to stay even so you don't wind up fatiguing the listeners," said Brown.

"When I listen to the podcast's audio contextually, overall, I will try to remove any type of crutch word, like 'um' or 'ah,' or any type of unwanted noise, like a cough or unpleasant static. For the most part, my biggest focus is to make the audio sound as natural as possible, so that it does not sound over edited. I believe podcasts should sound like the host is talking to the listener in person. Contextually, for me, that means leaving in breath sounds, so the host sounds natural. However, if there's a lot of rambling, that might get truncated a bit. For the most part, I only remove audio that would not be pleasing to the listener," explained Brown.

"I am a proponent of leaving breath sound in podcasts because humans breathe. This keeps the audio sounding natural when people in the podcast speak. I personally don't find breaths offensive when listening to someone speak. When someone's voice sounds natural in a podcast, I believe this causes the audience to feel more connected with that speaker. When breath sounds are removed, I personally believe this can make someone's audio sound too sterile. Some people want a more sterile-sounding podcast, but when breath sounds are removed, I think it makes someone sound robotic and less natural or relatable," he added.

If you were to research what constitutes the ideal podcast episode length, you'll see research supporting almost any length, based on the subject matter and target audience.

Based on Brown's experience, he believes, "Once you conveyed your key information or talking points, and you've provided the value your podcast episode is designed to offer, that episode is over. This might take anywhere from five minutes up to 60 minutes."

He added, "Based on my own experience, I have discovered that a 20- to 25-minute length seems to be the sweet spot for many podcasters. This is the duration that most people can remain engaged. It's also about the same length as a television sitcom, and about the same length of many commutes, walks, or workout regimens, which is often when people listen to podcasts. We love podcasts because it's a frictionless medium. We can listen to podcasts easily while doing other things. We can listen to podcasts that allow us to learn, grow, or be entertained while engaged in many other types of activities."

This recommended length for a podcast should include the intro, outro, and any ads that will accompany the episode. When it comes to choosing music to accompany a podcast, as part of its intro, outro, or as background while people are speaking, Brown is a firm believer that the selected music should match the vibe of the podcast.

Brown tries to choose music that matches the mood of the podcast as a whole and that will add a cinematic effect that generates excitement and captures attention, but won't distract the listeners or take away from the core content or whatever information is being conveyed. "Music can create emotion or excitement. My goal is to use music to make a podcast sound as radio-like or broadcast-like as possible," said Brown.

First and foremost, podcasts are a form of entertainment, like radio, TV, streaming videos, or audiobooks, for example. Brown added, "As a podcast producer, always keep the entertainment aspect in mind. If you want to sound professional, and you want to be a professional entertainer, the music you use will play a factor in that. That being said, I am seeing a turn where podcasters are keeping their intros and outros very short and to the point, so they can delve directly into their core content. Don't create a situation where a listener needs to fast-forward through an episode in order to get to the main content."

Using background music behind vocals is typically a mood or vibe-setting enhancement when the right music is selected and mixed with the voice track(s) at the appropriate level.

"However, if a podcaster has a powerful enough message and a commanding or attention-keeping voice, they can forgo using background music except in the intro, outro, and maybe for a transition. For the intro and outro parts of the podcast, using music is the norm," said Brown.

Countless music libraries are available to podcasters that provide a plethora of music selections from all genres and at all tempos. "I personally use music I write, record, and produce myself as a musician, or I rely exclusively on an online service called AudioJungle. net. This service has thousands of music tracks that someone can quickly search in order to find the perfect addition to their podcast. The service is super affordable. They work with many independent musicians, so you're able to find and use music that fits the vibe and style of any podcast quickly, and it won't sound like generic elevator music," said Brown.

When it comes to recording and producing ads that'll be heard within a podcast episode, Brown believes the host should record those ads themselves. He explained, "When someone subscribes to your podcast, they're falling in love with you and your voice. I always tell my clients, if you're going to include ads, record them using your own voice, especially if it's for your own product, because there's nobody better to talk about it to your audience than you. I also don't believe there's a need to use a professional announcer to record the intro or outro for a podcast episode. Those messages should also come from the host, because it's all part of the podcast's overall brand."

So as not to confuse the audience, there is something to be said for producing ads within a podcast in such a way that they sound different from the body of a podcast. "I have two thoughts on this. One is that the host can do what's called a live read, and naturally include some form of advertisement for a product or service within the podcast by reading an ad's script or ad-libbing using just talking points. This approach works when taking a natural, nonsales-oriented 'just so you know' approach to the ad's contents. I am also a big fan of producing ads using the host's voice-over, but with different music that will stand out from the rest of the content and also serve as a transition when presenting that content," said Brown.

One of the biggest challenges songwriters and music producers have is knowing when a song is actually done, perfect, and ready to release. This is the same challenge that podcast producers often face, since it's easy to listen back to a produced episode before it's published online and continuously make tweaks, edits, and second-guess creative decisions.

"When listening back to a podcast episode, I am a big fan of taking the approach that if it sucks, cut it out. If you're not being entertained when you listen to an episode before it's released, then you know it's not ready for your listeners to hear. An episode is done when you've told the audience what they're going to get from listening to the episode, and the content of the episode gives them exactly that. The episode then gives them an action step

tip

As a podcaster, it's possible to give your listeners aural fatigue if they listen to something for too long. Using music to break up segments in a podcast episode gives their minds a quick break from listening to content. It gets their minds ready to listen to the next section of the podcast. Brown explained that music can be used as a transition within podcasts when going from one topic or section of content to another.

related to how to utilize the information or what to do with it next. Once these three steps are efficiently included in a podcast episode, it's done," explained Brown.

Brown believes that podcasters need to adopt a nonperfectionist mindset when producing each episode. He stated, "Learn from your previous episodes, but don't keep second-guessing every creative or production decision you make. For me, if I listen to a podcast episode I am working on and it feels good to me, I know it's the right thing to do. If I find places in an episode where I think the listener might need a quick break, I'll often add transition music at those points. These are all creative and highly subjective decisions. Always listen to a podcast episode as the end user and ask yourself if, as an audience member, are you enjoying what you're hearing or are you bored? Put yourself in the audience's shoes when making creative and production decisions."

After years of experience producing podcasts, he's become a huge fan of making mistakes and learning from those mistakes, as well as asking for feedback from listeners. "Listening to listener feedback is a great way to optimize the format of your show," he explained.

As mentioned, Brown relies on Apple's Logic Pro as his podcast recording, editing, and postproduction software of choice. Now that he's become proficient using this software, editing and postproduction time takes him only about one-and-a-half times the length of a typical podcast episode.

"Don't take shortcuts when editing your podcast. For example, some people think they can save time by listening to the playback at one-and-a-half times the normal speed. When you do this, you can easily miss important nuances. After the recording process is done, I know it'll take me 90 minutes to edit and produce a 60-minute episode, so I plan my time accordingly. Until you get really good at using your audio workstation software, editing and postproduction will likely take much longer," said Brown.

The biggest mistake Brown often sees when up-and-coming podcasters edit and produce their own podcast episodes is that they overuse some of the audio processing tools available to them. "Using an EQ tool can be tricky and it can easily be overused. People also tend to utilize

tip ⓘ

In conjunction with his Podcast Buddy podcast production company and his "Shortcut to Podcasting" course, Travis Brown also offers a product called Pod Decks ($19.99–$39.99, www.poddecks.com). Three decks of 50 cards each (sold separately) offer creativity tools to podcasters. For example, one deck includes episode idea generators, and another offers insightful interview questions that work with almost any type of podcast.

volume levels that are too loud. Volume and quality are not at all related. Podcasters also tend to cut out too much of their personal vocal qualities, so the end product does not showcase what's actually them. Don't suck the life out of your podcast. Let it breathe. You, as the host, are a person. Your listeners want to hear you, not a sterile, overedited version of you that does not sound authentic. Don't get too surgical when editing your podcast, especially when it comes to how you sound."

Editing and handling the postproduction aspects of a podcast are skill sets that will require a lot of practice to master. "Every podcaster needs to develop their own personal workflow when it comes to producing their podcast. Your workflow has to work for you. In my three-and-a-half-hour video course, 'Shortcut to Podcasting,' I show people exactly how to edit a podcast episode from start to finish using Audacity," said Brown. "Producing a professional-sounding podcast is not difficult if you take time to learn all about the recording, editing, and postproduction aspects of creating your podcast."

When all the recording, editing, and postproduction for a podcast episode is done, the podcast needs to be published online. "For a podcast hosting service, I recommend Libsyn.com. This service offers a bunch of features and functions, including analytics, for a very low price. It also makes it very easy to publish your podcast quickly on all of the popular podcasting distribution services and directories using its one-click publish tool," said Brown.

As for where your podcast should be offered, Brown's top three choices include: Apple Podcasts (https://help.apple.com/itc/podcasts_connect/#), Stitcher (www.stitcher.com), and Spotify (www.spotify.com).

One of the biggest goals for a podcaster should be to make their podcast and their content unique. Brown's best advice to accomplish this is to be vulnerable as a podcaster. "Instead of trying to look like the king of the world, share your successes, as well as what you're struggling with. Unapologetically share your true self and lean into being you within your podcast. Don't be self-conscious. Share your passions and opinions. That's the most magnetic thing you can do. Don't try to be what you think your audience wants you to be. Just be you! Authenticity works."

Monetizing Your Podcast

The ultimate dream of almost every podcaster is to build a large and loyal enough audience so that advertisers come knocking on their door, offering to sponsor their podcast for an entire season or year at a time at a cost per thousands (CPM) rate that allows the podcast to be operated as a profitable business venture.

Yes, this does happen. Many of the podcasts currently available are generating revenue from sponsors and advertisers. The question is, How much money is actually being made? Unless the podcast is produced and hosted by a well-known celebrity or public figure, or supported by a well-established television network, radio network, movie studio, website, or other media outlet, realistically, it will take time—up to several years—to organically grow a podcast audience that's large enough to generate any significant income from it through advertising.

Those podcasters who are passionate, persistent, clever, and perhaps a little bit lucky will eventually grow their audience, and as a result, the potential to successfully monetize their podcast and earn a full-time income from it. Whether advertisers will be interested in supporting your podcast comes down to its audience size, the makeup of the audience, and the production quality of the content. Believe it or not, the topics covered within a podcast or the show format are of lesser importance to many advertisers.

Podcast Advertising's Industry Standards Are Still Evolving

Compared to virtually all other forms of advertising—on TV, on the radio, in print, on billboards, and even online—podcasting is still a relatively new advertising medium. As a result, there are not yet any industry standards. That being said, the podcasts that offer the best *value proposition* to potential advertisers, and that have a decent audience size, are the ones able to successfully monetize their content using advertising or sponsorships.

Advertisers typically have a specific goal in mind. They either want to sell their product/service or increase their brand awareness (or both) through paid advertising. The value proposition your podcast offers must be clearly presented to a potential advertiser. It should be custom-tailored to show how your podcast can help them achieve their advertising-related goals, and it can include a wide range of factors and information, such as:

▶ *Audience size.* The podcaster must present accurate statistics and analytics pertaining to the number of downloads/streams the podcast has on a weekly, monthly, and per episode basis.

▶ *Audience makeup.* This relates to the demographics of the audience (their age range, income, education level, etc.), combined with whether the podcast is reaching a niche or highly targeted audience of interest to particular advertisers.

▶ *CPM rate.* The advertising cost per thousand listeners. The rate to strive for is around $25 per thousand, until the podcast is well-established and the audience is massive. Realistically, a podcast might only be able to charge between $5 and $10 per thousand downloads/streams. This is a rate the podcaster sets, but it typically must be negotiable.

▶ *Reputation.* This refers to how the podcast is perceived as a whole, as well as the individual reputations of the podcast's host(s) and even its guests. Many advertisers want to stay clear of controversy, as well as podcasts that cover certain topics.

▶ *Audience loyalty.* The loyalty of the audience can be measured in many ways, such as social media interaction, the number of listeners donating to the podcast through Patreon (www.patreon.com), the number of comments podcast episodes receive, or the response rate to specific types of ads.

▶ *What else the podcast offers to advertisers.* Beyond featuring 15-, 30-, or 60-second ads within the podcast itself, what else does the podcast offer to its advertisers? Are the advertisers promoted on the podcast's web page and/or within the podcast's social media feeds? Does the advertiser gain access to the podcast's opt-in email list? In what other ways can an advertiser benefit by supporting a particular podcast?

▶ *Ad format(s) the podcast will accept.* Podcast (audio) ads can be pre-produced by the advertiser, custom-produced for the advertiser by the podcaster, or presented as a "live read" by the podcast host using talking points provided by the advertiser. This last ad format tends to generate the best response rate, especially if the podcaster is skilled at presenting "live read" ads in an attention-getting and authentic way that encourages a high percentage of the audience to respond to that ad's call to action.

▶ *Ad placement within each episode.* Advertisers want their ads to receive premium placement within each episode of a podcast that's being sponsored. Terminology including *pre-roll placement, mid-roll placement,* and *post-roll placement* are used to describe when an ad will be heard within an episode. Pre-roll refers to before the content begins (or just after the episode's intro). Mid-roll refers to somewhere in the middle of the podcast, and post-roll refers to the end of the podcast (in conjunction with or after the episode's outro).

▶ *Relationship between the podcaster and advertiser.* Advertisers are more apt to support podcasters who work hard to develop a positive and long-term relationship, who are attentive to the advertiser's needs, who are easily accessible, and who go out of their way to exceed the advertiser's expectations. If a podcaster develops a reputation for being difficult to work with, advertisers will seek out other podcasts to sponsor, regardless of the value proposition the podcast offers.

Set Your Podcast's CPM Rate

A podcast's *CPM* rate refers to how much it charges advertisers per thousand downloads/ streams of a podcast episode. This rate is set by the podcaster, but to allure advertisers, must be fair, negotiable, and based on reliable audience statistics. Most advertisers will only consider podcasts whose audience is measured using IAB certified tools that many (but not all) podcast hosting services offer.

In CPM, the *M* refers to the Latin word *mille*, which means thousand. Thus, the *C* stands for *cost*, the *P* stands for *per*, and the *M* stands for *mille*. In the podcasting world, each unique download or stream for an episode is considered one listen. A more detailed explanation of how CPM is set and how revenue is calculated can be found at: https:// adopter.media/podcast-advertising-rates-explained.

Podcasts with a small audience (below 5,000) can still potentially attract advertisers, especially if the podcast caters to a very niche (targeted) audience that can clearly be defined and that the potential advertiser is anxious to reach.

It's not until a podcast grows its audience to 10, 25, 50, or 100 thousand (or larger) that audience size is what will attract advertisers and allow podcasters to earn a premium CPM rate. As of late 2019, AdvertiseCast (www.advertisecast.com/podcast-advertising-rates) released statistics showing that the *average* rates for podcast ads were $15 per thousand listeners for a ten-second ad, $18 per thousand listeners for a 30-second ad, and $25 per thousand listeners for a 60-second ad. However, the ability to charge that average rate (or higher) depends on a wide range of factors, including the value proposition the podcast offers its advertisers.

As the popularity of podcasting continues to grow and more and more major companies and brands begin utilizing podcast advertising, "average CPM" rates will certainly adapt over time, and more industry standards will be established over time.

The chart in Figure 10.1 on page 141 showcases what a sample podcast (with 25-minute episode lengths) could potentially earn from advertising revenue, based on its audience size and CPM. For this example, the sample podcast accepts a maximum of five 30-second ads per episode.

Types of Ads

In terms of revenue, a podcaster can feature several types of ads within their podcast. Ideally, you want to accept ads where the advertisers pay a negotiated CPM rate to reach your audience. However, there are also ads where advertisers only pay for results. In this case, the podcaster receives a small percentage of the sale made as a result of a response ad, or a fixed price for

Sample Podcast ROI			
Audience Size	CPM Rate (per 30-second ad)	Revenue per Ad	Total Potential Ad Revenue per Episode (with five ad spots sold)
10k	$10	$100	$500
25k	$20	$500	$2,500
50k	$25	$1,250	$6,250
100k	$30	$3,000	$15,000
250k	$50	$12,500	$62,500

FIGURE 10–1: **Sample Podcast ROI**

every response to the ad, or a fixed price for every sale made as a result of a response from the ad. Payment for all podcast ads is typically made within 30 days after an episode is published online, not in advance.

How and Where to Find Potential Advertisers

Once your podcast is established, you have reliable audience data ready to present, and you've crafted a value proposition for your podcast that you believe will appeal to potential advertisers, you can reach out to those advertisers in a handful of ways, including:

▶ Contact the company directly and develop a relationship with the CEO or vice president of advertising, for example. Sell ads directly to the advertiser. To achieve the best results using this approach, only contact companies that will be interested in your podcast's niche audience, and then craft a personalized value proposition for each potential advertiser.

warning

For the podcaster, response-based ads (that are not paid for based on a CPM) are much easier to get (since there's little risk to the advertisers), but since the response rates for these ads will likely be very low, the revenue potential is also low. A 1 percent direct response rate from a podcast ad is considered very good. For a startup podcast with a small but growing audience, this type of ad is a place to begin, but there's no way to project in advance what the revenue from the ads will be.

- ▶ Work with established advertising agencies that are known for buying podcast advertising on behalf of their clients. Adopter Media (www.adopter.media) is an example of this type of ad agency.

- ▶ Work with an established agency or network that, for a fee or commission, matches up podcasters with advertisers. AdvertiseCast (www.advertisecast.com/podcast-advertising) is an example of this type of network.

- ▶ Focus on building a successful podcast with a large and loyal audience, and potential advertisers will likely approach you eventually. One of the biggest mistakes podcasters make, however, is making it difficult for potential advertisers to contact them. Make sure to include contact information for potential advertisers within your podcast's show notes, on its website, and within its social media profiles. Don't make it difficult for a potential advertiser or advertising agency to find and contact you!

- ▶ Work with your podcast hosting service to help you land advertisers/sponsors. Some services, like Libsyn and Blubrry, take a more active role in placing ads with podcasts hosted on their respective services (for a fee or commission, of course).

- ▶ Hire an experienced advertising salesperson to work on your podcast's behalf. This should be someone who understands podcasting and has preexisting relationships with potential advertisers, or who has the sales skills, reputation, and experience that allow them to reach out to potential advertisers and effectively sell ads. The ad sales rep may be paid a fixed salary, salary plus commission, or just commission. Commission-only salespeople tend to earn rather high commissions for each sale they make, but this is negotiable.

There's a Lot About Podcast Advertising You Need to Learn

Advertising is an industry unto itself that generates billions of dollars per year in revenue for all sorts of media outlets. Thus, some people spend their entire professional careers mastering the art of advertising. Podcast advertising is only one form of advertising that's internet-related, but it's a fast-growing one.

Before you start soliciting advertisers or sponsors for your podcast, do plenty of homework so you understand exactly how the process works, keeping in mind that with no real industry standards yet developed (as of early 2020), the intricacies of podcast advertising are continuously evolving. When the time is right for your podcast, if you don't want to invest the time to properly monetize it yourself, hire freelance experts to help you.

The more you understand about your own podcast and its audience, as well as how podcast advertising works in general, the better equipped you'll be to generate the most revenue possible from your podcasting efforts. Keep in mind, beyond selling advertising or sponsorships, numerous other revenue-generating opportunities are available to successful podcasters. Many of these are outlined within Chapter 11, "More Ways to Generate Income from Your Podcast."

Learn More About Podcast Advertising from One of the Industry's Leading Experts

Utilizing a professional mentor or seeking out advice and guidance from someone who is already successful in your field is always a great strategy. As a starting point for finding and working with your own podcast advertising expert(s) or mentor(s), the following is an exclusive and in-depth interview with Glenn Rubenstein, founder and CEO of Adopter Media (www.adopter.media), one of the world's foremost, full-service podcast advertising agencies.

Rubenstein is considered one of the world's leading experts when it comes to podcast advertising. Through his work, he deals directly with high-profile companies and brands looking to utilize podcast advertising as part of their overall advertising strategy. As a result, he has a unique understanding of what advertisers look for when choosing podcasts to sponsor. Thus, he can offer expert advice to podcasters about how to make their podcasts more attractive to potential advertisers.

When asked what it means to be a full-service podcast advertising agency, Rubenstein explained, "We work on the brand side. A brand like Pitney Bowes comes to us and says they want to advertise on podcasts and wants us to tell them what they should be doing. In turn, we do all of the research.

"We first study what all of the client's competition has already done in the podcast advertising space. We look at who the client's demographic targets are, and then we start putting together a media plan that includes anywhere from several dozen to hundreds of podcasts that we believe that client should advertise with over the course of six weeks to 12 months. We work everything from start to finish on behalf of our clients. We also do all of the in-depth research related to the podcasts we recommend that our clients sponsor. We then negotiate the ad rates, and help develop the talking points or production for the ads themselves," said Rubenstein.

As podcast ad campaigns are running (and immediately afterward), Adopter Media tracks and analyzes the performance of each ad and campaign and reports back to their clients. The ad campaign data is then used to grow, scale, and optimize the campaign moving forward, based on what's working, what's not working, and where the client should focus more of their dollars.

"We're very much *A* to *Z* in the podcast advertising process. Our clients typically want to outsource their podcast advertising activities to us, and then we do everything to make that advertising successful. As a result of our work, we have developed very close relationships with many podcasters that we work with on a regular basis. We study which podcasters do things well, and who does things right. We've also discovered the potential pitfalls to avoid for advertisers and podcasters, and how podcasters can set up their podcast so it has a highly engaged audience that can be monetized," added Rubenstein.

One of the most important lessons Rubenstein has learned related to podcast advertising is that everyone's success depends heavily on the relationship that's built between the podcaster and the advertiser. "The real money for the podcaster, when it comes to advertising, is from the repeat ad buys from advertisers. If you look at the effort that's involved in selling one podcast ad to one advertiser, for most podcasters, this is a break-even proposition in terms of the time, effort, and energy that's involved with securing the advertiser, getting the copy together, developing an understanding of the product, and actually doing the ad.

"Where the real profit potential lies is after that first initial test campaign runs and is successful. That's when the advertiser renews or expands the campaign for a full six months or year. The hard work has been done, so now the podcaster can benefit from the ongoing revenue," added Rubenstein.

The good news for podcasters is that more and more mainstream companies and brands are quickly turning to podcasting as a viable advertising vehicle and are increasing the ad dollars spent in this space. "The sky is the limit related to the types of companies that are starting to utilize podcast advertising. This type of advertising is very hot right now [as of early 2020], and there's a lot of buzz around it. Beyond that, once specific advertisers start to understand the benefits of podcast advertising, they see there's typically a strong one-to-one relationship or connection between a podcast host and a listener. Audience members often build a strong bond and trust with a podcast host, so when a podcaster tells them to do something, their listeners are very receptive to that messaging," said Rubenstein.

Thanks to the growing popularity of podcasting, some large companies and brands are actually turning away from other advertising media (like TV, radio, and print) and boosting their podcast-related ad budgets. This is also a highly targeted and affordable advertising option for smaller to midsize companies looking to reach their potential customers or clients. "For advertisers utilizing direct response ads, podcast advertising is often something they're willing to try, and then expand upon once their efforts are proven successful," added Rubenstein. "On the brand advertising side, companies are still experimenting with podcast advertising, but they're starting to see greater and greater success as more reliable data is now available pertaining to brand lift as a result of podcast advertising."

For startup podcasters, day one of their podcast's availability is not the best time to start seeking out advertisers. "Based on whether the podcast reaches a highly targeted, niche, and measurable audience, the best time to start monetizing a podcast varies greatly from podcast to podcast, and among other things, is based on audience size and makeup," added Rubenstein.

"Podcasts that reach a hyper-niche audience can start seeking out advertising a lot sooner, and with a smaller audience than typical podcasts. Podcast advertising is almost entirely purchased on a CPM basis. A $20 to $25 CPM is average, so at the very least, a podcast needs at least 1,000 streams/downloads before its audience is even measurable by advertisers," explained Rubenstein.

"The more you focus on audience development, the more payoff you'll receive when your podcast does start attracting sponsors. Once your podcast has 10,000 or more listeners, that's when ad revenue potential will start adding up, especially when you sell two to five ads per episode, and you're already doing something that you really love," he added. "The larger your audience grows, the less niche it has to be to attract advertisers, but it's still vitally important for a podcaster to know who their audience is and know who you're reaching, because that's information you need to craft a value proposition that advertisers will take notice of."

▶ What's IAB Certification?

This is an industry-accepted way podcast analytics are collected, measured, and reported. For an up-to-date listing of IAB certified podcast hosting services, visit: https://iabtechlab.com/compliance-programs/compliant-companies.

According to Blubrry Podcasting (a well-known podcast hosting service), "One podcast download in Blubrry Statistics is equal to one individual consuming the media. Unlike other podcast statistics systems, we analyze every download/stream/play request to arrive to a download number that equals the number of individuals who downloaded or streamed (played in a web page or mobile device) an episode." This data is collected in a manner that's consistent with IAB Tech Lab's Podcast Measurement Guidelines.

According to Rubenstein, when showcasing details about your podcast's audience to potential advertisers, it's essential to present data that comes from a third-party and highly reliable source. "If your podcast is hosted on a platform that's IAB certified with its Podcast Measurement Guidelines and downloads reporting, we take that very seriously. If you're not able to present reliable data, you're not going to be paid top dollar by advertisers," he said.

When it comes to podcast advertising, both the podcaster and advertiser want ads to achieve the best possible results which are measurable. As of early 2020, one ad format that continues to work very well involves the advertiser providing the podcaster with talking points for an ad, and then the podcaster ad-libs the ad "live" during the podcast recording process.

When a host is trusted and well-liked by their audience, and the host has honed their skills at presenting talking point-based ads, the results tend to be significantly better than utilizing prerecorded and highly produced ads within a podcast.

"I would recommend that podcasters develop and practice the skill required for taking talking points and transforming them into an attention-getting and credible ad on the fly. Listen to podcasts that include this type of ad and pay attention to how other podcasters use a specific rhythm and cadence to deliver the ads in an effective way to their audience," said Rubenstein.

"The advice I can offer is to imagine you're talking one-on-one to a close friend and telling them about a new product you just bought or a new restaurant you just tried and loved. Focus on the excitement in your voice as you talk about your experience and tell your friend that you need to experience it for themselves. That's the level of believability and enthusiasm a host needs to deliver when presenting talking point ads. It should sound like a personal recommendation from a best friend," he said.

"If you're a podcaster who is going after your own advertisers, go after companies whose products or services you're already personally passionate about and love, and that you think your audience will appreciate as well. This will make it much easier to present talking point ads during your podcast that are credible and that will generate results," explained Rubenstein.

In Rubenstein's opinion, audiences tend to tune out pre-produced or highly produced ads they hear within a podcast, which limits their results. "Talking point ads work well because they're spontaneous and come across as honest information coming from a trusted friend, who in this case is the podcast host," added Rubenstein. "When a host tries to prerecord an ad spot, they tend to overthink it, record multiple takes, spend a lot of time trying to get it right, and then wind up having an ad that has no passion behind it. I recommend that podcasters always present talking point ads live, during their recording process, if possible. It's going to sound more authentic and more ephemeral, and the audience will respond better to that."

Podcasters who pre-produce and prerecord ads tend to do it at a different time than recording their actual podcast episodes. This results in the host having a different mindset when recording the ads. Also, their voice might not be warmed up, and in many cases, the ad won't have the same energy compared to if it were recorded during the actual episode. "What we are seeing, based on what our advertisers are doing, is that highly produced and prerecorded ads within podcasts don't perform anywhere near as well as when a host does a live read or ad-libs an ad based on talking points," he explained.

First and foremost, anytime Rubenstein is evaluating a podcast on behalf of a potential advertiser, he pays careful attention to the audio production quality of the podcast and the professional appearance of the podcast's cover art. "Thanks to advancements in technology, a podcaster has no excuse for having a podcast that sounds bad or cover art that looks unprofessional," said Rubenstein.

He added that if a podcast sounds like it was recorded on an outdated cassette recorder in a noisy room, or if the artwork looks cheesy, his evaluation won't proceed any further, since these are two of what Rubenstein calls "Pass/Fail" podcast elements that can easily be analyzed.

As for a podcast's actual content, he looks for the energy and enthusiasm of the hosts and how the podcast is received by the audience. "If we have an advertiser who wants to use talking point-based ads that the podcast host will ad-lib and present during each episode, we evaluate things like the audience's loyalty to the podcast and host. If a podcast has a Patreon account and solicits donations from its audience, and that account has several hundred subscribers, meaning that a bunch of listeners are regularly donating money to the podcast, we look at that as very favorable audience engagement, which means that direct response ads will likely perform well on that podcast," explained Rubenstein.

Another thing that Rubenstein looks for when evaluating a podcast for his clients is whether that podcast has had the same group of advertisers for a long time, and whether those advertisers continue to renew their contracts. "This is a clear indication that the podcaster is easy to work with, professional, and cares about developing a long-term relationship with its advertisers," said Rubenstein.

One of the biggest mistakes Rubenstein continuously sees podcasters make when trying to land sponsorships and advertisers is that the podcasters make it almost impossible for potential advertisers or agencies to contact them. "You would not believe how many times we get a request from a client to pursue advertising on a specific podcast, and we have to invest over an hour simply trying to get in touch with that podcaster to discuss advertising opportunities," stated Rubenstein. "Every podcast's web page should have clearly displayed sponsorship information and contact details. You can even publish your audience size and ad rates since that's the first thing a potential advertiser will be asking for. Also share information about who your podcast's advertisers currently are, and which companies have sponsored the podcast in the past."

Beyond being easy to find and contact as a podcaster, Rubenstein also recommends that you always be very prompt to reply to advertising and sponsorship inquiries. "On the agency side, clients sometimes wait until the last minute to decide how much they want to spend on podcasting during the next quarter or 12-month period, for example. As a result, our agency is given a $100,000 budget, for example, that it needs to allocate within a few days before the end of the advertiser's current quarter. If we can't quickly make contact with the podcasts we're interested in for our client, we'll need to quickly go elsewhere in order to meet the deadlines we're presented with. If a podcaster waits a few days or a week to get back to me, that money has already been spent and allocated, and the campaign is already live on other podcasts," said Rubenstein.

Anytime a podcaster approaches Rubenstein looking for ads from clients to be placed with them, in addition to expecting a really well-crafted value proposition presented in a professional manner, Rubenstein expects to receive a well-written, highly personalized, and upbeat introductory letter, as opposed to a copied and pasted, pre-written solicitation email.

"Again, find brands that you're passionate about, and then write personal, concise, and excited emails that communicate your podcast's value proposition and explain why you're reaching out to that particular company. The most important thing you can do with a cold, unsolicited email is to put something in that first sentence that explains, in a personalized way, why you're reaching out to them," said Rubenstein.

As for whom to contact within a company you'd like to have advertise on your podcast, Rubenstein suggests trying to contact the company's CEO, and then work your way down as needed. He stated, "Always start with the CEO and then go down. If you reach out to the CEO, even if they don't respond directly, they might forward your correspondence to the right person within the company. That person is then more apt to get back to you if the correspondence is forwarded to them by their company's CEO. If you're writing to a company CEO, however, your pitch had better be good!"

Early on, as your podcast is getting established, be willing to start with a low CPM rate and potentially go even lower as a result of negotiating with potential advertisers. Also be extra creative when presenting your podcast's value proposition. Once you've fine-tuned your craft, achieved successes you can show, filled most of your available ad spots, and cultivated a growing and loyal audience, you can raise your CPM rate.

"As a podcaster, I would personally avoid dealing with affiliate marketing-type ads, although some podcasters do okay with them. Most performance marketing is not set up for podcasts. Anytime you can get advertisers to pay a set fee for ads on your podcast, in the long run, that will always work out better for you as the podcaster," said Rubenstein.

As of early 2020, most podcast advertising is direct response-style advertising, as opposed to brand awareness. Rubenstein stated, "Most advertising agencies that work in direct response advertising, particularly in the podcasting realm, know one another and communicate informally on a regular basis, even though we're technically competitors. As a podcaster, you want to be as honest and straightforward as possible with your potential advertisers and any agencies you work with. If as a podcaster you develop a poor reputation, that can have a very negative impact on your ability to sell ads to anyone moving forward."

One way to make your podcast more appealing to potential advertisers is to offer value-added opportunities and support through your podcast's web page, social media feeds, email list, or electronic newsletter, for example.

"The success of podcasts and podcast advertising is based on treating advertisers like a partner rather than a transactional relationship. The more that you can communicate that understanding with potential advertisers, the more eager they'll be to work with you," said Rubenstein. "When someone is unpleasant to deal with, or they adopt an attitude that says they're all about 'pay us the money and we'll do the bare minimum possible,' those are the podcasters we don't work with, or don't offer repeat business to moving forward. In your value proposition, make it clear that as a podcaster you're looking to become a partner

▶ Downloads and Streams Are More Important Than Subscribers

What advertisers ultimately pay for is based on the number of unique people who hear their ad when it's presented as part of your podcast. While having a lot of documented subscribers certainly helps boost your podcast's credibility, the data advertisers care much more about pertains to the number of downloads/streams each episode of your podcast receives. Presenting third-party data (from your podcast hosting services, for example) that accurately demonstrates your audience size and makeup is what will help you monetize your podcast with advertising.

with the advertiser, and you're willing to do what's necessary to make their ad campaign a success."

As you're about to discover, you can also monetize your podcast in other ways, in addition to or instead of accepting paid advertisements or sponsorships. That's the focus of the next chapter.

More Ways to Generate Income from Your Podcast

Until you build a respectable size and loyal audience for your podcast, directly selling 15-, 30-, or 60-second ad spots or sponsorship opportunities to other companies probably isn't a viable option. Companies that will pay big money to reach a specialized or niche group typically will only work with podcasts that already have a well-established audience of 10, 50, or 100 thousand, or even larger.

Once your audience grows into thousands of regular listeners, however, there are plenty of advertising agencies or podcast advertising networks that will bundle your podcast with many other podcasts, and then sell advertisers packages that include running ads on your podcast. Some revenue potential exists pursuing this opportunity.

Another option, as you learned from the previous chapter, is to accept per-inquiry ad deals or affiliate marketing deals from advertisers. In exchange for running a company's ads, you'll receive a small commission for every sale that's generated, for example. This type of ad, however, typically does not generate great results, since only a very small percentage of your audience will likely respond to the ads, and the commissions tend to be rather low.

While a podcast audience is still relatively small, but showing signs of continuous growth, some podcasters develop relationships with small to midsize local businesses or companies looking to reach the podcast's niche audience. Along with accepting traditional 15-, 30-, or 60-second ads, the podcaster sells sponsorship opportunities to those companies. How much you can earn from this option depends on the size of your audience and how much the sponsors are willing to pay to reach your podcast's niche audience.

When soliciting sponsors for your podcast, be creative in terms of what you offer as a podcaster, and seek out companies willing to support up-and-coming podcasts. As you're continuously working to expand your audience, however, other moneymaking opportunities are available. Whether any of these alternative options will work for you will depend on the type of podcast you're producing, the subject matter you cover, and the makeup of your audience.

This chapter discusses some of the additional revenue-generating options that may be available to you as a podcaster.

Create and Sell Branded (Podcast-Related) Merchandise

As you begin reaching audience members who are excited about your podcast, if you've developed a unique and identifiable brand around your podcast, one option is to create and sell branded, podcast-related merchandise that features your podcast's logo, your host's catchphrases, or your podcast's marketing slogan, for example.

In addition to providing a revenue stream for your podcast, selling merchandise like T-shirts, baseball hats, hoodies, stickers, and coffee mugs that feature identifiable graphics related to your podcast and/or its hosts will serve as a promotional tool once audience members begin wearing or using those products in public.

▶ Feature a Catchphrase or Slogan on Your Podcast-Related Merchandise

If your host(s) have created an original catchphrase that catches on with your audience, or your podcast has a unique and memorable slogan, printing that catchphrase or slogan in a visually appealing font and color scheme on merchandise could become as popular or more popular than similar merchandise that displays your podcast's logo.

Just as you would for a logo, consider hiring a professional graphic designer to create original artwork that showcases that catchphrase or slogan in a unique and visually interesting way.

Once a particular catchphrase or slogan is used and starts to catch on with your audience, be sure to get it copyrighted or trademarked, as necessary, to protect it legally. Details about how to file a copyright can be found at www.copyright.gov, while information about how to file a trademark is available from www.uspto.gov.

You can take two approaches when selling branded merchandise. One is considerably more profitable than the other, but the less profitable option is much easier and requires little or no upfront costs.

Option one for creating podcast-related merchandise that you'll promote and sell on your podcast, as well as through your podcast's website, for example, involves you (or a freelancer you hire) designing the merchandise. Working with a company that creates imprinted products, such as T-shirts, you'd prepurchase several dozen or more of each item. You'd maintain an inventory yourself and manually ship out individual orders as they're received.

The benefit to this option is that you'll keep the majority of the profit from each sale (minus the wholesale cost of the merchandise and shipping charges). To dramatically lower your upfront costs, you'll need to order larger quantities of each item, which means a more significant initial financial outlay. You'll also need to warehouse your inventory until it sells out.

For example, if you prepurchase two dozen T-shirts featuring your podcast's logo, you may pay $10 per shirt. You can then sell them for $20 per shirt (plus taxes, shipping, and handling) and earn approximately $10 per shirt. However, if you purchase five dozen T-shirts, your wholesale cost might drop down to $5 per shirt (or less), so now your profit will be $15 per shirt.

If you choose to pursue this option, first figure out the types of branded products you'd like to offer (such as T-shirts, hoodies, coffee mugs, stickers, pins, etc.), and then use the internet to find a company that sells wholesale imprinted products. Be sure to shop around for the best deals, and ask for product samples in advance to ensure you'll be offering the highest quality merchandise possible.

A much more affordable option is to work with a company that allows you to design your products online. That company then sets up an online store on your behalf, showcases and sells your branded merchandise online, plus handles all the payment processing and order shipments. In exchange, that company keeps a significantly higher percentage of each sale (between 40 and 80 percent). When you pursue this option, there are little or no upfront costs, and you don't have to maintain any inventory.

The company you work with creates the products on an on-demand basis, and all orders are received and fulfilled on your behalf. You, however, maintain all legal rights to your original artwork and product designs.

Using this type of print-on-demand merchandise company that handles all order manufacturing, printing, and fulfillment, you might have to pay $10 to $15 per shirt, and if you set your retail price at $20 (plus taxes, shipping, and handling) per shirt, your profit margins are much lower, regardless of the quantity you wind up selling. On the plus side, you don't have any upfront costs or financial risk, plus you don't have to invest the time needed to fulfill the orders yourself.

A wide range of merchandise printing companies specifically work with podcasters, YouTubers, and social media influencers to create and sell branded merchandise. You'll discover companies that create and sell imprinted products by entering the search term "imprinted products" within any search engine (such as Google).

Some of these companies include:

▶ Bonfire—www.bonfire.com
▶ CafePress—www.cafepress.com
▶ District Lines—www.districtlines.com
▶ Podcast Merch—www.podcastmerch.com
▶ PodSwag—www.podswag.com
▶ Printify—www.printify.com
▶ TeeChip—www.teechip.com
▶ TeePublic—www.teepublic.com
▶ Teespring—www.teespring.com

tip

If you plan to sell merchandise that features your podcast's logo or original artwork, hire a professional graphic designer to create that artwork for you. Starting for as little as $50, you can hire a freelance logo designer online, from a service like Upwork (www.upwork.com), and have that person create the artwork you need. Ultimately, having professional-looking graphics featured on your products will make them easier to sell and help to boost your podcast's credibility and reputation.

Before settling on which company you'll work with, shop for competitive prices, and determine your profit per sale. For example, you may only earn a $5 to $10 commission for a $40 hoodie sale. Also, acquire product samples to confirm quality, determine order fulfillment time for your customers, make sure the company does not charge excessive shipping and handling fees, and seek out a company that offers a broad range of products (available in a variety of size and color options).

The trick to selling branded, podcast-related merchandise is to set your prices high enough to make some money from each sale, but not set them so high that potential buyers lose interest.

Consider selling a variety of products at different price points. For example, offer stickers, pins, or posters for $5 to $10 each (or less), T-shirts in the $20 to $30 price range, and perhaps hoodies in the $35 to $45 price range. Try to keep your prices lower if you plan to add taxes as well as shipping and handling fees to each order.

One way to promote the sale of branded, podcast-related merchandise without blatantly selling it during your podcast episodes, for example, is to do a one-item giveaway during each episode. Talk about the product you're giving away to one lucky listener, but casually mention that everyone else can order the product from the podcast's website.

Additional Ways to Generate Revenue from Your Podcast

As you get to know your audience and establish your podcast, you'll likely discover new and interesting ways to earn money as a result of your efforts. Some will require you to think outside of the proverbial box, while other opportunities may be presented to you.

Solicit Donations from Your Audience

If you listen to public radio, you're probably familiar with their efforts to raise money by soliciting donations from listeners. For a podcaster not affiliated with a public

warning

Remember, don't get greedy and don't exploit your audience simply to earn an extra few dollars. If you're not producing your podcast for the love of the subject matter you're covering, and you're simply using the podcast as a moneymaking venture, you should probably seek out a different opportunity. For people who regularly listen to many different podcasts, it quickly becomes clear which podcasters have a passion for their work, and which are simply going through the motions to produce new content on a regular basis. Those in the second group tend to have trouble building and keeping their audiences.

radio broadcast, this can be a tricky endeavor. After all, people have become accustomed to listening to their favorite podcasts for free.

Trying to convince listeners to donate money to your podcast will likely fail. It'll also take more time during your podcast episodes to justify your request for money than simply running ads or including sponsorship messages.

Should you choose to solicit donations from your audience, make it very clear how the money will be used and exactly why it's needed. Also be sure to answer these two questions: How will audience members benefit by donating money to your podcast? What will they get out of it?

However, if you're producing a podcast and looking to raise money for a legitimate charity, requesting donations and promoting that charity will likely be looked upon favorably by your audience. Upon choosing to team up with a charity, make sure it's one that your audience will relate to and that you're truly passionate about. When trying to raise money, speaking from the heart will go a long way toward rallying the support of your audience.

A service called Patreon (www.patreon.com) allows podcasters and content creators to solicit and collect donations online, and then give back to donors by providing them with specific benefits more easily. In addition to one-time donations, Patreon allows for donors to automatically donate the same amount on a regular basis, such as monthly. The trick to raising a decent amount of money using Patreon is to offer enticing perks to people who donate. This might include access to exclusive content, a one-on-one phone call with the podcast's hosts, or some other experience that's not offered to the podcast's regular audience. You can also use services like PayPal or Apple Pay to easily accept donations electronically.

Charge Your Guests an Appearance Fee

Just like asking audience members to donate money to your podcast, trying to charge guests to appear on your podcast can be a bit tricky. By doing this, you run the risk of losing credibility with your audience, because your podcast's content will become more of an advertorial for the products and services your guests are endorsing. At the same time, your hosts will likely lose credibility, because audience members will think they're hearing biased information, thoughts, and opinions based on what the paying guests want audience members to hear.

With these potential drawbacks in mind, if your podcast's audience grows to a significant size, and it's very targeted, plenty of spokespeople from companies that would otherwise advertise to your target market will pay you (the podcaster) to be a guest. Assuming you're willing to follow the paying guest's agenda, ask them the questions they want to be asked, and give them the opportunity to share the talking points they want to promote, this does offer a revenue-generating option for your podcast.

Should you choose to pursue this option, seriously consider disclosing to your audience the fact that your guests are paying to appear on your podcast. One approach might be to only allow paying guests on your podcast who are also paid advertisers or sponsors. This gives you the opportunity to publicly thank the advertiser or sponsor for their support and allows the guest to share their talking points, but your audience already knows that the guest is paying to be featured within your podcast as a traditional advertiser.

Remember, charging guests to appear on your podcast can be a slippery slope in terms of maintaining your credibility and positive reputation. Proceed with caution and use your creativity to create a win-win-win situation.

Promote Yourself as an "Expert" Consultant Available for Hire

As the host of a podcast, you have an opportunity to promote and "sell" yourself as an expert in your field to an audience comprised of people who'd potentially want or need your services. Through your podcast, hopefully you're able to build a strong reputation, plus provide plenty of information about yourself and your services using a friendly, soft sell approach.

tip

One way to increase the value proposition you offer to your podcast's advertisers and sponsors is to give them the opportunity to have one of their spokespeople be a guest during one or more episodes of your podcast. As long as you make it clear that the guest is affiliated with a paying advertiser or sponsor (you offer full disclosure), this can be a win-win-win situation. Your advertiser/sponsor will get more airtime, your podcast will become more valuable to advertisers, and your audience will receive additional information/content from the guest that they might not otherwise receive.

During your podcast, or in the intro or closing of your show, take the opportunity to showcase your credentials, experience, and areas of expertise, plus briefly remind your audience that you're available for hire. To maintain the soft sell approach, encourage potential customers/clients to visit your website, email, or call you for details about the services you offer and the fees you charge.

Meanwhile, use the content of your podcast episodes to share your skills, experience, or areas of expertise in a way that'll set you apart from your competition and showcase you in a positive way to prospective customers/clients. After someone has heard a few episodes of your podcast, they'll feel as if they already know you. Thus, when they choose to hire you, it'll be more like hiring a friend whom they already know and trust.

If you're a tarot card reader and your podcast is all about new age topics, consider ending your podcast with a soft sell statement about your services. For example, you might conclude the show by saying "I'd like to thank you all for joining me for this episode of [insert podcast title]. If you liked what you've heard, be sure to subscribe to the podcast and stay tuned for the next episode that'll be released on [insert date]. The topic of the next episode will be [insert topic]. In the meantime, to schedule a personal tarot card reading with me, either in-person, by phone, or online, please visit my website at [insert website address] for details. Until next time, I'm [insert your name], and you've been listening to [insert podcast title]."

Participate in Live Events and Paid Appearances

Once your podcast becomes successful and builds a decent size audience, the host(s) will likely take on a celebrity status (at least in the podcasting community or the community in which your target audience belongs). Use this newfound popularity and credibility to book yourself as a paid guest speaker and/or to make in-person meet and greet appearances at special events.

If you're not able to actually get paid directly for your speaking engagements or appearances, arrange to sell podcast-related merchandise, or promote your own company's products/services to the audience. You can also use these appearances as a way to expand your podcast's audience.

Depending on your knowledge, experience, or area of expertise, trade shows, association meetings/gatherings, special events, or local events hosted by specific groups could all offer potential speaking or appearance opportunities.

Again, based on the size of your podcast audience, you might also make yourself available as a paid spokesperson for your podcast's sponsors, or another company that's somehow related to your podcast's topic. As a spokesperson, you'd get paid by a company to appear within its ads, participate in its public relations efforts, engage in media interviews to promote it, and make in-person appearances on the company's behalf to promote its brand, products, or services.

Anytime you accept money to appear in conjunction with a specific event or on behalf of a company or organization, for example, you're affiliating yourself and your professional reputation with that event, company, or organization, so choose your affiliations wisely.

In preparation for making yourself available as a paid public speaker, create a short video that showcases you in action. Consider including video clips of you hosting your podcast, along with footage of you speaking in front of a live audience. You also want to create the equivalent of a one-page information sheet about yourself and the topic(s) that you can talk about with credibility. This should include a professional headshot and a summary of your credentials.

Once you've gotten some public speaking experience under your belt (in addition to your podcast hosting experience), to help you find and book paid speaking engagements, consider working with a speakers bureau. These are agencies that match up speakers with companies, associations, trade shows, and groups looking for paid speakers.

To help you gain valuable experience speaking in front of a live audience, consider offering workshops or classes through adult education programs in your area. Local libraries, senior citizen centers, retirement communities, service clubs (such as local Rotary or Kiwanis chapters), your local chamber of commerce, and many colleges/universities offer speaking opportunities to experts in their respective field, but typically have low budgets (or no budgets) to pay speakers. Offering yourself as a speaker at an industry-oriented trade show is also a viable option.

To find well-established speakers bureaus you might want to work with, enter the search term "speakers bureau" into your favorite search engine, such as Google. How much you'll get paid for public speaking appearances will depend a lot on your experience, your level of popularity, the topics you're able to cover, the type of audience you'll appeal to, and where you'll be speaking. Your rate might be anywhere from $50 to thousands of dollars per appearance or lecture.

Produce and Sell an Online-Based Course

Another revenue-generating option that involves public speaking if you're an expert on a topic or in a specific field is to create a video-based how-to workshop or lecture that you sell online. A bunch of online-based services exist that invite experts and speakers to create, upload, and sell video-based classes, lectures, workshops, or courses online.

Some of these services include:

- ▶ Coursera—www.coursera.org
- ▶ edX—www.edx.org
- ▶ LinkedIn Learning—www.linkedin.com/learning
- ▶ Skillshare—www.skillshare.com
- ▶ Udemy—www.udemy.com

Once you've produced your online course, be sure to promote it within your podcast, as well as on your podcast's website and through its social media presence.

Offer Premium Content and Paid Subscriptions

Above and beyond the content you feature (for free) within your podcast episodes, your audience may be willing to pay for exclusive content that delves deeper into certain podcast-related topics.

For those listeners willing to pay an ongoing subscription fee, some of the exclusive content you offer could include:

- ► Outtakes from podcast episodes.
- ► The ability to listen to the podcast without hearing any ads or sponsorship messages.
- ► Extended interviews with podcast guests.
- ► Bonus episodes that are not offered as part of the regular podcast.
- ► The opportunity to hear each episode several days or a week before everyone else.
- ► A special email address where subscribers can send emails directly to the show's hosts/producers and get more personalized attention. You could also host invitation-only, online-based question-and-answer sessions with the podcast's hosts and producers.

Figure out what additional information or content you can offer that your audience will perceive as valuable and that they'd be willing to pay for. The more creative you are with what you offer specifically to your target audience, the easier it'll be to get them to subscribe. Keep in mind, however, that most people are already paying for a bunch of weekly or monthly subscriptions related to video and audio content. If you charge more than a few dollars per month, potential subscribers may have a difficult time justifying the cost.

Use Your Podcast as a Sales and Marketing Tool for Your Existing Business

If you own or represent an established business that offers products or services of interest to your podcast's target audience, build the podcast's content around what that company offers and position it as the sole "sponsor" of your podcast.

In addition to using the podcast as a soft sell sales tool and as a marketing tool targeted to potential customers/clients for the business, the same podcast can provide an easy way to informally communicate with existing customers and clients on an ongoing basis to build more trust and credibility, plus establish a stronger long-term relationship.

Be sure to use the same branding for your podcast as you've established for the company. Create a synergistic way to cross-promote the company's products, services, website, and social media feed(s) using the podcast, and position your podcast's host(s) as spokespeople for the company.

Build an Opt-In Email List

Encourage your listeners to subscribe to an opt-in email list related to your podcast. Promise the listeners a weekly or monthly newsletter (for free). In addition to providing a few informative articles, for example, within the email, be sure to promote upcoming episodes of the podcast and upcoming special guests, and include money-saving or promotional offers related to products/services your own company offers.

You can also use the email newsletter to promote products/services offered by the podcast's advertisers/sponsors. Consider working with your advertisers/sponsors to offer your audience exclusive discounts, and promote those discounts within the newsletter (and the podcast itself).

Using a specialized online service or software package, as a podcaster, you can easily create and format professional-looking electronic newsletters that'll be distributed via email, plus manage a podcast's opt-in email list. A few of the free and fee-based services that allow you to do this include:

▶ Benchmark—www.benchmarkemail.com
▶ Constant Contact—www.constantcontact.com
▶ Mailchimp—www.mailchimp.com
▶ Mailjet—www.mailjet.com
▶ Ontraport—www.ontraport.com
▶ OptinMonster—www.optinmonster.com

Creating an electronic newsletter for your podcast that's published on a weekly, biweekly, or monthly basis is a tool that can and should be used in addition to hosting a website for your podcast as well as a Facebook Page or Facebook Group. Each of these tools offers related but slightly different ways to interact with your audience (or potential audience) using text, photos, videos, graphics, and audio clips, outside of the actual audio podcast episodes.

Pursue a Television Series, Book, or Movie Deal Based on Your Podcast

Thanks to the popularity of podcasting and the need for new TV series, movie, and book ideas, more and more television networks, streaming video services (including Netflix,

Amazon Prime Video, Hulu, and Apple TV+), movie studios, and major book publishers are turning to established podcasts and podcasters for new programming and publishing ideas.

As a result, if you have a popular podcast, it might be in your best interest to team up with a professional and well-respected agent or entertainment attorney and pitch a TV series, movie, or book based on your podcast and its unique content.

In terms of pursuing a book, if you have a large and loyal audience, instead of working with a major book publisher, it might make financial sense for you to self-publish a printed book or ebook. This option requires a bit more work on your part (in addition to actually writing the book), but it allows you to keep much more of the book's profits.

The benefit of working with an established book publisher is that as an author you'll typically be paid an advance, plus a small royalty for each copy of the book that's sold. The book will then be published and distributed in printed form through traditional booksellers, as well as online booksellers, and could also be released as an ebook or audiobook.

If you choose to work with an established book publisher, you'll likely need to create a detailed book proposal and sample chapters, and then team up with a literary agent who will help sell your book idea to a publisher (in exchange for a commission). In today's economy, fewer books are being sold than ever before, so it's increasingly more difficult for first-time authors to get a book published by an established book publisher.

By self-publishing the book, you can sell the print-on-demand version, small print run version, or ebook version directly to your audience and keep a much higher percentage of the cover price per copy sold. While the book might not get bookstore distribution, it's relatively easy to get a self-published book listed on Amazon.com and BN.com, for example.

How well a self-published book sells will depend largely on your ability to promote it to an established

tip

The Vellum ebook publishing software ($199.99–$249.99, www. vellum.pub) that's available for Mac makes it easy to write, edit, format, and publish an ebook in a variety of popular ebook formats, so you can sell the completed ebook on Amazon.com (for Kindle), Apple Books (for iPhone, iPad, and Mac), BN.com (for Nook ebook readers), or Google Play Books (for Android-based devices). You can also use this software to create printed (print-on-demand) versions of your book to sell through several popular services, including Amazon's Kindle Direct Publishing.

and loyal following, such as the audience of your podcast. Keep in mind, while an ebook is faster, cheaper, and easier to publish than a printed book, some people still prefer purchasing printed books over ebooks, so they're easier to sell to a podcast audience. Through your podcast, you can also sell or give away autographed copies of a printed, self-published book, which is something you can't do with an ebook.

Many fee-based services will help you handle some or all aspects of writing, formatting, proofreading/editing, printing/publishing, distributing, and promoting a printed book or ebook. Depending on how much time and money you want to invest in a self-published book venture, some of the companies you might consider working with include:

▶ Amazon/Kindle Direct Publishing—https://kdp.amazon.com
▶ BookBaby—www.bookbaby.com
▶ iUniverse—www.iuniverse.com
▶ Lulu Press—www.lulu.com
▶ Page Publishing—www.pagepublishing.com/services
▶ Smashwords—www.smashwords.com
▶ Xlibris—www.xlibris.com

In printed book, ebook, or audiobook form, you can easily create original content based on your podcast, or repurpose your podcast transcripts, for example.

▶ Don't Forget About Audiobooks

Since your content is already in audio form, and since you already have the equipment needed to record, edit, and produce audio content, consider repurposing your podcast content into a longer audiobook format as well in order to earn additional money.

An audiobook might be an extended (audio) version of your podcast episodes that is several hours in length. Many services make it easy to record, edit, and publish audiobooks that then get listed with a variety of audiobook sellers. To learn more about these services, using an internet search engine, enter the search terms "audiobook production" or "audiobook distribution."

One of the largest audiobook sellers is Audible.com, although Apple Books, Google Play Books, Amazon.com, and BN.com also sell audiobooks from a wide range of major and independent audiobook publishers.

Don't Limit Yourself or Your Podcast

As you become experienced as a podcaster and really get to know your audience, you'll likely brainstorm many different ways to potentially earn additional revenue from your podcasting (and related) efforts. Be creative! Take a look at what other podcasters and content creators are doing, and determine ways you can do those things better or in a way that'll cater to the wants and needs of your audience.

Whatever you do, don't get greedy and sell yourself or your podcast in a way that you lose credibility with your audience or that could in any way damage your personal or professional reputation as the podcast's host/producer. The goals and revenue-generating plans you have for your podcast should all be long-term-based, as podcasting is not a get-rich-quick scheme. By remaining highly focused on creating new, original, engaging, and consistently high-quality content that caters to your podcast's target audience, over time, moneymaking opportunities will likely present themselves. Pursue only those opportunities that work well for you and your podcast, and that will be accepted by your audience.

Publish Your Podcast Online

After each episode is produced and ready to be heard by the masses, the process of publishing your podcast online is pretty straightforward, but it does require you to export your digital audio files into the appropriate file format once all postproduction work has been done. Your chosen podcast hosting service will provide the file format details you need to adhere to.

Before you can publish and distribute your podcast, you'll need to choose a *hosting service* and then decide where your podcast will be made available. Each podcast hosting service offers a slightly different selection of features for the podcaster, and monthly hosting prices vary. The podcast hosting service you choose will store all your digital audio files related to your podcast (in the cloud) and make them available to the podcast directories and distribution services that then make the content available to listeners.

The hosting service you select will likely offer a one-click or easy option for publishing your podcast episodes on multiple podcasting services, such as Apple Podcasts, Google Podcasts, Spotify, Stitcher, and TuneIn.

Each time you upload a new episode, you'll also need to compose text-based details about your podcast and each individual episode. This content will be in the form of a title and description. During the publishing process, you'll be prompted to choose an appropriate category for your podcast, supply contact information, and potentially provide a list of tags/keywords associated with its content.

You can also supply text-based show notes in conjunction with each episode during the podcast publishing process. These notes can include more details about the podcast itself, the individual episode, and contact information (including your podcast's website address, social media feed information, email address, etc.). Some podcast producers use show notes to provide listeners with additional topic-specific information that's not included within the podcast episode itself, such as links to additional resources, updated facts or statistics, or accompanying photographs. You're also able to publish an optional text-based, word-for-word transcript of each podcast episode, which is made available to listeners who want it.

Create Your Podcast Artwork

During the publishing process, you'll be required to upload podcast artwork (also referred to as cover art). This must meet the technical requirements of the podcast hosting service you'll be using, but it is usually based on industry standards. In general, artwork that is square-shaped, has a minimum resolution of 1,400 by 1,400 pixels and a maximum resolution of 3,000 by 3,000 pixels, and is saved in a JPG or PNG file format at 72 dpi using a 1:1 aspect ratio, will work fine. You also want to utilize the RGB color space when selecting colors that'll appear in your artwork to ensure the audience will see them as you intend them to be seen.

If you have basic artistic ability and know how to use a graphics program, such as Adobe Photoshop, you can easily create podcast artwork yourself. However, graphic arts is one of those skill sets that in addition to having natural ability, people train for years to perfect. You're typically better off paying between $50 and $200 for a skilled graphic artist to create professional-looking, attention-grabbing podcast cover art for you.

tip

Have your podcast artwork created at the maximum resolution requirements of 3,000 by 3,000 pixels (72 dpi) and provided to you in either the JPG or PNG file format.

While just about any graphic artist capable of designing a logo can create podcast artwork that meets the necessary specifications, some specialize only in creating this type of artwork for podcasters. Online-based services that, for a fee, allow you to create your own artwork are also available.

Refer back to Chapter 5, "Brand Your Podcast," for information about graphic arts services you can hire. In addition, the following services specialize in podcast cover artwork:

▶ Adobe Spark—https://spark.adobe.com/templates/topic/podcast/
▶ BrandCrowd—www.brandcrowd.com/maker/s/podcast
▶ Placeit—https://placeit.net/c/logos/stages/podcast-cover-art-logo-maker-a1184?

You may think that a podcast is all about creating top-quality audio content to attract an audience (which is 100 percent true), but to first grab someone's interest and draw them to your podcast, you'll need attention-getting artwork, along with a great podcast title and enticing description.

Quick Tips for Creating Eye-Catching Podcast Cover Art

Whether you hire a professional graphic artist or choose to create your own podcast cover art, the following tips will ensure the end result attracts the positive attention needed to lure in audience members:

▶ Use at least one bright and vibrant color in your podcast cover artwork to help it stand out visually. However, choose an overall color scheme that's pleasing to the eye and that'll appeal to your target audience.
▶ Don't forget to incorporate your podcast's branding into your artwork. The color scheme and overall appearance of the cover art should be consistent with your company or podcast logo and other graphic elements used to promote your company, yourself, and your podcast. Take a synergistic approach to all your visuals.
▶ Cover artwork utilizes a small space on someone's screen. Don't include too much text or it'll be too hard to read. If your cover art includes text, make sure

it can easily be read on all screen sizes. Don't mix and match more than two different fonts or typestyles.

► Remember that saying, "A picture is worth a thousand words?" The same holds true for podcast artwork. Use the artwork to convey a message to your potential audience that will help them determine what your podcast is all about with just one quick look.

► Be original! The goal of the cover artwork for your podcast is to capture attention in a positive way. If your artwork looks like the artwork used by many other podcasts, this won't help you in any way.

► Just like a company logo makes that company and its brand immediately identifiable in the mind of the viewer, you want your podcast's cover art to have the same effect on your (potential) audience. Remember, in addition to appearing as part of a podcast's listing within a directory, for example, listeners will see the cover art while the podcast plays on their smartphone, tablet, or computer.

warning

Poorly designed podcast cover art, or poor-quality art (from a resolution standpoint), will be detrimental to your podcast's success, as it could drive away potential audience members if it gives off an amateurish vibe. You want the artwork to convey a strong sense of professionalism so it helps you (the podcaster) quickly establish a positive reputation.

Whatever fee you agree to pay your graphic artist should include a bunch of revisions to the artwork before it's finalized. Once you settle on an overall design concept, have the graphic artist offer you at least five versions of the same artwork (using different fonts for text or different color schemes, for example), so you have a selection to choose from. Don't be afraid to make multiple revisions or tweaks before making a final selection. Creating and choosing the right cover art for your podcast is a process. Don't rush it or try to cut corners.

Create Show Notes for Each Episode

Again, the main focus of your podcast is the audio content that's provided to listeners. However, the text- and graphics-based support elements that go along with your podcast should be used as powerful tools to capture attention and provide additional information to your (prospective) audience and subscribers.

Show notes are optional for podcasters, but when used correctly, they provide a way to further communicate and interact with your audience, share additional information, and issue a call to action. Show notes can accompany each episode of your podcast. How you utilize this tool is entirely up to you, based on the goals for your podcast.

One of the benefits to incorporating show notes with each podcast episode is that the text within those notes becomes searchable (just like your podcast's title and description). When you use search engine optimization (SEO) strategies when composing the show notes, you increase your chances that your podcast will be found by potential listeners performing search engine or podcast directory searches using keywords that are relevant to your podcast episode.

Information to Include Within Show Notes

You might want to include the following information within show notes for each podcast episode:

- ▶ A more detailed description of the podcast itself and the individual episode.
- ▶ A listing of the episode's main points. (Provide a short, text-based recap.)
- ▶ One or two sentences about the show's host(s).
- ▶ A short bio (again just a few sentences) about the show's special guest, if applicable.
- ▶ A link to your podcast's website.
- ▶ Links to your podcast and/or host's social media feeds.
- ▶ Email addresses for your host(s) and producer(s) with an invitation for listeners, potential advertisers/sponsors, or potential guests to make contact.
- ▶ Links to websites, articles, additional resources, or bonus content relating to the episode's subject matter.
- ▶ Updated information, statistics, or facts. While content in your podcast episodes may become outdated over time, you can use the show notes to publish more current data as it becomes available.
- ▶ A few photos (or artwork) that relate to the show's subject matter.
- ▶ A specific call to action that encourages listeners to subscribe to your podcast, post comments, or review the podcast.

tip

Use bulleted lists within your show notes to make information, like a list of additional resources or contact information for the host(s) and guest(s), easier to access and read. To help organize the information for your audience, use multiple headings and subheads (as needed) to format the show notes information. Use a few photographs, charts, tables, or illustrations if they'll help you communicate information more efficiently.

As with everything else related to your podcast, the content within your show notes should be concise, easy to read, and specifically written with your podcast's target audience (and their short attention span) in mind. Spelling and grammatical mistakes within the text should be avoided, as they'll detract from your credibility. Meanwhile, using highly technical or difficult-to-understand vocabulary can also be detrimental if the majority of people reading it won't understand it.

Think of your show notes as an extension of your audio podcast. Thus, the content in the show notes needs to maintain the same quality as the podcast itself.

If you don't have the time or writing skills to compose and publish show notes, but you know your audience (and your podcast) will benefit from including them, consider hiring a freelance writer to create the show notes for your podcast in conjunction with each episode. You can find and hire a skilled freelance writer using a service like Upwork (www.upwork.com).

Agree to pay the freelance writer a flat fee per episode, with the understanding they'll need to get the show notes completed within 24 hours after your podcast episode's production is done, so the notes can be published at the same time as the episode. To save money, consider working with a college intern, and make compiling and writing the show notes one of their core responsibilities.

tip

Keep in mind that show notes and a show transcript are different, and both can be used in conjunction with each podcast episode to add value to the listener and improve the podcast's episode's ability to be found when people use a search tool. Show notes can contain whatever additional content you want to create. A show transcript is a word-for-word script in a text-based format.

▶ Consider Publishing a Text-Based Transcript

Depending on the subject matter of your podcast and its target audience, your listeners might appreciate the ability to download and print a word-for-word transcript of each podcast episode. This is not necessary for all podcasts, but it could be a valuable resource to your audience if the audio content you're offering would benefit.

Instead of manually transcribing your podcast (which can be a time-consuming task), transcription services that charge anywhere from 10 cents to $1 per minute are available. Some podcast hosting services offer automated transcription services as part of their subscription plan for podcasters.

Choose Your Podcast's Hosting Platform

Once the writing, recording, editing, and postproduction work on your latest podcast episode is done, it's time to publish it online and make it available to your audience. This process involves two core steps. First, you need to begin working with a podcast hosting service. Among other things, this service will store your podcast's digital audio files online.

Second, once podcast episodes have been uploaded to your podcast hosting service, you'll need to have that service distribute your episodes to the podcast directories and podcast listening services you choose. Your (potential) listeners and subscribers will then be able to stream or download the latest episodes as they're published.

Keep in mind, utilizing a podcast hosting service typically requires paying a low monthly or annual fee, although a few offer a free option for startup podcasters. Listing your podcast (and its latest episodes) with podcast directories is free. One podcast hosting service can distribute your podcast to multiple podcast directories, typically with a few clicks of the mouse, on the dates and times you stipulate.

Podcast Hosting Service Options

Choosing the best podcast hosting service requires you to do a bit of online research to find a company that offers the features and functions you want and need for your particular podcast.

Five features you'll probably want are:

1. Unlimited bandwidth (allowing for any number of people to download or stream your podcast episodes simultaneously).
2. Full analytics tools (to determine who is listening to your podcast).
3. Plenty of online storage space for your digital audio files. (However, if you have a podcast with episodes that are five to ten minutes in length, and you only release one episode per week, for example, your online storage needs will be minimal.)
4. The ability to format and distribute your podcast episodes to individual podcast directories, including Apple Podcasts, Google Podcasts, Spotify, Stitcher, Amazon Alexa, iHeartRadio, TuneIn, and a handful of others, with a few mouse clicks.
5. Unlimited phone support, 24/7.

Other features and functions offered by some podcast hosting services include the tools needed to create and host a podcast-related website and/or branded mobile app, the ability to include ads from independent advertisers within your episodes (along with other monetization tools), the ability to host live broadcasts, and tools to help you more effectively promote your podcast and its new episodes via the internet.

Most podcast hosting services have multiple subscription-based plans to choose from, which range in price. The plan you choose determines which features and functions will be unlocked and accessible to you. To save money, instead of paying month-to-month, many services offer a discount if you prepurchase a plan one year at a time. Only agree to this, however, once your podcast is established and you know you'll be sticking with it. Look for a service that offers no long-term commitments and the ability to cancel or upgrade your plan anytime.

The easiest way to discover the many different podcast hosting services available to you is to launch your favorite web browser, and within the search field, enter "podcast hosting services." Figure 12.1 shows some information about a few of the more popular services, listed in alphabetical order, to help you jump-start your research.

Popular Podcast Hosting Services

Podcast Hosting Service	Website	Price Range*	Notes
Blubrry	https://blubrry.com/services/podcast-hosting/	$12–$80/month	All plans offer unlimited bandwidth and a free WordPress website. The higher-priced plans include more storage space, full analytics, and a variety of other services.
Buzzsprout	www.buzzsprout.com	Free–$24/month	Includes podcast analytics, a hosted podcast website, custom embed players, ability to list on multiple podcast directories, 250GB bandwidth per month. Additional features, like 192K stereo optimization and episode transcription, cost extra. No long-term contracts.

FIGURE 12–1: **Popular Podcast Hosting Services**

Popular Podcast Hosting Services

Podcast Hosting Service	Website	Price Range*	Notes
Captivate	https://my.captivate.fm/login	$49–$99/month	Limits the number of episode downloads for your podcast to between 50K and 150K, depending on the plan you choose. However, it offers an impressive selection of features and functions for managing all aspects of your podcast, including distribution, analytics, and promotions.
Libsyn	https://libsyn.com	$5–$40/month	Four plans are available. Each offers a different amount of storage space, and higher-priced plans offer a better selection of useful features. Analytics are only offered with the $20–$40/month plans, for example. Some plans allow a podcast to have its own mobile app.
Podbean	www.podbean.com	Free–$99/month	Offers four different plans. The more you pay, the more features/functions, online storage space, and bandwidth you receive. This service includes the ability to join advertising networks to increase income. A mobile app is also available.

FIGURE 12–1: **Popular Podcast Hosting Services,** continued

Popular Podcast Hosting Services

Podcast Hosting Service	Website	Price Range*	Notes
Simplecast	www.simplecast.com	$15–$85/ month	Along with all the features you'd expect, some of the more unique features include the ability to have multiple account managers and analytics that allow you to compare the performance of multiple episodes.
SoundCloud	https://creators. soundcloud.com/ podcasting	Free–$12/ month	Paid plans offer full analytics, unlimited upload time, the ability to schedule episode releases, and the ability to distribute through all major podcast services.
Spreaker	https://try.spreaker. com/starting-a-podcast/	$6–$45/ month	Analytics, easy distribution tools, 100 hours (or more) of audio storage, episode scheduling, and monetization options, plus the ability to host (stream) live podcast episodes.

FIGURE 12–1: **Popular Podcast Hosting Services,** continued

Popular Podcast Hosting Services			
Podcast Hosting Service	Website	Price Range*	Notes
Transistor	www.transistor.fm	$19–$99/ month	Limits the number of episode downloads per month to between 15K and 200K depending on the plan. For a startup podcast, this is more than enough, however. One unique feature is that it allows podcasters to manage private (paid) subscribers so they can offer premium content to that audience.

(*) Features, functions, and price vary by service plan selected. Most services offer a free 7-, 14-, or 30-day trial.

FIGURE 12–1: **Popular Podcast Hosting Services,** continued

Where to Distribute Your Podcast

After you've hired a podcast hosting service, set up an account, and started uploading your individual episodes, you'll need to decide where to make your podcast available to listeners for streaming or downloading.

While literally dozens of podcast directories are available, the majority of your audience will come from the most popular services, which include:

▶ *Amazon Music.* The popular Amazon music service offers the ability for subscribers to find and listen to podcasts using whatever equipment they'd typically use to listen to their favorite music via this streaming service.

▶ Distribution Is Key

Make your podcast available through podcast directories that have the broadest reach. To reach the largest possible audience, choose one or more directories that have a proprietary mobile app for iOS and Android devices, a web browser plug-in (for computers), online compatibility accessible from a web browser without a plug-in, smart TV compatibility, smart speaker compatibility, and compatibility with the latest vehicle infotainment systems.

Remember, people who listen to podcasts do so from home, at work, while in their cars, during walks or workouts, or while traveling/commuting, for example. It's important that the podcast directories that make your podcast available are accessible from whenever and wherever a listener wants to listen, using the equipment that's at their disposal.

With smart speaker technology now built into a wide range of smart appliances, many podcast directories make podcasts accessible when someone requests them by talking to their refrigerator, smart TV, or smartwatch, for example. The infotainment systems (screens) built into the dashboards of most new vehicles also offer compatibility with a growing number of podcast directories, meaning a listener can download or stream a podcast to be heard while driving (via their internet-connected smartphone or their car's built-in internet connectivity).

Based on your target audience, make sure you develop an understanding of where, when, and how they'll want to hear your podcast, and then be sure to make it available through podcast directories that cater to the necessary technologies and accessibility options.

In addition to the analytics tools offered by most podcast hosting services, many of the individual podcast directories offer podcasters their own analytics tools for measuring and tracking their listeners and subscribers.

▶ *Apple Podcasts.* Apple now offers the free Apple Podcasts app as part of macOS, iOS, watchOS, and tvOS. Thus, from Apple's podcast directory, anyone with an iMac, MacBook, iPhone, iPad, iPod, Apple TV device, Apple Watch, or HomePod can find and stream on-demand podcasts, or when applicable, download podcast episodes to listen to at their leisure when offline. Apple Podcasts is also compatible with CarPlay, so it can be used with a vehicle's infotainment system when an iPhone is connected.

▶ *Google Podcasts.* From the Google Play store, the free Google Podcasts mobile app is readily available on all Android-based smartphones and tablets, as well as on other compatible devices. In 2019, a web-based version of Google Podcasts was launched, making this massive and extremely popular podcast directory accessible to almost any computer or mobile device's web browser (including Chrome).

▶ *iHeartRadio.* This company owns and operates thousands of terrestrial AM and FM radio stations, which are available to stream via the iHeartRadio website or mobile app (available for iOS and Android). The iHeartRadio Podcast Directory (www. iheart.com/podcast/) gives listeners access to thousands of podcasts, and like all other podcast directories, offers more than 21 different podcast subject categories, including the Podcast Top 100 listing and iHeartRadio Podcast Awards Winners. More traditional categories, like Comedy, Music, Entertainment, News, Crime, Science and Technology, Politics, Sports, Health, and Business and Finance, are also featured.

▶ *SoundCloud.* This platform can serve as a podcast hosting service, but any podcaster can potentially get their podcast listed within its directory. For listeners, SoundCloud can be accessed via the web, on iOS or Android-based mobile devices, as well as from compatible smart speakers, smart TVs, and streaming devices (such as Chromecast or the Xbox One video game system). That being said, SoundCloud's focus is primarily on music and allowing independent artists and musicians to showcase and share their work. Visit https://creators.soundcloud. com/podcasting for more information on how podcasters are using SoundCloud. (At the time this book was being written, SiriusXM satellite radio made a substantial financial investment in SoundCloud. This could provide SoundCloud with the means to establish more dominance in the podcasting world.)

▶ *Spotify.* Available as an optional and free mobile app for all iOS and Android-based mobile devices, as a web browser plug-in for computers, and as an app on some smart devices (including compatible smart TVs and smart speakers), this popular podcast directory reaches a vast and ever-growing audience of podcast listeners, although Spotify is best known as an on-demand music streaming service that has both a free and a paid subscription option. As of late 2019, Spotify had more than 200 million listeners across more than 75 countries worldwide.

▶ *Stitcher.* Since 2007, Stitcher has been one of the most popular podcast directories on the internet. It has a free app available for iOS and Android-based mobile devices, a web browser plug-in for computers, an optional app for some smart TVs, plus it works seamlessly with some smart speakers. Thus, the service is available and used daily by millions of podcast listeners from around the world.

▶ *TuneIn/Alexa.* Just like Stitcher, for example, TuneIn offers free apps and accessibility from smartphones, tablets, smart TVs, smart speakers, smartwatches, vehicle infotainment systems, and compatible smart appliances. Like other podcast directories, TuneIn offers tools to help listeners quickly find and then stream or download podcasts that'll appeal to them. Podcasts are divided into categories by subject matter, but TuneIn also showcases popular podcasts within Editor's Choice picks and the service's This Week's Top 25 Podcasts list, for example. This is one of the most popular podcast directories and has millions of dedicated listeners and users. Listeners can use their Amazon smart speaker to seek out and stream your podcast using a voice command. For example, the user would say "Alexa, play the latest episode of [insert podcast title]," and it would start playing immediately.

Some podcast directories offer special incentives to podcasters willing to promote and share their podcast exclusively through just one directory. Each directory has different criteria for a podcast to be considered for an exclusivity deal, and in exchange offers specific perks (mainly relating to extra promotion of your podcast). If you're offered an exclusivity deal with one podcast directory, weigh your options carefully based on what's being offered and the value to you as the podcaster.

tip

Sirius/XM Pandora (www.siriusxm.com/pandora) is also now focusing heavily of becoming a prominent podcast directory, so it makes sense to get your podcast listed here as well. Overcast (https://overcast.fm) is also becoming a popular podcast directory. This one allows podcasters to use paid advertising to promote their podcast (in addition to free inclusion within the service's database).

13

12 Ways to Promote Your Podcast

Producing and publishing your podcast online is just the beginning. If you want to establish and grow your audience, you'll need to invest time, resources, and potentially some money into continuously promoting it. As soon as you stop promoting your podcast, the number of new listeners will dwindle, potentially down to none.

Once you develop a clear understanding of your podcast's target audience and their media consumption habits, for example, it'll be easier to promote your podcast to those people. Ideally, you should take an ongoing and multifaceted approach to your promotional efforts. In other words, find at least three different and effective ways to promote your podcast, and keep utilizing those multiple efforts.

Of course, you'll want to analyze the ongoing impact your promotional efforts are having, tweak your promotional campaigns and efforts as needed, and periodically experiment with new ways to get the word out about your podcast to your target audience, based on new trends or changes in that audience's habits.

For example, as of early 2020, Instagram is a popular social media service that offers both free and paid ways to promote a podcast to a highly targeted audience. Over time, your audience may move away from Instagram and find themselves using other social media services. It's important to stay up-to-date on the latest trends and utilize them to your advantage whenever possible.

If you'd like to establish a large audience quickly, utilizing paid advertising (online and in the real world) is a proven way to do this, but it's going to potentially be expensive. You can spend a lot less money using other promotional tools and opportunities at your disposal.

Taking a lower-cost, more organic approach to podcast promotion will require patience and consistency in your efforts. It'll likely take you six months to a year before you start seeing significant audience growth, and up to three years to expand your audience to the point where you're able to monetize the podcast and operate it as a viable business that could potentially support you financially with a full-time income.

When it comes to promotional opportunities for a podcast, the potential is limited only by your creativity, time commitment, and resources. This chapter offers a collection of promotional ideas to get you started. However, based on the focus and subject matter of your podcast, your target audience, and your ingenuity, you can develop promotional campaigns that are customized to help you achieve your personal podcasting goals.

1: Your Podcast Needs Its Own Website

It does not need to be fancy, but every podcast will benefit from having a website as a promotional tool to attract new listeners, as well as provide a way to interact with existing listeners. Many podcast hosting services include the online tools to design and manage a basic website for a podcast. If yours doesn't, many inexpensive options exist through companies like WordPress (www.wordpress.com), for example, that offer online-based tools to design and manage a website without requiring any programming know-how.

How a podcast can benefit from a website will vary, based on the podcaster's goals. However, some of the key elements a podcast's website might offer include:

▶ A detailed description of the podcast.

▶ Bios of the podcast's host(s) and producer(s).

▶ Contact information for the host(s) and producer(s).

▶ Advertising/sponsorship information.

▶ Previews of upcoming episode(s).

▶ Summaries of past episodes.

▶ Access to show notes and/or episode transcriptions.

▶ Additional (bonus) content pertaining to individual episodes, such as audio out-takes, extended interviews, photos, video clips, articles, or other information listeners would be interested in.

▶ An interactive and moderated message board allowing listeners to interact (publicly) with the show's host(s), producer(s), and other listeners.

▶ The ability to order podcast-related merchandise, such as T-shirts, baseball hats, stickers, or hoodies that display the podcast's logo and/or catchphrase.

▶ Online editions of PR materials related to the podcast, including downloadable press releases.

▶ The ability to opt into an email list to receive a free podcast-related newsletter, ebook, or other downloadable content. (The goal is to build an email list of your listeners, which you can later use for email marketing to promote your podcast and potentially your podcast's advertisers.)

Ideally, your podcast's website address (URL) should be your podcast's title followed by ".com." While plenty of other website extensions are available, most web surfers tend to automatically use the .com extension when manually entering a URL into their web browser, so keep things simple for your audience.

You'll want to include your podcast's website address within the show notes of every episode, within all other promotional materials for your podcast, and within the profiles of your podcast's social media feeds. During the outro of each episode, be sure to invite listeners to visit your website for a preview of the next episode or to access bonus content related to the current episode.

2: Fully Utilize Social Media

As you do your research to learn all that you can about your target audience, figure out which social media services they're apt to use, and then make sure your podcast has its

▶ Facebook: Public or Private?

A podcast or company-specific Facebook Page or Facebook Group can be public, allowing anyone to join and participate, or it can be private, meaning that either the group's leader needs to send individual invites or a podcast listener needs to request an invitation that will require approval. Which option you choose should be based on your objectives and audience. A private, invitation-only group offers a sense of exclusivity, but a public group is more readily accessible by anyone.

own presence on those services. Social media habits change. If you discover your audience utilizes Facebook, your podcast should maintain a moderated (and free) Facebook Page or Facebook Group, for example.

Likewise, if your listeners seem to spend time using Twitter, Instagram, LinkedIn, Pinterest, or Snapchat, for example, you'll want to allocate some of your online promotional efforts to those platforms by establishing and maintaining accounts for your podcast.

Your podcast should have its own social media account(s), with the podcast's title used as the username on each platform. Maintaining a presence on social media is free, but it does require a time commitment to continuously post new content and interact informally with your podcast's (prospective) listeners.

The profile associated with your podcast should include details about the podcast and include links for streaming/downloading the latest episode. It should also promote the podcast's website.

On an ongoing basis, use your podcast's social media presence to:

▶ Allow for informal interaction with the host(s) and producer(s).

▶ Preview upcoming episode(s).

▶ Share details about past episodes.

▶ Provide additional (bonus) content pertaining to individual episodes, such as audio outtakes, extended interviews, photos, video clips, articles, or other information listeners would be interested in.

▶ Promote the sale of podcast-related merchandise, such as T-shirts, baseball hats, stickers, or hoodies that display the podcast's logo and/or catchphrase.

▶ Share news or articles related to your podcast's topic or subject matter.

▶ Maintain an open, public, but moderated discussion related to your podcast's subject matter.

▶ Encourage engagement by hosting contests or prize giveaways. (Make sure any contests or prizes offered are legal in the state or country where you're operating.)

▶ Seek out ideas from listeners for future podcast episodes or potential guests.

3: Publish Your Podcast on Multiple Directories

Your podcast hosting service will likely offer one-click publishing or the ability to easily distribute your podcast to multiple podcast directories. If your goal is to build the largest audience possible, make sure your podcast is offered through the most popular podcast directories/distribution services, including: Apple Podcasts, Google Podcasts, Spotify, TuneIn, Stitcher, and Amazon Alexa.

By offering your podcast via Amazon Alexa, anyone with a compatible smart speaker can simply say "Hey Alexa, play the latest episode of [insert your podcast title]," and it'll instantly start playing.

Apple Podcasts gives easy access to your podcast to iPhone, iPad, Mac, Apple TV, Apple Watch, and Apple HomePod users. Google Podcasts works with all Android-based mobile devices, the Chrome web browser (on computers and Chromebook devices), Google smart speakers, as well as Chromecast TV devices, for example. The other popular podcast directories offer a wide range of ways for people using various types of equipment to access, stream, download, and subscribe to your podcast.

Unless you have a specific reason to offer your podcast exclusively through one directory or podcast distribution service, make it available on as many directories and distribution services as possible. Otherwise, figure out where your audience is most apt to listen to podcasts, and make sure your podcast is available through directories that support their equipment, whether it's a computer, smartphone, tablet, smart TV, smart speaker, smartwatch, or the infotainment system in their vehicle.

4: Take Advantage of Paid Advertising

In conjunction with all the promotional opportunities you take advantage of which are free, but require your time to manage, one of the fastest ways to establish and grow an audience for any podcast is to utilize paid, highly targeted advertising both online and in the real world.

Social media advertising (on Facebook, Instagram, or Twitter, for example) and search engine advertising (via Google Ads, for example) cost money, but they can help you quickly reach potential listeners that fit your target demographic. Keep in mind, every

▶ Be Careful Whom You Trust

If you seek out the help of advertising sales representatives from specific online services, their goal is to sell you as much online advertising as possible. These people won't necessarily understand what your podcast is all about or who the target audience is that you're trying to reach, and they'll always try to make you believe that their service offers the very best place for you to spend your ad dollars.

If you're new to online advertising, consider hiring an independent online advertising expert to help you design and manage your campaign, and leverage your spending in the best way(s) possible to achieve your objectives. Taking this approach can save you a lot of time, money, and potential aggravation.

Whether you work with an online advertising expert or decide to create and manage your own campaigns, pay careful attention to the analytics data provided by the ad service as your ads run in real time. This will help you better fine-tune the campaign, determine what's working, and reallocate money when a campaign is not achieving the desired results.

online advertising opportunity works slightly differently, so before investing a lot of money to launch a campaign, make sure you fully understand how advertising on each online service works, and that you're using the best possible ad(s) that'll appeal to your audience.

In general, display (banner) advertising on the internet no longer works. However, in addition to social media and search engine advertising, you could advertise on other well-established podcasts that reach the same target audience as yours, but that cover a noncompeting topic or subject.

How quickly you're able to grow your podcast's audience using paid online advertising will depend on how well you design the campaign, how effectively you're able to reach your target audience, and how much money you're willing to spend. Keep in mind that for advertising to work, someone typically needs to see your ad multiple times before they'll respond to it. Achieving multiple ad impressions costs money, so if you plan to use online advertising, make sure you have the budget to keep it going long enough to have the desired impact.

Beyond the advertising opportunities available in cyberspace, countless ways to use different types of advertising in the real world exist. However, your budget will best be spent on those opportunities that allow you to reach a highly targeted audience that matches the audience profile for your podcast. Thus, consider advertising in special-interest or topic-specific publications, for example.

▶ Consider Low-Cost Billboard Ads

If your podcast will appeal to commuters or a broader audience that you know will want to hear your podcast in their car (or while riding a bus, for example), consider low-cost billboard advertising. A company called Blip sells digital billboard advertising that's displayed on billboards you choose (almost anywhere within the United States).

Instead of having your ad continuously displayed on a billboard (which can be expensive), Blip allows many ads to scroll in between 7.5- and 10-second intervals for a very affordable rate. Thus, if you display your ad on billboards along busy streets or highways used by commuters, you can promote your podcast pretty inexpensively. For more information about Blip billboard advertising, visit: www.blipbillboards.com.

If you advertise in a general-interest publication, on a radio show, on a TV show, or in a movie theater, for example, only a small portion of the audience you reach will likely be in your podcast's target audience. The same is true if you advertise in mass-market consumer-oriented newspapers or magazines. These advertising options work best if your podcast truly caters to a broad mass-market audience, as opposed to a niche audience.

Again, figure out the media consumption habits of your target audience, and try to reach them using ads in media outlets you know those people read, listen to, or watch regularly.

5: Have Your Podcast Broadcast on the Radio

It's true that the internet, streaming music services, and podcasting are causing radio audiences to dwindle quickly. However, the Public Radio Exchange (PRX) network, which airs on local terrestrial public radio stations as well as on SiriusXM satellite radio (nationwide), actually broadcasts a wide range of independently produced podcasts as part of its programming.

Once your podcast becomes well-established, consider contacting PRX as well as any local radio stations around the country to determine if your podcast episodes could be broadcast as part of the station or network's programming.

In general, you'll want to contact the program director at a local radio station or network. To contact PRX, visit: www.prx.org/exchange.

6: Use Public Relations to Position Your Hosts as Experts

If your podcast's host(s) are experts on a specific topic, consider utilizing traditional public relations efforts to reach out to a wide range of media outlets to make your host(s) available as guests or interview subjects in conjunction with current news or human-interest stories.

The best way to reach out to media outlets is to create and distribute a press release, or to create a full digital press kit related to your podcast that you send to guest bookers, reporters, producers, and journalists that cover a specific subject matter for their newspaper, magazine, radio show, or TV show. Of course, you can also get your host(s) booked as guests on other podcasts, featured on YouTube channels, or interviewed within blogs that reach an audience that would be interested in their area of expertise.

Composing a press release is a skill. The one- or two-page (maximum length) press release must be written in a specific format and then distributed to a highly targeted list of people in the media. In other words, if your podcast is all about healthy cooking, you'd never send your press release to the sports or news editor at a newspaper. Instead, you'd send the press release to the food editor.

Getting booked as a guest or interviewed by another media outlet using public relations costs very little money if you do it yourself, but it can be done more effectively (if you have the budget) by hiring a freelance public relations expert or full-service public relations agency to help you.

What is required is the ability to write well-written, attention-getting press releases, and then investing the time to contact and develop relationships with people in the media that have the ability to offer your host(s) and podcast free publicity.

Once you've composed one or more press releases that are perfectly formatted, be sure to make them available on your podcast's website (in a For the Media or Press) section. This section of your podcast's website should also include a detailed description of the podcast, biographies of your podcast's hosts, a podcast episode list, and other resources relating to your podcast that someone in the media might find useful.

When it comes to compiling a targeted media list to distribute your press release to, you can invest the time to research and compile your own list, hire a PR specialist

tip

Using any internet search engine (such as Google), enter the search phrases "how to write a press release" or "press release writing tips" to learn how to write a correctly formatted press release that will generate the desired results.

and take advantage of their already-created list(s) and relationships, or purchase a media directory (or access to an online-based media directory database).

Fee-based press release distribution services that will distribute your pre-written press release(s) to specific types of media outlets that you request are also available. Some of these services include:

▶ EIN Presswire—www.einpresswire.com

▶ eReleases—www.ereleases.com

▶ Newswire—www.newswire.com

▶ PRWeb—www.prweb.com

▶ PR Newswire—www.prnewswire.com

▶ Send2Press—www.send2press.com

Keep in mind, it's always easy to obtain free publicity or get your host(s) interviewed or booked as guests within niche-oriented blogs, on other podcasts, and on YouTube channels, for example, so these are good places to begin. Many blogs, podcasts, and YouTube channels that cover specific topics have as large of an audience as more mainstream media outlets (such as newspapers, magazines, radio shows, or TV shows).

The tricks to getting media attention from your press release include:

▶ Composing a well-written and concise press release. It should quickly answer the questions who, what, where, when, why, and how, as those questions relate to your podcast or host(s).

▶ Formatting your press release properly.

▶ Sending the press release to the appropriate journalists, reporters, editors, producers, guest bookers/talent coordinators, or media professionals who cover the specific subject matter your press release relates to.

▶ Making sure the targeted list you create and distribute your press release to is up-to-date and accurate.

▶ Not harassing the people you send the press release to with lots of follow-up calls or emails.

▶ Making it very easy for media people to contact you and quickly obtain any additional information they need, such as a host's bio, photo, or podcast episode list, from your podcast's website, for example.

▶ Making it clear that your podcast's host(s) or producer(s) are available for in-person or phone interviews. You might also include a list of sample interview questions that are insightful and relevant to the talking points you're trying to convey.

7: Produce and Distribute Audiograms

In Chapter 9, "Edit Your Podcast Like a Pro," Travis Brown, the president of Podcast Buddy, described how his company produces Audiograms and uses them as a powerful promotional tool for podcasts. An Audiogram takes about 60 seconds of an episode's best and most compelling audio content, combines it with an animated graphic and subtitles, and then packages it into a single digital file that can easily be posted on social media, used as a digital ad, shared via a podcast's website, or embedded within an email.

The goal of an Audiogram is to capture the viewer's attention with the animated graphic, encourage them to read along using the subtitles, be intrigued enough to listen to the audio, and then compelled to click on the included link that leads directly to the podcast episode so the person experiencing the Audiogram can immediately listen to the podcast.

Podcast Buddy's research shows that using multiple forms of digital media at once—an animated graphic, text-based captions, and audio—can increase the chance of someone listening to the promoted episode by five times, compared to just using a stagnant social media post, for example.

Using the right tools, anyone can produce their own Audiograms for their podcast episodes and then come up with creative ways to distribute and share them online to attract an audience. Podcast Buddy creates Audiograms for all the clients it does podcast production for, plus any podcaster can purchase fully produced Audiograms for their own podcast episodes on an a la carte basis. For more information, visit: www.podcastbuddy.co.

Other tools you can use to create your own Audiograms include Wavve (www.wavve.co) and Headliner (www.headliner.app).

8: Be a Guest on Other Podcasts and Cross-Promote

Using public relations efforts is one way to approach other podcasters to get your host(s) booked as guests on their podcasts in order to promote your podcast. However, if this is your primary goal, a more direct approach would be to research podcasts that cover a similar subject matter as yours (and that reach a similar audience), and then contact those podcast producers directly to suggest a mutually beneficial cross-promotion.

This cross-promotion might include your host being a guest on their podcast and then having that podcast's host(s) featured as guests on your podcast, with the agreement that you'll each promote the other's appearance and podcast to your respective audiences. Consider spreading out the appearances by a few weeks, and brainstorm other ways your two podcasts can benefit by working together to build both your respective audiences.

▶ Avoid Pay-to-Appear Guest and Interview Opportunities

Some podcasts, radio shows, and other media outlets use a "pay to appear" business model. They'll invite almost anyone to appear as a guest if they're willing to pay an upfront appearance fee. In most cases, this won't be too beneficial, and the audiences of those podcasts/programs often know that guests are paying for their attention, which takes away from the credibility of those guests as well as the podcast that accepts payment for the appearances. In other words, the listeners know they're being exposed to advertorial-like content as opposed to truly unbiased and useful information.

You're better off appearing on podcasts, YouTube videos, TV shows, radio shows, and other media outlets that have a lot of credibility with their audiences and don't charge their guests. By sharing useful information as the guest or person being interviewed, as well as promoting your own podcast, you're more likely to recruit new audience members for your podcast and be perceived as an expert on the topic being discussed.

The easiest way to find contact information for other podcasters is to visit the respective websites for those podcasts and either utilize the "contact us" option or send an email to the address that's provided.

9: Focus on Word-of-Mouth Promotion

The best promotion your podcast can receive is when your audience members voluntarily boast about it to others, including their online friends, fellow club/group members, family members, and/or co-workers. The first step is to offer content that your audience loves and truly appreciates. This alone should encourage people to talk about your podcast. Next, however, come right out and ask for the help of your listeners.

During each episode's outro, for example, have your host say something like "Thanks so much for listening. If you haven't already done so, please subscribe to this podcast. It'll also really help us out if you review the episode, post comments, and share information about [insert your podcast title] with your friends."

You can also ask for the support of your listeners using informal interactions through social media, plus on your podcast's web page. For example, provide one-click hyperlinks that allow people to post a pre-written message about your podcast (including a link) on their social media feeds without having to actually type anything.

▶ Give Your Audience Something Positive to Talk About

The content of your podcast should focus on giving listeners something positive to talk about, and then encourage them to talk. Be creative in how you do this, since research shows that word-of-mouth promotion is far more effective than most other types of advertising and promotion. This is because people trust their friends more than they trust ads. In addition, word-of-mouth promotion typically allows you to reach more people in your podcast's target audience. Just make sure people have positive things to say about your podcast.

People will also talk about negative aspects of a podcast, such as any controversy or juicy gossip. There's a saying that "no publicity is bad publicity," but this is not always true. Try to keep word-of-mouth promotion about your podcast positive.

10: Leverage the Popularity of Your Guests

If the format of your podcast includes featuring special guests, chances are you've chosen those guests because they're popular, well-respected, credible, and entertaining. Perhaps they're a public figure, celebrity, author, business leader, or someone who already has their own popularity, fan base, or following.

At least a week before a guest's appearance on your podcast, start promoting that guest to your audience. At the same time, use keywords and SEO-friendly search phrases when publicizing your guest on social media or your podcast's website, for example, so fans of that guest will find your podcast.

SEO stands for search engine optimization. When writing in an SEO-friendly format, you purposely include keywords or search phrases within your text that you anticipate people will enter into a search engine or a search field (of a podcast directory, for example) in order to find your podcast.

Within your podcast or episode title, in your description(s), or when describing/promoting a podcast episode's guest, use keywords people would search for that are directly relevant. In the case of a guest, this would include their name and details about their qualifications or why they're famous.

In conjunction with the title, description, and show notes for the podcast episode the guest appears on, be sure to include their name and the keywords associated with that guest that their fans are likely to use to find more information about them. This will help the guest's established following find and listen to your podcast. If they like what they hear, they're likely to become subscribers to your podcast and continue listening to other episodes.

As you build a professional relationship with your podcast's guests, request that they promote their upcoming appearance on your podcast with their established following by posting announcements about it on their social media feeds and website, for example.

By allowing your guests to promote themselves and their company, product, or service on your podcast, they'll be more apt to help you promote their appearance to increase the number of listeners who will ultimately hear it. This creates a win-win situation for your podcast and the guest.

One way to attract extremely popular and otherwise hard-to-book guests on your podcast is to contact their personal publicist (when applicable) to seek out an interview. If that fails, attend a public appearance, press conference, trade show, or other public event where that guest will be, and ask if you can record a quick "on the spot" interview, or extend an in-person invitation to them when you meet them. When you do this, be sure to present yourself as a professional, so you're not misinterpreted as a stalker or overzealous fan.

11: Build a Targeted, Opt-In Email List or Publish an Online Newsletter/Blog

As you go about producing your podcast episodes, you'll no doubt gather or create a lot of extra content that doesn't actually make it into the podcast itself. One way to utilize this content is to offer a free newsletter, weekly email, or blog for your listeners. In addition to providing information that your audience will perceive as valuable within the newsletter, email, or blog, you can also informally promote upcoming episodes of your podcast, offer podcast-related merchandise you're selling, or share more details about your podcast's advertisers/sponsors. You can also host contests, give away prizes, or offer exclusive discounts from your podcast's advertisers/sponsors.

The goal is to get your listeners to voluntarily opt into your podcast's email list in exchange for something of value you'll be offering them for free on a regular basis. Yes, producing a weekly or monthly electronic newsletter, email, or blog takes additional time and effort, but you can utilize this additional contact with your loyal listeners in many ways that'll ultimately prove beneficial for your podcast.

Many software and online-based tools are available that can help you gather and manage an opt-in email list, plus format professional-looking electronic newsletters, blog posts, or emails. Some of these tools include:

- ► Constant Contact—www.constantcontact.com
- ► GetResponse—www.getresponse.com
- ► Mailchimp—www.mailchimp.com
- ► MailUp—www.mailup.com

12: Make Public Appearances

Building on the fact that your podcast's host(s) will likely become "online famous," or popular within the community that your podcast's subject matter relates to, use this newfound popularity to make in-person appearances whenever and wherever you can in order to promote the podcast to potential new listeners.

Be a guest speaker at special interest group meetings, trade shows, colleges, adult education programs, senior centers, church/community group meetings, organization or service club meetings (such as Rotary, Kiwanis, or a local chamber of commerce), bookstores, libraries, or wherever you can find an audience that would be interested in hearing about your podcast's subject matter or learning from the expertise of its host(s).

To make it easier to get booked for appearances or as a speaker, put together an information packet about the podcast's host(s) that includes a detailed bio, professional

► Repurpose Your Podcast Content

Once you've published a bunch of episodes of your podcast, you'll have amassed a nice collection of valuable content in an audio format. To extend the reach of your podcast to an even broader audience, consider repurposing that content into other formats, such as a full-length printed book, e-book, or audiobook.

You can either self-publish this content and sell it, work with a literary agent to pitch it to a major publishing house, or offer it as a free giveaway to your audience members who opt into your podcast's email list. Choose an option that best aligns with your podcast's goals.

If you want to repurpose content that includes appearances from special guests or copyrighted material you don't own, be sure to seek out written permission to use that content for other purposes (beyond your audio podcast).

Also, keep in mind that more and more TV and movie producers and studios are seeking out unique podcast concepts to transform into TV series and movies, so this might be a viable option, assuming your podcast offers something special that would fit one of these media formats.

headshot (photo), information about the podcast, and a summary of other appearances they've done. Providing a three-to-five-minute video clip of the host making an in-person appearance or speech will help, too.

Consider the in-person appearances and speaking engagements to be part of your podcast's promotional efforts, and don't expect to be paid. When you're using them as a grassroots, no-cost way to promote your podcast, don't look at public speaking or appearances as moneymaking opportunities, especially when reaching out to nonprofit organizations or small groups.

Avoid the 12 Biggest Podcasting Mistakes

Once your podcast is established and published online, with new episodes being introduced on a regular schedule, you may not experience the success you initially anticipated. First off, be patient. It could take weeks, perhaps months, to start building a loyal audience for your podcast. That's to be expected. If after two to

▶ Define What Podcasting Success Means to You

Before you can measure your podcast's success, you need to define what success means to you as a podcaster. In other words, make sure you have a clear understanding of your podcast's goals. Are you hoping to build a large audience, sell sponsorships or ads, and generate revenue? Instead of using ads, are you looking to sell branded merchandise related to your podcast directly to your audience? If the podcast is being created to promote a preexisting company, product, service, or association, after two to six months, are you experiencing the added sales or brand recognition you hoped to achieve? Right from the start, determine what you want to get out of the podcast, and understand how you'll measure the results you're able to achieve.

three months you don't see your audience growing, you need to figure out why and fix the problem(s).

What you'll discover from this chapter are a dozen of the biggest mistakes first-time podcasters often make. Any one of these mistakes (or a combination of them) will likely have a negative impact on the success of your podcast. Upon discovering you've made one or more of these mistakes, take immediate steps to fix them, so that you can get your podcast back on track and achieve the success you desire!

Mistake 1: The Scope of Your Content Is Too Broad (or Not Broad Enough)

Creating what you believe to be compelling and top-notch content simply isn't enough. Your audience needs to share that same belief. For your podcast to be successful, your audience needs to listen to your podcast episodes in their entirety, subscribe to the podcast, and ideally interact by reviewing it, leaving comments, and sharing details about it with their friends. Most important, they need to listen to all new episodes moving forward, and perhaps check out older episodes as well.

Knowing who your audience is and understanding what they want out of your podcast is essential. If your subject matter is too broad, you won't be able to consistently provide content that's of interest to your niche target audience. Too often, your focus will go beyond what certain audience members are interested in, so you run the risk of losing them.

Equally important is to not have a focus that's too narrow. In this case, enough people might not be interested in the topic, so your audience will stay small, or you may quickly run out of relevant content after a handful of episodes and have nowhere to go in future episodes.

As a podcaster, you'll experience an ongoing juggling act. You need to keep tabs on who your audience is and what they're looking for, and make sure you're providing enough relevant and interesting/entertaining content to keep those people coming back for more.

► Study the Analytics

Solicit feedback from your audience, and at the same time, study the analytics provided by your podcast hosting service, website hosting service, and social media services. Among other things, podcast analytics measure audience engagement with your podcast and its individual episodes.

These analytics, which are continuously updated in real time, will give you a clear understanding of who's listening, how long they're listening, which app(s)/service(s) they're using to listen (and with what equipment), when they're listening, and their level of ongoing engagement. You'll also be able to quickly determine how each episode is performing compared to your other episodes.

Other data that's collected and measured includes: the number of plays/streams per episode during a specific time period (such as a day, week, or month), the number of downloads per episode, and the number of ad impressions (if applicable). Each podcast hosting service and podcast analytics tracking service collects, analyzes, and displays the data slightly differently, so choose tools that provide the information you want and need related to your podcast. If the analytics data is IAB certified, you'll know it's accurate and can be trusted.

If you notice people are listening to your 30-minute podcast episodes, but a high percentage of the audience drops off after 20 minutes, this is a clear indication that your episodes are too long. For podcasts hosted on Apple Podcasts, for example, podcasters can use iTunes Connect Podcast Analytics to view the Average Consumption statistic to see the average amount of time the audience listens to each episode. In this case, a 100 percent consumption rate is what you're striving for.

Likewise, if people are listening to one episode of your podcast, but not subscribing or returning for more, this indicates a lack of understanding on your part about who your audience is and what they're looking for.

Meanwhile, if you discover people are listening to the same podcast episodes over and over, this could mean one of two things. Either you're creating amazing content and people love it enough to repeat their listening experience, or you're confusing people and they need to hear the same content several times in order to fully understand it.

Use the analytics feedback, along with direct feedback from your audience, to your advantage on an ongoing basis. Make adjustments in your content as needed to accommodate the largest number of people. Of course, if just one person has a complaint or provides feedback that's different from everyone else's, consider what's being said, but you don't necessarily need to take any drastic actions. However, if you start receiving the same type of feedback over and over from different people, and a trend can be identified, you'll likely want to take action and address that feedback.

Understanding and using your podcast's analytics can also help you charge more money when selling advertising and sponsorships. After all, you want to be able to prove (using third-party statistics and data) that your podcast is reaching a specific size audience. Showing potential advertisers your podcast's third-party analytics that demonstrate 10,000 or 25,000 unique weekly listeners with an 80 to 100 percent average consumption will be appealing, especially if you're able to clearly define your podcast's target audience and match that with the audience your potential advertisers/sponsors are looking to reach.

If your podcast is only published on one platform, such as Apple Podcasts, for example, using iTunes Podcast Analytics makes perfect sense. However, if you're publishing your podcast on multiple hosting services, you'll want to use a third-party analytics tracking service that will simultaneously monitor your podcast on all platforms. This will provide you with the reliable and comprehensive information that potential advertisers and sponsors will be looking for.

In addition to the analytics information provided by your podcast hosting service, a wide range of third-party companies can offer additional insight into your podcast's audience and listening habits, based on the real-time performance of your individual episodes.

As a podcaster, determine how to access the analytics data that's provided by your podcast hosting service or podcast distribution sites. For example, if your podcast is listed with Apple Podcasts, analytics information is accessible from Apple's iTunes Connect website (https://itunesconnect.apple.com). Log in using the same email address and password you use

▶ **Study the Analytics,** continued

to publish your podcast on Apple Podcasts. From the iTunes Connect menu, select the Podcast Analytics option.

Using any internet search engine, enter the search phrase "podcast analytics" to discover services like: Backtracks (www.backtracks.fm), Podtrac (https://analytics.podtrac.com), Anchor (https://anchor.fm/features#analytics), Chartable (www.chartable.com), Transistor (www.transistor.fm), and Podbean (www.podbean.com). Some of these analytics services are free. Others charge a monthly fee.

In addition to all the other data that's tracked, Podtrac (https://analytics.podtrac.com), for example, calculates a "Unique Monthly Audience" metric that shows the demographics of a podcast's audience (including age range, gender makeup, education level, income, and listening behavior), not just the audience size.

Mistake 2: You're Targeting the Wrong Audience

During the early stages of planning your podcast and choosing a focus for it, you'll need to do a bit of research and guesswork to figure out your target audience. However, once one or more episodes of your podcast are published online, use the analytics information and feedback from your audience to determine exactly who is listening.

If you're spending a lot of time, money, and resources promoting your podcast, but those efforts are not helping you expand your audience, it's very likely there's a disconnect between whom you believe your target audience is and who is actually interested in your podcast. You may discover once your podcast is published online that you need to fine-tune your target audience or tweak the scope of your content.

Should you discover there's a disconnect between your intended target audience and your actual audience, you can do one of two things. Either tweak your future content to better appeal to the audience your podcast is actually reaching, and then adjust your marketing and promotional efforts according to the actual audience, or keep your content as is, but change your marketing and promotional efforts to cater to the group of people who would be more interested in what you're already offering.

You'll know you're doing things correctly once you determine that the people listening and subscribing to your podcast are actually the group of people you're targeting the content for and marketing your podcast to.

Mistake 3: You're Utilizing the Wrong Show Format for Each Episode

As you discovered from Chapter 3, "Choosing Topic, Title, Format, Length, and Frequency," once you choose the subject matter and focus of your podcast, there are many different ways to package that information to appeal to your target audience. For example, you'll need to choose an appropriate show format.

The goal of your podcast should be to convey your information in the most entertaining and efficient way possible. To do this, select a show format that'll allow you to share your content in a way that'll appeal to your audience and give you, the podcaster, the best possible forum to communicate with your audience effectively and efficiently. Keep in mind, almost all podcast listeners have a very short attention span. In most cases, if you can share your information in a shorter length format, do so. Select a show format that allows you to convey the most information in a clear way in the shortest time possible. That being said, however, stay true to your podcast's focus and objectives.

If you plan to adopt a show format that includes one or two hosts, along with a panel of experts sharing their information and opinions as part of a discussion that focuses on a specific topic, your podcast episode needs to be long enough to hold that conversation and give everyone a chance to speak and get their points across. Likewise, if your podcast revolves around soliciting questions or comments directly from listeners, you need ample time in each episode to bring on multiple callers or read multiple emails or incoming messages and then address them.

Should you adopt a show format with just one host presenting their own monologue or two co-hosts conversing about a specific topic, you'll discover you're able to pack a lot of information into a shorter length show. To hold the attention of your audience, keep the episode length down to 15 to 30 minutes.

As you get to know your audience and clearly define the goals for your podcast, create a show format that caters to your audience yet allows you to achieve your podcast's objectives. Creating a hybrid show format is fine, as long as you offer some level of consistency from episode to episode. Plus, if your podcast will feature ads or sponsorship messages, be sure your show format allows for this content to be presented in a way that won't alienate or distract your audience.

Mistake 4: Poor Audio or Production Quality

Numerous times throughout this book, including within several of the interviews with the featured podcasting experts, you'll read that showcasing professional-quality production throughout every episode of your podcast is an absolute must! If you're not able to produce a podcast that sounds amazing using your current recording/broadcast location and equipment, you need to upgrade your recording and editing equipment and/or invest more time learning how to use that equipment to achieve the quality that's expected.

warning

If the first few episodes of your podcast are published online, but the audio quality is poor, you'll likely alienate that initial audience. Those people will find other podcasts to listen to instead of sticking with yours. This will slow down your podcast's growth and make it harder to build a positive reputation or generate positive word-of-mouth from listeners.

One of the biggest causes of poor production quality is using a low-quality microphone or the wrong type of microphone to record your content. If you don't start out with crystal clear recordings of your hosts, guests, and announcers, for example, it'll be difficult (perhaps impossible) to create a professional-sounding podcast during postproduction.

Make sure you're using the right type of microphone to do your recording/broadcasting and that you're using all your equipment correctly. Even a several-hundred-dollar microphone could wind up making your audio sound awful if you adjust the recording levels incorrectly, set it up wrong, or try to use the microphone in a way that it wasn't designed for.

To achieve great sounding audio, you don't need to spend a fortune on equipment. In most cases, you just need to ensure your recording environment is appropriate and that you know how to use your microphone and recording equipment (as well as your postproduction editing software) correctly.

If you try recording and editing your podcast on your own, but you're not achieving the quality that your audience desires and expects, seriously consider working with a professional audio engineer/podcast producer to record and edit your podcast episodes.

Mistake 5: You're Allowing Your Episodes to Run Too Long

You may have a lot to say and a lot of really great content to share with your audience. However, don't let your ego determine the length of each podcast episode. This should be something that your audience directly or indirectly dictates. In most cases, you're better off removing all ancillary or repetitive information from each episode during postproduction, and then breaking down an episode that runs very long into two or more shorter episodes.

► Know When to Offer More

If your average consumption analytics are consistently close to 100 percent (across numerous episodes), this could be an indication that your audience is craving more. Congratulations! You could now consider increasing the length of each episode a bit. Another option that'll often work better, however, is to increase the frequency that you release new episodes. Remember, it's sometimes very difficult to come up with the perfect episode length, give the audience exactly what they want during each episode, and consistently leave them wanting more after each episode.

Chances are, in addition to studying your podcast's analytics, you'll need to do some experimentation to come up with a show format and episode length that work perfectly for your podcast.

Pay attention to your podcast's Average Consumption analytics to help you determine the ideal length for each podcast episode after you've published a handful of episodes. If you notice your audience consistently drops significantly after 15, 20, or 30 minutes, this is a clear indication of what your ideal episode length should be.

Mistake 6: Under Utilizing the Postproduction Tools at Your Disposal

Every podcast recording and postproduction (editing) application offers a different collection of features and functions. As a podcaster, first choose software that provides the functionality you need, based on the type of content you'll be recording. Next, whoever will be editing the podcast episodes and handling postproduction tasks needs to become an expert using the selected software and truly understand what's possible using it.

Then, it's important to utilize the right collection of tools, in the right way, to make each podcast episode sound as professional and clear as possible. Depending on what software you're using, optional third-party plug-ins are likely available for it that allow you to expand its capabilities by adding specific functionality.

If you'll be using the free Audacity software (Windows PC or Mac) to record your podcast and handle many postproduction tasks, be sure to visit https://www.audacityteam. org/download/plug-ins/ to discover an ever-growing collection of free plug-ins available for this application. You'll discover plug-ins that allow you to add audio effects during postproduction, as well as plug-ins that allow you to convert and export your audio files into a wider range of popular file formats.

Depending on the quality of the voices of your podcast's host(s) and guest(s), as the producer, you might opt to utilize the editing/postproduction software's ability to alter an audio track's (or entire recording's) pitch and/or tempo. This will change how the people speaking actually sound. If you decide to use these editing tools, it's important to stay consistent throughout all your episodes.

One audio editing feature you'll definitely want to utilize during postproduction is noise reduction. When used properly, this will remove static, unwanted hisses and hums, and most other constant background noises that were captured during the recording process. This feature alone, which takes seconds to administer to a podcast episode during the editing process, will make your recordings sound more professional, especially if the recordings were not made in a soundproof recording studio.

Meanwhile, if you'll be mixing different audio tracks together, you'll also definitely want to use the editing/postproduction software's Normalize tool. When mixing multiple voice-over tracks together, or combining voice-over tracks with background music, for example, utilizing the Auto Duck feature that's likely built into your audio editing/ postproduction software will help you quickly level out tracks you want or need to be heard at different levels simultaneously.

► Learn to Use Your Audio Editing/Postproduction Software

In addition to reading the printed or online-based manual for the software you'll be using, be sure to check out free tutorials that are likely available on YouTube. Within YouTube's search field, enter a phrase like "podcast editing using Audacity tutorial," for example. Start by watching videos that have titles and descriptions related to the skills you're looking to learn.

When watching tutorial videos or reading tutorial information pertaining to any audio recording, editing, or postproduction application, be sure the information pertains to the version of the software you're using. Many applications get updated on a regular basis. Keep in mind, the YouTube videos with the most views and "Likes" are often the ones that offer the best information.

Mistake 7: You're Promoting Poorly Worded Episode Titles and Descriptions

Each time you upload a new episode of your podcast to a hosting service, or details about a podcast and its episodes to a podcast directory, as the podcaster, you'll be prompted to provide a podcast title, episode title, and related description(s). It's this information that'll allow potential audience members to find your podcast, and then attract their attention to it.

Consider the wording you use carefully. In many cases, you're given a limited amount of space. For an episode title, you may be limited to just 255 characters, for example. Titles and descriptions should always be concise, descriptive, straightforward, accurate, and attention-grabbing. Put time and thought into composing your titles and descriptions. Keeping in mind that a potential audience member might spend just two to five seconds scanning your title(s) and descriptions before deciding whether to listen to your podcast, make sure that the information you choose to convey caters specifically to your target audience and will be appealing to that group of people.

A catchy podcast episode title might capture someone's attention, but its description is what will likely convince someone to listen. Spelling and grammar mistakes are a no-no and will detract from your podcast's credibility.

Before uploading each episode of your podcast, write several drafts for its title and description. As you're brainstorming and editing, remove words or phrases that are repetitive or irrelevant. Consider showing your drafts to co-workers, friends, and people who would be in your target audience to get their feedback. Composing effective podcast episode titles and descriptions is a skill unto itself, and one that'll take practice, yet this is an important skill to master since it'll directly help you expand and grow your podcast's audience.

Within your podcast episode titles and descriptions, use as many keywords or search phrases as you can, based on what you believe potential audience members would enter into the search field of a podcast directory to find a podcast that covers your podcast's subject matter. Be specific!

If an episode of your podcast features a well-known guest, be sure to list that guest's name in the episode title and/or description, as this is something people might be searching for. Thus, if someone enters your guest's name into a search engine or podcast directory, your podcast listing should show up as a search result.

The more keyword matches your title and description contain, the better placement your podcast will receive as a result of someone searching online for it.

If your podcast is serialized, and you release new episodes on a regular basis, be sure to number your episodes as well as give each of them unique titles. When applicable, use a season number, episode number, and a title. For example, use this format: "Podcast Title: Season Number/Episode Number: Episode Title." This will make it easier for prospective listeners to determine the order they should listen to your episodes in.

tip

To help you compose short but catchy podcast episode titles, consider using an online-based title generator to help. You'll find this type of online tool at: www.tweakyourbiz.com, www.portent.com, or www.title-generator.com.

Some podcast episode titles speak for themselves, convey all the information necessary, and don't require potential listeners to read a detailed description to discover what an episode is all about. Brevity is important, so if this is the case, focus on highly descriptive titles. You can always add as much additional detail as you deem necessary within each episode's show notes, which an audience member can access before, during, or after listening to the episode.

An episode's show notes typically include production credits (a listing of the episode's cast and crew), an in-depth description of the episode, website links to relevant information, relevant photos, and links to the podcast's website and social media feeds. Use show notes as yet another way to communicate with your audience and share relevant information in a text-based format that might not have been covered within the podcast episode itself.

Mistake 8: You're Not Taking Advantage of Social Media to Promote Your Podcast

As you learned from Chapter 13, "12 Ways to Promote Your Podcast," you have many options for promoting your podcast with the goal of reaching new listeners, building your audience, and then retaining your listeners and subscribers. Based on your podcast's target audience and the goals you have for your podcast, taking full advantage of social media should be part of your overall promotion strategy.

By learning as much as possible about your target audience, you should be able to determine which social media service(s) they're most active on. Obviously, that's where you want to focus the majority of your social media efforts. This might include Facebook, Twitter, Instagram, LinkedIn, Snapchat, or YouTube, for example.

It's important to set up separate social media accounts for your podcast, and then brand those accounts using your podcast's logo/cover art and name. You should also register your podcast-specific social media account(s) using an email address for that podcast (not a personal email address). This way, as your podcast grows in popularity, you can easily delegate social media promotional responsibilities to someone else, without having to give that person access to your personal email or social media accounts.

In addition to choosing which social media services to become active on based on your target audience, consider what functionality you want available and how much interaction you want to have with your audience (and potential listeners), and then adjust the settings for each social media account accordingly.

For example, if you're looking to quickly and easily create an online, interactive community based around your podcast, setting up a Facebook Page or public Facebook Group is the way to go. Managing a Facebook Page or Group will require an ongoing time commitment, as you'll want to publish fresh content on a regular basis, plus moderate the posts from others. Facebook is a great forum for establishing and managing an informal, interactive community where you can communicate with your audience, your audience can communicate with you (the podcaster), and your audience members can interact with each other.

Based on the level of interaction you want with your social media followers, modify the account settings. For example, in relation to your posts, turn on or off the ability for people to publish comments. Allowing comments provides a way for people to give you feedback or communicate with you in a public forum. Depending on your target audience, allowing comments also typically means you'll need to actively moderate posts to ensure everything stays friendly and related to your podcast's subject matter.

The great thing about using social media as a promotional tool for your podcast is that it's free! Yes, a time commitment is involved, but it won't cost you money. Using social media also allows you to reach very niche audiences and interact with those people in an easy and informal way. When you utilize social media to promote your podcast and communicate with your (potential) audience, take a synergistic approach. The branding of your social media accounts should be consistent with the branding of your podcast, as well as everything else you're doing online and in the real world.

15 Ways to Promote Your Podcast Using Social Media

In addition to using social media to promote the podcast itself and to make your podcast's host(s) and producer(s) more readily accessible to listeners, the following are 15 ways to use social media to interact with your podcast's (potential) audience members:

1. Share details about your podcast as a whole.
2. Promote upcoming episodes and offer sneak previews (perhaps one- to three-minute audio clips).
3. Promote upcoming guests.

4. Solicit feedback from your audience, and ask for suggestions related to future episodes or guests.

5. Have audience members post questions for the host(s) and/or guest(s) that will be answered online and/or within an upcoming podcast episode.

6. Post updates related to past episodes, as applicable.

7. Share links to your podcast's latest episode(s) as well as to the podcast's website.

8. Encourage listeners to share your podcast's social media posts with their online friends.

9. Host contests and give away prizes to audience members who are active on your social media pages. (Keep in mind, in some countries and states, restrictions apply when hosting a contest or offering giveaways, including cash or prizes. Research what's legal before proceeding.)

10. Create a detailed account profile that's keyword-oriented and makes your podcast and its hosts easy to find using the social media service's search tool.

11. Create original content related to your podcast's subject matter that your audience will perceive as valuable, but that you didn't include in actual podcast episodes. You can also share outtakes. For example, include segments from interviews that were originally edited out of the podcast episode, but that your audience may find interesting.

12. Engage your audience in public (but moderated) discussions about relevant topics. Encourage people to voice their opinions, share their own knowledge, make recommendations to others, and provide you (the podcaster) with useful insight.

13. Sell podcast-related merchandise, such as branded T-shirts or coffee mugs.

14. Develop cross-promotional relationships with your podcast's guests, other podcasters, advertisers, sponsors, or other companies that reach the same target audience as your podcast. Be creative and come up with plans that are mutually beneficial for all parties involved.

15. Share photos, artwork, and/or video clips directly related to your podcast.

Using analytics data provided by Facebook, Twitter, Instagram, LinkedIn, or whichever social media platforms you're using, figure out what content people enjoy and utilize, and focus your energies on providing additional content that's similar and equally appealing. Stop wasting time and resources creating content for social media that isn't getting proper traction.

In addition to continuously monitoring your podcast's social media accounts and moderating discussions and posts, get into the habit of posting original content on a regular basis. Create a schedule for yourself, and plan out what you'll post and when, in advance. As you're brainstorming and scheduling upcoming podcast episodes, think about relevant content you'll post on social media in conjunction with each episode. People will be more willing to engage with you online if you're regularly active and readily accessible.

Mistake 9: You're Promoting Your Podcast to the Wrong People

Promoting and advertising your podcast will take a considerable amount of time (and in some cases money and other resources). Promotion is something that needs to be done on an ongoing basis. You should take a multifaceted approach to your efforts.

Regardless of what promotional efforts you choose to pursue, make sure you're allocating your time, money, and resources to reaching people who directly fall into your podcast's target audience and demographic, otherwise, you'll just be wasting your time and money.

If you have additional time, money, and resources at your disposal, consider dedicating them to reaching a secondary target audience for your podcast. However, keep your efforts as focused and niche-oriented as possible to achieve the best results.

Mistake 10: Your Podcast's Branding Isn't Appealing to Its Target Audience

As you learned from Chapter 5, "Brand Your Podcast," a lot goes into creating and maintaining your podcast's recognizable brand and positive reputation. If your branding doesn't appeal to your podcast's target audience, you could actually wind up driving potential audience members away. Consider every aspect of your branding, from the fonts, wording/vocabulary, and color schemes used in the visuals to the background music people hear during your podcast episodes. All the branding elements should appeal to your target audience and be consistent across all platforms and media. If your intended audience doesn't relate to your branding, you'll lose them.

Mistake 11: You're Not Taking Advantage of the Potential Revenue Streams Your Podcast Offers

Once your podcast develops a decent-size and continuously growing audience, a wide range of revenue-generating opportunities will become available to you. Many of these moneymaking opportunities were discussed within Chapter 10, "Monetizing Your Podcast," and Chapter 11, "More Ways to Generate Income from Your Podcast."

Based on the overall goals for your podcast and the size of its audience, pick and choose moneymaking opportunities that make sense and that your audience won't find objectionable or distracting. Also, be sure to use these various opportunities in moderation. In other words, if each episode of your podcast lasts 15 minutes, allocating more than two minutes to advertising or messages from sponsors will likely be considered excessive and annoying.

Likewise, if you're going to sell products or services directly related to your podcast's subject matter, make sure whatever you're selling will be in demand by and of interest to your target audience. Don't waste time promoting products or services that won't appeal to your audience.

Sure, you want to take full advantage of the revenue-generating opportunities available to you once your podcast becomes successful, but you don't want to alienate or exploit your audience in the process. By demonstrating that, as a podcaster, you're very selective in terms of the advertising opportunities or sponsorships you accept, over time, your audience will trust you more and be more loyal to you and whatever you ultimately choose to sell or promote.

Mistake 12: Inconsistency and Lack of Synergy

Once you create and establish a brand for your podcast, choose a show format, and define the podcast's overall sound and attitude, stick with it and be consistent. Sure, you might make minor tweaks here and there, but maintaining a synergistic approach across your podcast, its website, and all its social media, advertising, and promotional efforts will serve you well.

Using different logos or typestyles/fonts that don't match, constantly changing the color scheme in visual content, or using vastly different styles of background music during podcast episodes are all ways you'll wind up confusing or alienating your audience.

After a while, you want someone to be able to just glance at your podcast's listing or listen to a few seconds of your podcast and immediately recognize it as uniquely yours. Likewise, after someone listens to one episode of your podcast, you want them to experience a sense of familiarity when they listen to future or past episodes.

At the same time, if they visit your podcast's website, check out your podcast's Facebook page, and then listen to your podcast episodes, they should feel like all that content was created by the same team, for the same purpose, and that it was targeted to the same audience. The more synergistic your approach is, the easier time you'll have building a loyal audience.

Learn from Your Mistakes!

As a first-time podcaster, you will make mistakes, make a few bad decisions, and take incorrect actions. When you do something wrong, figure out:

- ► Exactly what you did wrong.
- ► Why you did what you did.
- ► How you'll prevent the mistake in the future.
- ► What needs to be done to correct the mistake.
- ► Whether you need to apologize to anyone you might have offended.
- ► How you'll recover from any damage caused by the mistake.

► Enhance Your Public Speaking Skills as Part of Your Ongoing Training

If you lack the confidence or skill required to be a compelling public speaker and ultimately a good host for your podcast, you can enhance your public speaking skills and experience.

For example, consider joining a local chapter of Toastmasters International (www.toastmasters. org) and attending meetings. This is a nonprofit organization that helps everyday people become better speakers.

Of course, you can also rehearse before recording each episode of your podcast. Another option is to work with a professional vocal coach to help perfect your vocal tone, timing, vocabulary, and pronunciation.

Countless (free) tutorials are available on YouTube that cover how to become a better podcast host. Plus, either for free or a small fee, you'll find many public speaking courses available from online services including: Effective Presentations (www.effectivepresentations. com), Udemy (www.udemy.com), Dale Carnegie (https://www.dalecarnegie.com), and LearnOutLoud (www.learnoutloud.com).

To find additional resources and public speaking training programs, within any search engine (such as Google), enter "public speaking skills training" or "public speaking workshops."

Over time, you'll gain firsthand experience handling every aspect of your podcast's preproduction, production, postproduction, promotion, and management. You'll learn what works and what doesn't, again based on your audience and your overall objectives as a podcaster. Moving forward, make sure you understand that becoming a successful podcaster means you'll always need to continue learning, and that based on what you learn, you may need to tweak your actions to achieve bigger and better results.

Be sure you invest the necessary time to stay up-to-date on the latest podcasting trends, the latest technologies and tools used by podcasters, and the latest trends that pertain to your podcast's subject matter and target audience.

Always be honest with yourself in terms of what you don't know or understand and what skills you lack, and then take steps to expand your knowledge and skill sets so you're constantly striving and working toward becoming a better podcaster.

Interviews with Podcasting Pros

By now, you should clearly understand that there's no such thing as a guaranteed formula for success when it comes to producing your podcast. Many factors go into a podcast's success (or failure). To achieve your podcasting goals, you'll definitely want to follow the steps outlined throughout this book, but also learn as much as you can from the producers and hosts of popular and well-produced podcasts.

This final chapter offers a collection of exclusive interviews with podcasters from many walks of life, with varying podcasting goals, and who have already achieved some level of success producing and distributing at least one podcast.

Within these interviews, podcasters share their real-world experiences and offer their own advice and opinions about what it takes to follow in their footsteps, produce an attention-getting podcast, and then build and continuously grow an audience. Keep in mind that everyone's experiences, goals, and approach to podcasting are different. Be sure to utilize the advice that relates most to your own project(s) and use this chapter as a chance to learn from the valuable experiences of others, while avoiding their mistakes.

Tom Scarda, Creator/Host of *The Franchise Academy* and *Franchise FrontRunner*

When it comes to franchise-based business opportunities, Tom Scarda, CFE, is a leading expert. To share his knowledge and promote his business, he produces and hosts two podcasts.

Launched in 2014, with two episodes released per week, *The Franchise Academy* is a general show about franchising. It acts as a resource for anyone who wants to buy a franchise, learn best operations practices, sell a franchise, or turn their existing business into a franchise.

His second podcasting venture is called *Franchise FrontRunner*. It's a ten-minute show dedicated to showcasing top franchise owners across all 90 industries in franchising. Its objective is to fill a void in best practice information for franchise owners. Both podcasts are distributed via his website (www.tomscarda.com), as well as through Apple Podcasts, Spotify, iHeartRadio, Pandora, and Google Podcasts.

Scarda explained, "I am using these platforms because they are free and have the most listeners. *Franchise FrontRunner* can also be heard on Alexa news briefs."

Why did you decide to become a podcaster and create these two podcasts?

Scarda: "*Franchise Academy* started as a radio show in New York. I decided on a whim to upload the MP3s to iTunes. I slowly started to realize that the radio listenership was close to zero, but the podcast was getting a lot of play. I ultimately stopped the radio broadcast and built a professional podcast studio in my home."

When you started the podcast, what was the biggest challenge you faced and how did you overcome that challenge?

Scarda: "My biggest challenge was figuring out the best technology that helps sound quality. I watched a ton of YouTube videos and tried different platforms to get it right. To achieve the best audio quality possible, I ultimately hired an audio editor using the Upwork website [www.upwork.com] to handle postproduction."

What are your best tips for building and retaining an audience for a new podcast?

Scarda: "The quickest way to build an audience is by having guests who have a following. To retain an audience, it will all come down to producing great, interesting, and well-produced content."

What equipment and software do you use to produce your podcast?

Scarda: "I currently use Zoom video [www.zoom.us] calls to record shows. My podcasts offer video on my website and via YouTube."

How long did it take before you were able to generate a respectable income from the podcast? How does your podcast currently generate revenue?

Scarda: "I offer sponsorship opportunities; however, I have not yet accepted any deals. I don't want to lessen the value for the listeners."

In your opinion, what's the biggest misconception startup podcasters have about podcasting?

Scarda: "Many think all they need to do is record it and the audience will automatically come. Unless your podcast is just a hobby for you, it's necessary to treat it like a business. Have a business plan and a marketing strategy."

Is there a piece of information you wish you knew when you started podcasting that you had to discover the hard way?

Scarda: "Keep the audio of your show saved on an external drive. You never know when a sinister technology monster will rear its ugly head and you'll lose the content because of a glitch. Create backups of everything!"

What are some of the biggest mistakes you've seen podcasters make? How can these mistakes be avoided?

Scarda: "I think mistakes come from not having a plan, not knowing who your audience is, or not understanding what information your listeners are looking for. Again, have a business plan for the show."

What are your top five tips for producing an amazing, professional-quality podcast?

Scarda: "First, the sound quality must be great. Invest in good equipment. If you're not an audiophile, hire a great audio engineer or podcast editor. There is more to the sound than just volume. A podcast also must have an attention-grabbing logo. They say having the host's face on it is worthwhile. I recommend creating a good website for the show, where folks can get more information about your topic. Have a marketing plan. Never just upload the show and hope for the best."

What are some of the personal qualities and core skills someone needs to become a top-notch podcaster?

Scarda: "Think about a podcast as a web-based radio show. However, instead of broadcasting, a podcast is a narrowcast aimed to a specific audience. To be a top-notch podcaster, you must be a good interviewer or storyteller. Listen to great broadcasters, like Edward R. Murrow, Walter Cronkite, and Anderson Cooper. If your show is a story podcast, learn great storytelling. Think about producing your podcast as audio-only, before expanding into video."

How do you generate original ideas for your content on an ongoing basis? What are some of your best brainstorming techniques?

Scarda: "My podcasts are franchise business specific. I find that most podcasts in this arena talk about specific franchise companies because they are probably paying for the placement. I keep my podcasts as a pure educational resource. That is why I don't want to have sponsors that could skew the information I can put out for my listeners. My topics are generated by the most frequently asked questions, or what people are asking me to cover via comments."

Is there any other advice you can share that would benefit startup podcasters, based on your own experiences?

Scarda: "It's one thing to do a podcast for fun, because you're passionate about a hobby or an activity. However, if you're thinking about monetizing the show or having it be picked up by Hollywood to become a movie or a TV show, you must have a plan. Don't just wing it."

Lucas Rockwood, Creator, *The Lucas Rockwood Show*

According to Lucas Rockwood, *The Lucas Rockwood Show* is a weekly health and wellness show for anyone looking to live a radiant life. It's been in existence since 2012 and is currently distributed via Apple Podcasts and Spotify, and is syndicated. "I started this podcast as a way to talk to my yoga students around the world," he explained.

When you started your podcast, what was the biggest challenge you faced? How did you overcome that challenge?

Rockwood: "My biggest challenge initially was finding great guests who were well-spoken, entertaining, informative, and that added value to my show."

What are your best tips for building and retaining an audience for a new podcast?

Rockwood: "Understand that building an audience is a slow grind. It took me years. However, once your audience begins to tune in because they are getting something of value, they often stay for life."

What equipment and software do you use to produce your podcast?

Rockwood: "I utilize Skype in conjunction with MX Skype Recorder, along with an Audio-Technica ATR2100-USB cardioid dynamic microphone."

How long did it take before you were able to generate a respectable income from the podcast?

Rockwood: "Five years. However, today it's a profitable venture."

In your opinion, what's the biggest misconception startup podcasters have about podcasting?

Rockwood: "They assume they can build an audience or generate revenue quickly. It takes years. There are few shortcuts like in other media."

Is there a piece of information you wish you knew when you started podcasting that you had to discover the hard way?

Rockwood: "Early on, I would have focused more on booking great guests."

What are some of the biggest mistakes you've seen podcasters make? How can these mistakes be avoided?

Rockwood: "I've put some boring people on the show as guests. I should have cut them."

What are your top best tips for producing an amazing, professional-quality podcast?

Rockwood: "Serve your audience. Give them value. Clean up your vocal tracks, and keep the content focused."

What are some of the personal qualities and core skills someone needs to become a top-notch podcaster?

Rockwood: "I think podcasters need to ask good questions when interviewing guests. It's also important to have and share your own opinions and have something interesting to say."

How do you generate original ideas for your content on an ongoing basis? What are some of your best brainstorming techniques?

Rockwood: "I'm not original, but on my podcast, I strive to interview people who are."

Is there any other advice you can share that would benefit startup podcasters, based on your own experiences?

Rockwood: "I would try to go small, not go big. The more niche, the better. Audio is culty."

David Hooper, Host/Producer, *Build a Big Podcast– The Marketing Podcast for Podcasters*

David Hooper refers to himself as a marketing expert, whose clients (who include authors and people in the entertainment industry) are themselves experts in their respective fields. He has been involved with podcasting since 2005.

"I currently host and/or produce a few different podcasts. The main one right now is called *Build a Big Podcast—The Marketing Podcast for Podcasters* [https://podcast.bigpodcast.com]. Most of the time, I produce two to three episodes per week; however, I recently produced 30 episodes in 30 days, as part of a 30-in-30 challenge."

How long has the podcast been in existence?

Hooper: "*Build a Big Podcast—The Marketing Podcast for Podcasters* was started in 2017, but I have been podcasting since 2005. My first podcast was a show called *Music Business Radio*, which is also on broadcast radio."

Where is your podcast distributed? How did you choose that distribution outlet?

Hooper: "*Build a Big Podcast* is available wherever you can get podcasts, including Apple Podcasts, Google Podcasts, Spotify, iHeart, and Amazon Alexa."

What made you start podcasting?

Hooper: "I started *Music Business Radio* back in 2005 as a way to market myself and my music marketing company. I was looking to break away from working exclusively in the music industry and talk about other marketing-related topics. People were always asking me about getting involved in radio and podcasting, so I started *Build a Big Podcast* to help establish myself with nonmusicians."

When you started the podcast, what was the biggest challenge you faced? How did you overcome that challenge?

Hooper: "I'm going to give you two answers—one for 2005, and one for 2014. When I started *Music Business Radio* in 2005, the biggest issue was convincing radio professionals that podcasting was a worthwhile way to distribute the content we made for the broadcast airwaves. In general, it wasn't taken very seriously.

"Fortunately, I worked with a production team that let me run with it. Now, because we've been at it so long, the naysayers are coming to us to find out how to do podcasting themselves.

"Later, in 2014, when I started to branch out from music and work with entrepreneurs and companies, the biggest challenge was educating people on what podcasting was. Even though podcasting was 10 years old at that time, there were still technical hurdles to overcome for most people, and it wasn't as easy as radio to listen to.

"Fortunately, over the last few years—thanks largely in part to Apple, which now includes the Apple Podcasts app on every iPhone, iPad, or Mac—more people are aware of how to listen to podcasts. We still have a long way to go to match the ease and reach of traditional radio, however."

What are your best tips for building and retaining an audience for a new podcast?

Hooper: "Be consistent and take the work seriously. However, don't take yourself too seriously. Beyond that, get to really know your audience. Get on the phone with them, go to related events, read books on the subject, and do whatever you can to get connected with your audience in a meaningful way."

What equipment and software do you use to produce your podcast?

Hooper: "Coming from radio, I had access to a lot of great broadcast gear. But I wanted to own 'podcasting,' and show that it could be done without much money. My first podcast setup was a $70 mic, the ATR2100 by Audio-Technica, that could plug directly into a computer via USB. As far as recording, I love Audacity [www.audacityteam.org], which is open-source audio recording software, for a PC or Mac, that's free. My podcast's website [https://www.bigpodcast.com/resources] has the full list of equipment we currently use."

How long did it take before you were able to generate a respectable income from the podcast? How does your podcast currently generate revenue?

Hooper: "I've always used podcasting/broadcasting as a way to promote an existing business. When it comes to marketing yourself, podcasting is amazing. It showcases you and presells people who are interested in working with you. By the time I have somebody approach me about working together, they're already sold, because they feel like they know me . . . and they do!"

In your opinion, what's the biggest misconception startup podcasters have about podcasting?

Hooper: "It can take years to develop a great podcast personality and have a focused and compelling message. My first podcast-only show, which was not also produced for radio, was created after ten years of me hosting a weekly, long-format interview show, so I was pretty established as a host before the first episode.

"I still had to work through kinks to let that show emerge and find its own voice. This isn't instant or easy, but because most shows are established and very slick by the time a big audience hears them, or some hosts are established from radio or other media, there's a misconception that success in podcasting happens quickly."

Is there a piece of information you wish you knew when you started podcasting that you had to discover the hard way?

Hooper: "I wish I'd started a podcast-only show way earlier than I did. Working on a broadcast/podcast hybrid has been great, but the flexibility you have just releasing content via podcast is so much greater. With just podcasting, whether you succeed or fail is all on you, which is very scary to some people, but I find that to be empowering."

What are some of the biggest mistakes you've seen podcasters make? How can these mistakes be avoided?

Hooper: "The biggest mistake podcasters make is related to organization, planning, and polish. Many podcasters don't plan. They also don't do preinterviews, and they don't properly edit their content. Because of this, there are a lot of sloppy podcasts.

"Fortunately, some real broadcast talent is getting into podcasting now, which is upping the reputation of podcasting and showing amateur/beginning podcasters what is possible. You can also find some great online tutorials that show people how to shortcut the process."

What are your top five tips for producing an amazing, professional-quality podcast?

Hooper: "First, have high standards for guests and episode topics. Your podcast is your home, so don't open it to people who won't take care of it. Next, always preinterview guests or somehow vet them. Also, always outline your episode before going into the studio, and then invest the time to properly edit your episodes. If something doesn't move an episode forward, cut it. Finally, be open to feedback. Not everybody will like what you do, but if you keep hearing the same feedback, consider listening to it."

What are some of the personal qualities and core skills someone needs to become a top-notch podcaster?

Hooper: "The biggest thing is having curiosity. Be genuinely interested in whatever you're talking about. Ask insightful questions, and then follow up on those questions whenever it's appropriate. Podcasting is a great place to go beyond surface-level conversations and reporting that we see in our day-to-day lives when consuming many other forms of media.

"You also have to know how to listen. Way too many podcasters neglect this, talk over their guests, and miss big opportunities because they're too worried about having the last word or getting through a list of prepared questions.

"The tech stuff related to producing a podcast is relatively easy and can always be hired out. Curiosity, however, can't be delegated, and neither can the personality of the host. The podcasting world doesn't need another nameless and faceless radio host. What's needed are people who aren't afraid to express themselves, have opinions, and be bold."

How do you generate original ideas for your content on an ongoing basis? What are some of your best brainstorming techniques?

Hooper: "I am always looking for episode ideas. I keep a notebook with me and also have a spreadsheet where I record stories of things that happened to me on a daily basis. There are stories and lessons everywhere if you look for them and pay attention. I actually just did an episode on my podcast about this topic [https://podcast.bigpodcast.com/day-29-where-to-get-unlimited-podcast-ideas]."

Is there any other advice you can share that would benefit startup podcasters, based on your own experiences?

Hooper: "You're not going to get it right, but you're not going to screw it up. Jump in, have fun with it, and take chances. This advice may sound cliché, but you learn more by doing than thinking about it or talking about it. Hit record and just do it. If you don't like what you record, try again using a different approach."

Anielle Reid, Editor/Producer, *Magick and Mediums*

By now, you should understand that podcasts work best when they cater to a niche audience, and that there are already podcasts that cover just about every topic imaginable. Anielle Reid describes her 3-year-old podcast as "A magical place on the airwaves for pagans and occult authors to share their firsthand accounts of real magic. I started this podcast because I love speaking to witchy people and to the creators of the books that I love."

Magick and Mediums is distributed on virtually every popular podcasting platform, including Spotify, Apple Podcasts, Stitcher, and Google Podcasts. She initially chose these platforms by researching where other successful podcasts could be found. The website for her podcast and online shop is www.magickandmediums.com.

When you started the podcast, what was the biggest challenge you faced? How did you overcome that challenge?

Reid: "First, I invested time learning about the setup and production aspects of podcasting by watching a lot of YouTube videos."

What are your best tips for building and retaining an audience for a new podcast?

Reid: "I suggest that as a podcaster, you ask your listeners to email you with their feedback, thoughts, and ideas. I also recommend producing a weekly newsletter which you email to audience members who opt into your email mailing list. I find it very useful to post on multiple social media outlets about my podcast at least two times per week, while engaging with my audience via comments throughout each week."

What equipment and software do you use to produce your podcast?

Reid: "To record and edit each podcast episode, I use the free Audacity software [www.audacityteam.org]. I record using an Apple MacBook laptop computer in conjunction with a Blue Yeti microphone [www.bluedesigns.com/products/yeti] that plugs into the computer via its USB port."

How long did it take before you were able to generate a respectable income from the podcast? How does your podcast currently generate revenue?

Reid: "It took about one year of dedicated work. The way I generate revenue from the podcast is that I use it to market my own oracle deck, The Magick and Mediums Oracle, as well as my other services, which include personalized card readings and membership to the Magick Book Club. In addition, I generate some additional revenue from affiliate marketing, and also solicit donations from the audience via PayPal [www.paypal.com] and Patreon [www.patreon.com]."

In your opinion, what's the biggest misconception startup podcasters have about podcasting?

Reid: "People think that podcasting is quick and easy, and that it doesn't actually involve time-consuming work."

Is there a piece of information you wish you knew when you started podcasting that you had to discover the hard way?

Reid: "I'd have to suggest that you initially set up retargeting ads at the same time you launch your podcast."

What are some of the biggest mistakes you've seen podcasters make? How can these mistakes be avoided?

Reid: "They don't have a theme for each episode. Be sure to outline and plan each episode first, so you don't waste a lot of time recording and editing, and then potentially wind up with something your target audience won't be interested in."

What are your top five tips for producing an amazing, professional-quality podcast?

Reid: "I suggest that you learn how to make useful edits using Audacity or recording and editing software and take full advantage of the noise removal feature. Also be sure to edit out the distracting breath sounds and the 'ums.'

"I also found that it's useful to have intro music, but to keep it short. Then, within each episode of your podcast, talk about something specific that you care about or are knowledgeable about. Most importantly, if you're hosting the podcast, be yourself!"

What are some of the personal qualities and core skills someone needs to become a top-notch podcaster?

Reid: "Be persistent with your efforts. Have a good voice and be willing to learn all about content marketing."

How do you generate original ideas for your content on an ongoing basis? What are some of your best brainstorming techniques?

Reid: "I am a part of the community that I created and seek out their feedback and input. I also follow news that is relevant to my listeners. I always research what new books are coming out that may be of interest to my audience. My best brainstorming technique is to listen to my heart over my brain."

Is there any other advice you can share that would benefit startup podcasters, based on your own experiences?

Reid: "Yes. Be yourself! Don't try to copy a podcasting trend or format just because it is popular now, especially if you don't like that trend or format. Choose the best way to share your unique content with your target audience, in a way that works best for you."

Sharvette L. Mitchell, Host, *The Sharvette Mitchell Radio Show*

Launched in February 2008, *The Sharvette Mitchell Radio Show* is an interview-style show that features guests that include celebrities, artists, authors, small-business owners, public speakers, consultants, media personalities, and other influential people. The show airs live, every Tuesday at 6 P.M. EST, and is then immediately available as a new podcast episode that can be streamed or downloaded. The show's target audience is emerging and established women in business.

Currently, BlogTalkRadio (www.blogtalkradio.com) is the main distribution outlet for the podcast, but it's also available from Apple Podcasts and from Mitchell's own website (www.sharvette.com). She explained, "I chose to distribute the podcast via BlogTalkRadio because it had the best capabilities for allowing callers to call during the live show."

What made you start the podcast?

Mitchell: "I actually started a small 15-minute radio show on a local station in Richmond, Virginia, back in 2007. At the time, I was all about promoting my web design business. A few months into hosting that show, people kept asking me if they could be a guest on the show, so I needed to figure out a way to have guests and also extend the length of the show. This is when I found out about BlogTalkRadio and discovered podcasting. I transitioned my show to the internet in February 2008."

When you started the podcast, what was the biggest challenge you faced?

Mitchell: "My biggest challenge was getting listeners on the internet vs. people who had listened to the show in their car on traditional radio. I overcame that challenge by falling in love with MySpace and promoting like crazy on that platform." [Back in 2008, MySpace was the most popular social media platform.]

What are your best tips for building and retaining an audience for a new podcast?

Mitchell: "Consistency and content are the two main keys to building and keeping an audience. Listeners want to know exactly when they can hear your podcast, just like they watch their favorite show on TV and they know the channel, day, and time it comes on every week. Your podcast must be just as consistent. After consistency is content. You must talk about information that is interesting, intriguing, and enticing to your ideal listener and target audience."

What equipment and software do you use to produce your podcast?

Mitchell: "I just need a computer with internet access to connect to the BlogTalkRadio service, as well as a telephone."

How long did it take before you were able to generate a respectable income from the podcast?

Mitchell: "My podcast has been used mainly to promote my brand and draw attention to my web design services. I left my corporate job in February 2018 to operate my own web design business full-time. The podcast plays a role in helping to obtain web design clients, coaching clients, speaking engagements, and in generating ticket sales for my annual conference."

In your opinion, what's the biggest misconception startup podcasters have about podcasting?

Mitchell: "They believe they will have millions of listeners from the first episode. In reality, you must build your listener base over time."

Is there a piece of information you wish you knew when you started podcasting that you had to discover the hard way?

Mitchell: "I would have pushed Apple Podcasts subscriptions sooner rather than later. When I first started, podcasting was rather new and so was internet radio. I drove traffic to my website, mobile app, and to BlogTalkRadio. Today, Apple Podcasts is really the main channel for podcasts, so for most podcasters, I believe their attention should be there."

What are some of the biggest mistakes you've seen podcasters make?

Mitchell: "The biggest mistake is inconsistent podcasts. Releasing just one podcast episode here and there is not going to build listeners. To avoid this, set a realistic schedule for your podcast, even if you just operate in seasons. If the listener knows season one starts on a specific date and then ends on a specific date, they will come back and look for season two. This also helps to give the podcaster a break.

"No matter what, show up for your podcast! The other mistake is rambling on and on during an episode, which is probably an indication that you're not prepared. To avoid this, select one topic and three talking points associated with that topic. Have this information written down before you start the episode. This will help to keep you focused. When you have covered your points, wrap up the podcast. You don't need to have the same length podcast each time. Quality of content is the most important thing."

What are your top five tips for producing an amazing, professional-quality podcast?

Mitchell: "First, have great sound quality. Second, include intro music that's 30 seconds or less. Third, include outro music. Fourth, have an amazing podcast graphic with a professional picture. Finally, include a great show topic and description with each episode."

What are some of the personal qualities and core skills someone needs to become a top-notch podcaster?

Mitchell: "You should have energy in your voice so that the listener can visualize you and the content. It's helpful if you love words, because you will use a lot of them while hosting a podcast.

"Reading books and looking up the definition of words is a good back-pocket tip. Lastly, staying up-to-date on social media is a core skill for the marketing of your podcast and for building your personal brand as a podcaster. At the end of the day, your listener is connecting to you, not just the podcast title, content, or interview guest. They are buying into what you have to say. Social media helps them get interested in you."

How do you generate original ideas for your content on an ongoing basis? What are some of your best brainstorming techniques?

Mitchell: "I have a new guest every podcast. My content and questions are based on them and their business or story. I use the guest's bio to help formulate my talking points. To brainstorm show topics, content, and guests, I first think of main categories, such as authors, speakers, businesses, events, health, wellness, and/or relationships. Then, on a consistent basis, I leverage social media to identify guests that fit in my selected podcast categories or topics. Facebook Groups are a terrific resource for finding guests and potential topics. Since I have hosted my podcast for a while, I also receive submissions from people who want to be a guest. This gives me a consistent flow of guests and topics. Each new podcast guest also brings new listeners."

Is there any other advice you can share that would benefit startup podcasters, based on your own experiences?

Mitchell: "When you become a podcaster, you turn into the media. Not only that, but most people will see you as somewhat of a celebrity. Use that to your advantage to spread your message. Share your voice to impact the world."

Marla Goldberrg, Founder and Host, *Guided Spirit Conversations*

Guided Spirit Conversations is produced as a live, weekly audio and video-based podcast that's targeted to a primarily female audience between the ages of 25 and 80, although Goldberrg has seen her male audience expanding as well. The podcast was launched in April 2018 as a prerecorded show, but when she began working with VoiceAmerica (www.voiceamerica.com) in August 2019 to host and distribute the podcast, she changed the show to follow a live format.

In addition to the VoiceAmerica website (www.voiceamerica.com/show/3900), *Guided Spirit Conversations* is also available as an audio podcast via Apple Podcasts, Google Podcasts, iHeartRadio, and Spotify. The video version of the podcast can be streamed from YouTube.

According to Goldberrg (www.marlagoldberrg.com), who is an accomplished energy healer, intuitive, teacher, speaker, and author, "Offering the show as a streaming video on YouTube allows the audience to see the behind-the-scenes activities as the audio podcast is being broadcast."

She added, "*Guided Spirit Conversations* is an interactive show where I have insightful, informative, and fun conversations with my guests. These guests include energy healers, psychics, mediums, spiritualists, and thought leaders from all over the world. Each weekly program offers the audience easy-to-use methods that they can bring into their own daily practice to help them enhance or shift their current life experience. My guests share what they do and offer tips, tools, and techniques. My goal is to spotlight individuals that the audience may not have learned about otherwise."

What made you start the Guided Spirit Conversations *podcast?*

Goldberrg: "I truly felt guided to start the show. Anyone who knew me before the show knew that I was not comfortable in front of the mic or the camera, so taking this leap was huge for me."

When you started the podcast, what was the biggest challenge you faced? How did you overcome that challenge?

Goldberrg: "Using technology was and still is one of my greatest challenges. I overcame it by hiring a producer who edits my show, as well as puts in the intro and outro, and then uploads it to the appropriate places. My assistant is also very adept with technology, which helps strengthen my area of challenge."

What are your best tips for building and retaining an audience for a new podcast?

Goldberrg: "I feel that the best way to build your audience is to market, market, and market the show! I post to all popular social media outlets and have been active on social media since the beginning of my podcast. About a year ago, I started a private group on Facebook where I go live each Monday and chat with my audience. I have learned that it is important to put your name and face in the public as often as possible to build momentum for a podcast."

What equipment and software do you use to produce your podcast?

Goldberrg: "When I'm in my home studio, I use a Behringer mixer box and an Audio-Technica mic and headphone combination. On the road I use a PreSonus mixer box, PreSonus headphones, and an Audio-Technica microphone."

How long did it take before you were able to generate a respectable income from the podcast? How does your podcast currently generate revenue?

Goldberrg: "At this time my podcast is just starting to make money. I don't believe in charging my guests to be on my show. Revenue is generated by sponsorship and ad sales."

In your opinion, what's the biggest misconception startup podcasters have about podcasting?

Goldberrg: "I believe that there don't need to be misconceptions about anything. All the information one needs to learn related to how to record, produce, and market their show can be found through books, as well as from Google and YouTube. There is an investment one needs to make to educate themselves and to determine their show format, as well as who their target demographic is."

Is there a piece of information you wish you knew when you started podcasting that you had to discover the hard way?

Goldberrg: "I've been lucky. I found a producer who was patient with me and who got me up and running. I also have an assistant who is my godsend, and who is educated in areas that totally perplex me."

What are some of the biggest mistakes you've seen podcasters make? How can these mistakes be avoided?

Goldberrg: "I feel that one mistake that a host of an interview can make is talking too much, while not allowing their guest to share the messages that they were brought on the show to discuss. I also don't believe in being too scripted. I like when my shows have an organic flow to them.

"I believe that the host needs to know how to pull back a show that is going in a direction that is off message, and that the host needs to be present and aware of how much to pontificate, as well as how to veer the show back to topic."

What are your top five tips for producing an amazing, professional-quality podcast?

Goldberrg: "First, know your topic and, if applicable, as much as possible about your podcast's guests. Second, be authentic. Today's audiences are very savvy. I have found that they prefer someone who is real. Third, be relaxed. It's important to stay grounded while hosting a show. Fourth, if you have a recorded show and you're not technologically astute, find someone who is. There are many people out there who are willing to start with a show and want to grow with it. Finally, always try to enjoy yourself. True enjoyment comes through to the listening audience."

What are some of the personal qualities and core skills someone needs to become a top-notch podcaster?

Goldberrg: "I feel that a host of a show needs to be passionate about the focus or topic of their podcast. For example, I would never podcast about sports or technology. The disingenuousness of my interest would be too transparent.

"I believe that a host must be somewhat outgoing and have a pleasant tone to their voice. They should exude a kind of warmth and engaged tone, especially if the show follows an interview-style format. Someone who speaks too slowly and is tentative in their delivery might have a hard time convincing the audience that they're into or enjoying themselves and their work."

How do you generate original ideas for your content on an ongoing basis? What are some of your best brainstorming techniques?

Goldberrg: "Since my podcast is an interview-oriented show, I try to book my guests based on their specialty and the time of year. For example, I had a psychic medium and a paranormal investigator on my Halloween episode, and then a guest on the last show of the year spoke about predictions for the following year. I also generate ideas based on intuitive messages I receive.

"For the most part, I brainstorm mostly through conversation. It's not unusual for me to be chatting with someone who I trust and have an idea come forth. I look to those around me for inspiration."

Is there any other advice you can share that would benefit startup podcasters, based on your own experiences?

Goldberrg: "I love my podcast and find it to be a great format for people to share their knowledge, beliefs, and abilities with others. I would suggest that if you're on a limited budget, start by offering Facebook Live, or use YouTube Live to get your feet wet and to begin to build a following before committing to the production for a podcast."

Final Thoughts . . .

While thousands upon thousands of new podcast episodes are published each week, the podcasting world is still very much in its infancy. Every day more people from around the world are listening to podcasts for the very first time.

As a result, podcasting offers a tremendous opportunity for those with something to say or with content to share, and who are willing to tap their creativity to present their podcast in a new and interesting way.

There's no room for podcasters who simply copy other people's content. However, if you're able to present information in a way that's appealing to your unique target audience, and you're able to make your podcast stand out, that's where the true potential lies.

With ongoing persistence and hard work, once you build a loyal audience for your podcast, you'll then be able to benefit from monetizing it or using it as a powerful marketing/promotional tool.

Remember, it's your responsibility as a podcaster to stay informed about up-and-coming podcast-related trends and new technologies being used by podcasters. Even once you identify the ideal show format for your podcast, over time, you'll likely need to make some tweaks in order to keep everything fresh for your loyal listeners.

Moving forward, always remember to have fun, be passionate about what you're doing, stay relevant to your audience, and be yourself! It'll likely be your unique personality, perspective, qualifications, and/or talent that'll allow you to set your podcast apart and stand out. Combine what makes you unique with professional-level production quality, unique content, and an understanding of your audience, and you'll have what it takes to succeed.

Welcome to the exciting world of podcasting!

Glossary

Ad placement: The point within an episode when an ad will be heard. Pre-roll ads are played at the very start of a podcast (in most cases even before the episode's intro). Mid-roll means an ad is heard during a podcast, and end-roll means the ad is heard immediately after an episode ends. Advertisers often request specific ad placement (or multiple ad placements) within an episode.

Ad rate: The price per thousand streams/downloads that an advertiser pays to have their ad featured within a podcast episode. This rate is set by the podcaster, but often gets negotiated.

Ad spot: An individual 15-, 30-, or 60-second commercial (advertisement) that's played during a podcast episode. It can be an ad that's pre-produced, an ad that the host reads live (word-for-word) from a script, or an ad that the host ad-libs based on talking points provided by the advertiser.

Advertiser: A company that pays a podcaster to include its advertisement(s) or sponsorship message(s) within a podcast.

An advertiser can be a company, organization, or individual that wants to promote a brand, product, or service.

Amazon Alexa: Smart speakers (or smart hubs) manufactured by Amazon that utilize the Alexa virtual assistant. This virtual assistant also serves as a podcast directory, allowing users to use verbal commands to find and listen to a podcast's episodes.

Analytics: Data compiled by podcast hosting services, podcast directories, and third-party services that measures the audience size and makeup for a podcast.

Apple Logic Pro software: Professional-level audio workstation software for the Mac that can be used to record, edit, and produce an audio podcast. This software is sold by Apple and available from the Mac App Store.

Apple Podcasts: The podcast directory and podcast player app operated by Apple. The app now comes preinstalled with iOS, iPadOS, and macOS, and is also available for the Apple Watch, HomePod, and Apple TV device. The app is free and can be acquired from the App Store (iOS) or Mac App Store (Mac).

Audacity: Free, open-source audio workstation software that can be used to record and edit a podcast, plus handle much of the postproduction needed to create a podcast episode. It's available to download for Windows PCs and Macs from www.audacityteam.org.

Audio Editing Workstation software: Computer software (or a mobile app) used to record, edit, and handle postproduction aspects of an audio-based podcast.

Audio interface: A piece of equipment that connects between microphones and a computer or digital audio recorder. It converts the audio signal from a microphone into a digital format that can be stored (and edited) as a digital audio file. An audio interface can have one or more audio inputs. It allows the user to handle tasks like manually adjusting the recording levels during the recording process.

Audiogram: A promotional tool used by podcasters to promote a podcast or individual podcast episodes. It combines video (or an animated graphic) with text-based captions and audio content in a way that is designed to capture someone's attention. Audiograms can be shared via email or text message, posted on social media, or featured as ads on websites, for example.

Background music: The music that is heard in the background as part of a podcast's intro, outro, or within the actual episode. It can also be used during ads. Podcasters need permission to use copyrighted music within their productions, and often seek out royalty-free music that requires a low, one-time licensing fee to use a music track.

Copyright-free or open-source music is also available, which requires no payment. Using music from a popular band or recording artist is typically not allowed, however, without paying high licensing fees.

Call to action: A request by the podcaster to their audience to perform some type of task, such as review/rate the podcast episode after listening, subscribe to the podcast, post comments about the podcast on social media, or support the podcast's advertisers.

Cover art: The artwork that represents a podcast. It's displayed as part of a podcast's listing within a podcast directory. It's also seen when someone listens to a podcast using a compatible podcast player on their smartphone, tablet, smartwatch, smart TV, computer, or car infotainment system, for example.

CPM rate: The cost per thousand listeners (streams/downloads) that an advertiser pays to a podcaster to have their ad included within a podcast. The rate is set by the podcaster. Even for a widely popular podcast, an average CPM rate is typically around $25. Thus, if a podcast episode's audience comprises 10,000 listeners, the cost of one 60-second ad with a CPM of $25, for example, would be $250.

Digital audio recorder: A recording device used to record a podcast. A computer or mobile device with a microphone attached can be used as a digital audio recorder; however, handheld, battery-powered digital audio recorders are also available (some with built-in microphones) that can capture professional-quality audio while you're on the go. Often, a digital audio recorder allows a podcaster to record and control multiple audio tracks at once via separate audio inputs.

Direct response ad: A commercial that's designed to generate an immediate response from the customer—to place an online order or call a toll-free number, for example. The response rate for these ads can easily be measured and tracked to determine their level of success. Branding is another common podcast ad type, used purely to establish or improve brand recognition for a company or its products/services; no response from the listener (potential customer) is expected.

Download: A podcast episode that a listener downloads and stores on their computer, mobile device, or compatible podcast player. The internet is used to acquire and store the audio file, which can later be listened to anytime—with or without an internet connection.

End-roll ad: An advertisement that plays at the very end of a podcast, either right before or typically right after the closing credits or outro.

Fair use: A legal concept in U.S. copyright law (Section 107 of the Copyright Act) that allows certain types of copyrighted material to be used for certain purposes without first obtaining written permission or a license from the copyright holder. For a podcast, fair use typically applies when the content is used within a review, as part of news reporting, or as part of educational material. For more information, visit: www.copyright.gov/fair-use/more-info.html.

Google Podcasts: One of the most popular podcast directories. It is created and maintained by Google. The Google Podcasts mobile app can be used to stream and/or download podcast episodes to compatible devices, such as Android-based smartphones or tablets. A free Google Podcasts plug-in can also be added to popular computer web browsers (including Google Chrome).

Host/co-host: The person or people who host a podcast.

Intro: The first few seconds (typically less than one minute) of a podcast episode that often includes background music and someone introducing the audience to the podcast and its host(s). It also previews what will be covered within the episode and sets the audience's expectations about what to expect.

Microphone: Condenser and dynamic are the two main types of microphones used to record audio for a podcast. Choose the type of microphone that's best suited to your unique recording needs and recording environment. Keep in mind that in most recording situations, every person who will be speaking should use their own microphone.

Mid-roll ad: An advertisement that plays somewhere in the middle of a podcast episode—not before the intro or after the outro.

Outro: The closing portion of a podcast episode (typically less than one minute) that offers a summary statement. The host(s) often use this time to thank the audience for listening, to promote the next episode, and to offer a call-to-action requesting that listeners do something immediately (such as subscribe to the podcast, review the podcast, post social media comments about the podcast, or support the podcast's advertisers, for example).

Patreon: An online service that can help a podcaster solicit and collect one-time or ongoing financial donations for their podcast. In exchange, the podcaster offers some type of exclusive perk or reward to benefactors.

Podcast: A serialized (episode-based) audio program offered via the internet that can be streamed or downloaded using a podcast player on a computer, smartphone, tablet, smartwatch, smart speaker, smart TV, or car's infotainment system, for example. A podcast episode can be anywhere from a few minutes to one or two hours long. A podcast consists of a series of episodes, which differentiates it from a long-form audiobook, for example.

Podcast Advertising Agency: A full-service agency that works with advertisers to develop, place, manage, and then track highly targeted direct response or branding ad campaigns on podcasts. Podcasters can promote their podcasts to these agencies in hopes of having the agencies purchase advertising or sponsorships on behalf of their clients.

Podcast category: All podcast directories and podcast distribution services organize podcasts into subject-based categories to make them easier for listeners to find. Each directory uses several dozen separate categories.

Podcast description: The text-based description of a podcast that explains what a podcast is all about and what listeners can expect from it. It's featured within podcast directories, for example, as part of a podcast's listing. It is typically accompanied by the podcast title, and perhaps a listing of individual episodes.

Podcast directory/distribution service: A directory where potential listeners can find and listen to podcasts by streaming or downloading individual episodes or subscribing (for free) to a podcast. Apple Podcasts, Google Podcasts, Stitcher, TuneIn, Spotify, Pandora, Amazon Alexa, and SoundCloud are among the most popular podcast directories. Like an internet search engine, a podcast directory allows listeners to use a search field to find a podcast based on a keyword or search phrase, or view a listing of podcasts divided into subject-based categories, for example.

Podcast editing: The process of taking the raw recordings for a podcast, editing the content, and then performing postproduction tasks to clean up the quality, remove unwanted elements, or add content (such as background music or sound effects).

Podcast hosting service: An online-based service a podcaster uses to store and distribute or promote their podcast and related content to podcast directories and distribution services. Two popular podcast hosting services include Libsyn and Blubrry.

Podcast monetization: The process of selling advertising or sponsorships within a podcast in order to generate money. Many other ways to earn money from podcasting activities also exist, keeping in mind that audio podcasts are typically distributed to listeners for free.

Podcast player: An app or web browser plug-in used by podcast audiences to find and listen to podcasts. Depending on the hardware used with the podcast player, it may stream the audio content (requiring continuous internet access) or allow podcast episodes to be downloaded and played later (on-demand). Downloaded episodes do not require the internet to play the content after it has been downloaded. Podcast players also allow users to subscribe to their favorite podcasts for free, and manage all saved content.

Podcast producer: The person who handles the ongoing (behind-the-scenes) operation and management of a podcast. Responsibilities might include managing the entire production team, editing episodes and handling postproduction activities, selling advertising/sponsorships, booking guests, managing interactions with listeners, and handling promotional activities for the podcast.

Podcast production service: A fee-based agency that will help a podcaster record, produce, distribute, and promote their podcast. These agencies team up podcasters with professional producers and audio engineers who handle virtually all the technical aspects of producing podcasts, allowing the podcaster to focus almost exclusively on creating their unique and targeted content.

Podcast recording/production: The process of recording a podcast episode and handling all the postproduction activities required to prepare the podcast for online distribution to its audience.

Podcast season and episode number: A way to organize and identify individual podcast episodes. In addition to using their unique titles, some podcasters choose to divide their episodes into seasons and/or label them by number. For example, an episode might be called "Season 1, Episode 3—[Insert Episode Title]." This helps listeners determine the order they should listen to past episodes.

Podcast subscriber: Someone who clicks or taps on the "subscribe" button for a podcast in order to download each new episode as soon as it's published online and be notified by email or via a notification from the listener's podcast player.

Podcast title: The text-based title of a podcast. The best titles are descriptive, short, and memorable.

Podcaster: A person who hosts and/or produces a podcast.

Postproduction: This encompasses everything a podcaster must do after recording each podcast episode to prepare it to be published online. This includes editing, mixing in sound effects and background music, incorporating any other production elements, and then uploading the completed episode (along with related content) to the podcast hosting service.

Preproduction: This includes everything a podcaster must do prior to actually recording each episode of their podcast, such as brainstorming episode topics, creating episode rundowns, writing scripts, booking guests, and scheduling recording sessions, for example.

Pre-roll ad: An advertisement or sponsorship message that runs at the very beginning of a podcast episode, typically before the intro.

Recording engineer: The person in charge of operating the recording equipment during the production of a podcast's episode and then handling the postproduction work, including editing. This person has experience using audio workstation (recording and editing) software and understands how to achieve the best quality audio using the microphone(s) and other equipment being used.

Royalty-free music: Professionally composed and recorded music that a podcaster can pay a one-time licensing fee to utilize within their podcast.

Show format: The format a podcast episode follows to convey its content to an audience. Examples include a question-and-answer format, one host interviewing a guest or panel of guests, or two hosts conversing with each other about a specific topic. A podcast can follow a wide range of traditional show formats. Many of the most popular podcasts tend to adopt a hybrid or original show format.

Show notes: Additional information (usually text-based) that can be composed by a podcaster and shared with listeners in conjunction with a podcast episode. Show notes can include photos, video clips, links to related articles, a more in-depth description of the podcast and the episode, a short bio for the podcast's host(s), a list of podcast credits, or bonus information not included within the actual audio episode. Podcasters utilize show notes in many ways to share additional content with listeners.

Show rundown: A detailed, minute-by-minute timeline created during the preproduction of an episode that helps a podcaster plan each episode and then stay on track during the recording process and postproduction.

Social media advertising: Paid advertising on social media platforms designed to help promote a podcast and build its audience.

Social media marketing: Nonpaid activities done on social media to promote a podcast, with the goal of building and maintaining its audience. This can include running a Facebook Page or Facebook Group for a podcast, sharing podcast-related content, and communicating informally with listeners.

Stinger: A produced snippet of audio (usually just five to ten seconds in length) that's often used as a radio station or podcast show ID. It typically includes a digitally enhanced and altered voice-over in conjunction with sound effects or impactful music designed to get attention and reinforce a brand or identity. Some audio production houses, such as Radio Voice Imaging (www.radiovoiceimaging.com), specialize in creating stingers for radio stations and podcasters.

Stitcher: A popular podcast directory available via a mobile app, website, or web browser plug-in, for example. Separate apps to access Stitcher are available for many smart TVs, vehicle infotainment systems, smartwatches, and smart speakers.

Stream: The ability for a podcast listener to access and listen to a podcast using a podcast player without downloading its digital audio file. A continuous internet connection is required.

Talking points ad: An advertisement within a podcast recorded extemporaneously by the host(s) using a series of talking points provided by the advertiser. This type of ad is typically recorded live, without a script, and takes on a more conversational or personal endorsement style, as if the host were recommending a product or service to a close friend.

Target audience: The specific, identifiable, and niche audience that a podcast is being produced for and is designed to appeal to.

TuneIn: A popular podcast directory available via a mobile app, website, or web browser plug-in, for example. Separate apps to access TuneIn are available for many smart TVs, vehicle infotainment systems, smartwatches, and smart speakers.

Value proposition: A personalized "sales pitch" that a podcaster presents to prospective advertisers. It outlines all the benefits of sponsoring their podcast. This includes details about the audience size and makeup, as well as any unique ways a podcaster is able to share the advertiser's message with the podcast's target audience.

Word-of-mouth promotion: A way to promote a podcast by getting loyal listeners to share details about the podcast with friends, family members, and co-workers, for example, both online and in the real world. This is perhaps the most powerful marketing tool a podcaster has at their disposal to grow their audience organically and for free.

About the Author

Jason R. Rich (www.jasonrich.com) is a highly accomplished and globally recognized author, journalist, photographer, and public speaker. In conjunction with Entrepreneur Press (https://bookstore.entrepreneur.com) he has written *The Ultimate Guide to YouTube for Business, 2nd Edition,* as well as several books in the popular *Start Your Own* series, including:

- ▶ *Start Your Own Etsy Business*
- ▶ *Start Your Own Import/Export Business*
- ▶ *Start Your Own Photography Business*
- ▶ *Start Your Own Travel Hosting Business*

As a public speaker, Jason R. Rich frequently lectures aboard cruise ships around the world, and as a writer, he regularly contributes to a handful of major daily newspapers, national magazines (including *AARP the Magazine* and *AARP Bulletin*), and popular websites. In the past, he served as an associate producer and/or co-host for two Peabody Award-winning radio shows.

Launched in March 2020, his podcast (which he writes and produces himself), is of interest to all smartphone users. It's called *Jason Rich's Featured App of the Week* (http://www.featuredapppodcast.com), and it's available on all popular podcast directories, including: Apple Podcasts, Google Podcasts, Pandora, iHeartRadio, Spotify, Stitcher, Amazon Music, and Outcast.

You can follow Jason R. Rich and his global travel adventures on Facebook (www.facebook.com/JasonRich7), Twitter (@JasonRich7), Instagram (@jasonrich7), and LinkedIn (www.linkedin.com/in/jasonrich7).

Index

CPSIA information can be obtained
at www.ICGtesting.com
Printed in the USA
JSHW030121190421
13613JS00006B/6

9 781642 011128